PROFILES IN AMERICAN HISTORY

Significant Events and the People Who Shaped Them

Volume 3: *Indian Removal to the Antislavery Movement* *(1825-1852)*

Indian Removal
Black Hawk, John Ross, Winfield Scott

Industrialization
Samuel Slater, Eli Whitney, Harriet Hanson Robinson

Women and Reform
Sarah Grimké and Angelina Grimké Weld, Susan B. Anthony, Amelia Jenks Bloomer

Plantation System
James Henry Hammond, Harriet A. Jacobs, Mary Boykin Chesnut

Slave Resistance
Denmark Vesey, Nat Turner, John Quincy Adams

Antislavery Movement
David Walker, William Lloyd Garrison, Frederick Douglass, Sojourner Truth, Harriet Beecher Stowe

Volume 4: *Westward Movement to the Civil War* *(1829-1865)*

Westward Movement
Christopher "Kit" Carson, Marcus Whitman and Narcissa Prentiss Whitman, John Augustus Sutter

Mexican War
José Antonio Navarro, Sam Houston, Zachary Taylor, John Charles Frémont and Jessie Ann Benton Frémont

Transcendental and Romantic Movements
Henry David Thoreau, Margaret Fuller, Nathaniel Hawthorne

Pre-Civil War Controversies
Stephen A. Douglas, Dred Scott, John Brown

Civil War
Abraham Lincoln, Robert E. Lee, William Tecumseh Sherman, Martin Robinson Delany, Anna Ella Carroll, Mathew B. Brady, Walt Whitman

(Continued on inside back cover)

PROFILES IN
AMERICAN HISTORY

Great Depression to the Cuban Missile Crisis

1929
▼
Stock market crash of October 24 sparks Great Depression.

1933
▼
Franklin D. Roosevelt commences twelve years as president. Adolf Hitler takes control of Germany.

1945
▼
Atom bombs are dropped in Japan, ending the war. Yalta conference divides Europe.

1944
▼
Dwight D. Eisenhower commands the invasion of Normandy in France.

1941
▼
United States enters war after Pearl Harbor bombed.

1939
▼
Germany invades Poland; World War II begins.

1935
▼
Dorothy Thompson begins anti-Nazi broadcasts.

1946
▼
George F. Kennan sends "long telegram" to the State Department; begins policy of containment and the Cold War.

1948
▼
Harry S Truman officially ends segregation in the armed forces.

1950
▼
Joseph McCarthy begins Senate investigations of communism in America. Ethel and Julius Rosenberg are executed as spies.

1954
▼
In *Brown* v. *Board of Education* the U.S. Supreme Court strikes down "separate but equal" policy.

1962
▼
United States achieves removal of atomic warheads from Cuba.

1961
▼
John F. Kennedy elected president. Bay of Pigs invasion of Cuba fails.

1959
▼
Allen Dulles and the Central Intelligence Agency plan to overthrow Cuba's Fidel Castro.

1957
▼
Martin Luther King, Jr., organizes Southern Christian Leadership Conference. First of a series of Civil Rights Acts is passed by Congress.

1955
▼
Rosa Parks challenges segregation in public transportation.

PROFILES IN AMERICAN HISTORY

Significant Events and the People

Who Shaped Them

Great Depression to the Cuban Missile Crisis

JOYCE MOSS

and

GEORGE WILSON

AN IMPRINT OF GALE RESEARCH INC.
AN INTERNATIONAL THOMSON PUBLISHING COMPANY

$\mathcal{P}$ROFILES IN AMERICAN HISTORY:
Significant Events and the People Who Shaped Them

VOLUME 7: GREAT DEPRESSION TO THE CUBAN MISSILE CRISIS

Joyce Moss and George Wilson

Staff

Carol DeKane Nagel, *U•X•L Developmental Editor*
Thomas L. Romig, *U•X•L Publisher*

Christine Nasso, *Acquisitions Editor*

Shanna P. Heilveil, *Production Assistant*
Evi Seoud, *Assistant Production Manager*
Mary Beth Trimper, *Production Director*

Mary Krzewinski, *Cover and Page Designer*
Cynthia Baldwin, *Art Director*
Arthur Chartow, *Technical Design Services Manager*

The Graphix Group, *Typesetting*

Library of Congress Cataloging-in-Publication Data

Profiles in American history : significant events and the people who shaped them.

Includes bibliographical references and index.

Contents: v. 1. Exploration to revolution. 7. Great Depression to the Cuban Missile Crisis.

1. United States—History—Juvenile literature. 2. United States—Biography—Juvenile literature. 3. United States—History. [JUV] 4. United States—Biography. [JUV] I. Moss, Joyce, 1951- . II. Wilson, George, 1920- .

E178.M897 1994 920.073 94-6677

ISBN 0-8103-9207-0 (set : acid-free paper)
ISBN 0-8103-9211-9 (v. 1 : acid-free paper)
ISBN 0-8103-9214-3 (v. 7 : acid-free paper)

∞™ This book is printed on acid-free paper that meets the minimum requirements of American National Standard for Information Sciences—Permanence Paper for Printed Library Materials, ANSI Z39.48-1984.

Printed in the United States of America

Published simultaneously in the United Kingdom by Gale Research International Limited (An affiliated company of Gale Research Inc.)

I(T)P™

The trademark ITP is used under license.

Contents

Great Depression and the New Deal 1

World War II 58

Cold War 140

McCarthy Era 196

Desegregation 226

COLORED ONLY

Cuban Missile Crisis 256

Reader's Guide

The many noteworthy individuals who shaped U.S. history from the exploration of the continent to the present day cannot all be profiled in one eight-volume work. But those whose stories are told in *Profiles in American History* meet one or more of the following criteria. The individuals:

- Directly affected the outcome of a major event in U.S. history
- Represent viewpoints or groups involved in that event
- Exemplify a role played by common citizens in that event
- Highlight an aspect of that event not covered in other entries

Format

Volumes of *Profiles in American History* are arranged by chapter. Each chapter focuses on one particular event and opens with an overview and detailed time line of the event that places it in historical context. Following are biographical profiles of two to seven diverse individuals who played active roles in the event.

Each biographical profile is divided into four sections:

- **Personal Background** provides details that predate and anticipate the individual's involvement in the event
- **Participation** describes the role played by the individual in the event and its impact on his or her life
- **Aftermath** discusses effects of the individual's actions and subsequent relevant events in his or her life
- **For More Information** provides sources for further reading on the individual

Additionally, sidebars containing interesting details about the events and individuals profiled, ranging from numbers of war casualties to famous quotes to family trees, are sprinkled throughout the text.

Additional Features

Maps are provided to assist readers in traveling back through time to an America arranged differently from today. Portraits and illustrations of individuals and events as well as excerpts from primary source materials are also included to help bring history to life. Sources of all quoted material are cited parenthetically within the text, and complete bibliographic information is listed at the end of the entry. A full bibliography of scholarly sources consulted in preparing the volume appears in the book's back matter.

Cross references are made in the entries, directing readers to other entries in the volume that elaborate on individuals connected in some way to the person under scrutiny. In addition, a comprehensive subject index provides easy access to people and events mentioned throughout the volume.

Comments and Suggestions

We welcome your comments on this work as well as your suggestions for individuals to be featured in future editions of *Profiles in American History*. Please write: Editors, *Profiles in American History*, U·X·L, 835 Penobscot Bldg., Detroit, Michigan 48226-4094; call toll-free: 1-800-877-4253; or fax: 313-961-6348.

Preface

"There is properly no History; only Biography," wrote great American poet and scholar Ralph Waldo Emerson. *Profiles in American History* explores U.S. history through biography. Beginning with the first contact between Native Americans and Vikings and continuing to the present day, this series offers a unique alternative to traditional texts by emphasizing the roles played by individuals, including many women and minorities, in historical events.

Profiles in American History presents the human story of American events, not the exclusively European or African or Indian or Asian story. The guiding principle in compiling this series has been to achieve balance not only in gender and ethnic background but in viewpoint. Thus the circumstances surrounding an historical event are told from individuals holding opposing views, and even opposing positions. Slaves and slave owners, business tycoons and workers, advocates of peace and proponents of war all are heard. American authors whose works reflect the times—from Walt Whitman to John Steinbeck—are also featured.

The biographical profiles are arranged in groups, clustered around one major event in American history. Yet each individual profile is complete in itself. It is the interplay of these profiles—the juxtaposition of alternative views and experiences within a grouping—that broadens the readers' perspective on the event as a whole and on the participants' roles in particular. It is what makes it possible for *Profiles in American History* to impart a larger, human understanding of events in American history.

Acknowledgments

For their guidance on the choice of events and personalities, the editors are grateful to:

Jonathan Betz-Zall, Children's Librarian, Sno-Isle Regional Library System, Washington

Janet Sarratt, Library Media Specialist, John E. Ewing Junior High School, Gaffney, South Carolina

Michael Salman, Assistant Professor of American History, University of California at Los Angeles

Appreciation is extended to Professor Salman for his careful review of chapter overviews and his guidance on key sources of information about the personalities and events.

For insights into specific personalities, the editors are grateful to Robert Sumpter, History Department Chairman at Mira Costa High School, Manhattan Beach, California.

Deep appreciation is extended to the writers who compiled data and contributed the biographies for this volume of *Profiles in American History:*

Diane Ahrens
Lisa Gabbert
Erika Heet
Colin Wells

The editors also thank artist Robert Bates for his research and rendering of the maps and Kathleen Witman at U•X•L for her careful copy editing.

Introduction

From the Great Depression of 1929 to the Cuban Missile Crisis of 1962, the United States underwent pivotal changes in its history. The power of national government expanded greatly under the direction of Franklin D. Roosevelt, the only four-term president in the nation's history. Women and African Americans won appointments to national positions in greater numbers than ever before, and government began to respond to the needs of workers, farmers, and the poor. But there was also tremendous racial and social controversy during this period, as Americans continued to struggle over segregation, equal rights, and the organization of labor.

World War II brought far-reaching international and domestic changes. Contributing greatly on the battlefields and in military supplies, the United States emerged as the leader of the victorious Allied powers. But there were, at the same time, abuses and conflicts over civil rights within the United States. Its government called on the whole population to join in the war effort but fell far short of fulfilling its own promise of liberty and justice for all in America. Among both Japanese and African Americans, leaders surfaced to protest the inequalities suffered by their groups as war raged in Europe and in the Pacific. Meanwhile, U.S. scientists invented the world's first nuclear weapon, the atom bomb. It brought an abrupt end to World War II but then led to a costly forty-five year race between the United States and the Soviet Union for world power. Called the Cold War, their competition threatened the survival of humanity.

The Cold War also threatened liberty within U.S. borders. Suddenly Americans became suspect for having joined, or just for having contact with others who had joined, leftist organizations in the past. The ranks of these organizations swelled in the 1930s, when the nation was groping for ways out of the Great Depression. Now the rights of these citizens were violated. Communist-hunters made accusations based on little evidence that turned into accepted facts that ruined careers as well as lives. Victims endured trials, some lost their jobs, and a few died. Other citizens who worried about the dangers of atomic weapons, opposed wars, and supported equal rights for workers and minorities were often labeled "communists" by their opponents.

Curiously, the Cold War had some positive effects on civil rights. The Soviets and some of the newly independent African and Asian nations ridiculed the United States for calling itself a democracy but allowing racism to exist by law and custom. Indirectly, then, the Cold War worked against segregation in America. This added to the pressure being exerted by civil rights workers who brought cases before the Supreme Court. Then direct action by blacks and whites in the larger population was added in the crusade against segregation in America. The struggle for civil rights grew as the 1960s dawned.

At the same time, the Cold War escalated. It reached a climax in 1962, when the Cuban Missile Crisis placed the United States and the Soviet Union on the brink of nuclear war. After this crisis, the two superpowers began to restrain themselves in their race for world supremacy. U.S. president John F. Kennedy and others became convinced that humans must start to put an end to war or it would put an end to them. It was a lasting recognition, yet many lives and billions of additional dollars would be spent on the Cold War in the years to come.

Picture Credits

The photographs and illustrations appearing in *Profiles in American History: Significant Events and the People Who Shaped Them,* Volume 7: *Great Depression to the Cuban Missile Crisis* were received from the following sources:

On the cover: **courtesy of the National Portrait Gallery:** John Steinbeck; **Courtesy of the Library of Congress:** Eleanor Roosevelt; **courtesy of True Yasui:** Minoru Yasui.

Courtesy of the Library of Congress: pages 3, 11, 13, 28, 30, 47, 64, 108, 119, 147, 161, 200, 228, 245, 263, 273; **courtesy of University Research Library, Department of Special Collections, University of California at Los Angeles:** pages 9, 158, 224; **courtesy of the Department of the Navy:** pages 20, 154; **courtesy of the National Portrait Gallery:** pages 23, 83, 171, 241; **courtesy of the Oakland Museum:** pages 35, 39, 41, 42; **courtesy of the San Diego State University Press:** page 50; **courtesy of the Dwight D. Eisenhower Library:** pages 67, 77; **courtesy of the United States Coast Guard:** page 74; **AP/Wide World Photos:** pages 90, 179, 207, 215, 221, 233, 238, 253, 259, 281; **courtesy of True Yasui:** pages 95, 98; **courtesy of Dorothy Thompson Papers, Syracuse University Library, Special Collections Department:** page 131; **courtesy of the United States Information Service:** page 149; **courtesy of the State Department:** page 185; **courtesy of the Department of Agriculture:** page 249.

Great Depression and the New Deal

1929
▼
Stock market crashes on October 24, triggering a nationwide economic depression.

1933
▼
Eleanor Roosevelt writes *It's Up to the Women,* about women's role in carrying the nation through the depression.

1933
▼
Dorothea Lange photographs the human consequences of the depression in "White Angel Breadline."

1933
▼
FDR becomes president, guides fifteen new laws through Congress in first 100 days.

1932
▼
Franklin D. Roosevelt (FDR) runs for president of the United States, promises Americans a new deal.

1933-1935
▼
FDR concentrates on relief and recovery from the depression.

1934
▼
First exhibit is held of Lange's depression photographs.

1934-1935
▼
John Steinbeck writes *Tortilla Flat,* a novel about Mexican American peasants during the depression.

1935
▼
Eleanor Roosevelt begins "My Day" newspaper column.

1940
▼
Steinbeck's *Cannery Row* is published, describing workers in Monterey, California, during the depression.

1940
▼
Depression ends.

1939
▼
Steinbeck's *Grapes of Wrath* is published, a novel about Oklahoma migrants in the depression.

1935-1936
▼
FDR moves from relief and recovery to reform measures to combat the depression.

GREAT DEPRESSION AND THE NEW DEAL

On October 24, 1929, the value of stock—or shares in American corporations—began to drop tremendously. The stock market crash was the first disaster in perhaps the greatest crisis to hit the United States since the Civil War. Lasting from 1929 to 1940, a panic that became known as the Great Depression gripped the nation. Businesses collapsed, and millions lost their jobs. Caused in part by economic problems that resulted from World War I, the crisis hit Europe, too. Economic ties around the world prompted the depression to spread across continents, throwing societies into turmoil.

Desperately hungry, some Americans were reduced to eating weeds. In cities, men tried to sell apples on street corners for five cents apiece, and thousands lined up every day in breadlines that stretched for blocks. Crops went unharvested because prices were too low to make selling them profitable. So produce rotted in the fields while people in the cities went hungry. In Kentucky, coal miners had no income at all and lived on a diet of dandelions and wild blackberries. All over, gas and electricity were shut off because people could not pay utility bills, and many lost their homes, farms, and businesses because they could not pay their debts. Homeless men welcomed arrest since jail meant they would have a bed and food for a time. Poverty was suddenly a reality or real possibility for most Americans.

▲ **A midwestern family during the Great Depression**

Serving as president at the time was Herbert Hoover, who tried to remedy the catastrophe with emergency measures. He did not, however, believe in direct government aid for the unemployed. Meanwhile, the jobless rate swelled from 1.5 million in 1929 to 12.1 million in 1932. And more than a million homeless roamed the nation in search of work. "Hoovervilles"—communities of shacks or shanties—sprang up near large cities of the nation. As suggested by the name, Americans started to blame Hoover for their ongoing poverty.

It was at this point that **Franklin D. Roosevelt** (FDR) stepped onto the scene. Crippled with polio, he could actually, and only with difficulty, stand but not walk. Warm and confident, Roosevelt was blessed with a personality that calmed the nation and was in obvious contrast to Hoover's. When nominated for president, FDR stood determinedly at a podium, leaning on his two strong, well-exercised arms, and promised his fellow Americans a new deal. He would try some of the same controls Hoover had tried and more, winning confidence in a way that Hoover could not.

The phrase "new deal" caught on, coming to stand for the package of measures FDR put into effect from 1933 to 1939. It focused first on relief and recovery measures and later on reforms. Unlike Hoover, Roosevelt believed in direct aid for the unemployed. He experimented freely to end the depression, comparing himself to a quarterback in football who tried first this play and then that one to score points. In his first one hundred days, Roosevelt, with the help of his cabinet and an informal team of advisers known as his "Brain Trust," guided through Congress fifteen major laws, providing unemployment relief, farm aid, loans to home owners, and more. Some 1,300 banks had closed their doors in 1930 alone. To restore America's willingness to place money in banks, the government created the Federal Deposit Insurance Corporation (FDIC) so that citizens would no longer lose their savings if a bank failed. The government would, through the FDIC, guarantee that depositors could always get their money back. This, and a flurry of other measures, brought new hope.

The Depression Strikes

"Newspapers under the shirt would temper the winter cold ... gunny sacks wrapped around the feet would mitigate [ease] the long hours in the frozen fields outside the factory gates ... children worked for pennies after school, not understanding the fear that was touching them, knowing that they must do what they could to help buy bread and coffee.

"As savings end, borrowing begins. Wedding rings are pawned, furniture is sold, the family moves into ever cheaper, damper, dirtier rooms ... dark cold rooms, with the father angry and helpless and ashamed, the distraught children too often hungry or sick, and the mother, so resolute by day, so often, when the room was finally still, lying awake in bed at night, softly crying." (Arthur M. Schlesinger, Jr., *The Crisis of the Old Order*, Vol. 1 of *The Age of Roosevelt* [Boston: Houghton Mifflin, 1957], pp. 167-168)

FDR himself went far in renewing faith in the American system, speaking directly to the nation over the radio. In a confident, winningly warm voice, he addressed average workers as his friends in "fireside chats" that explained what he was doing to solve the nation's problems.

Roosevelt had critics. Charles E. Coughlin, a Roman Catholic priest, attacked the New Deal programs as being too favorable to businessmen. Father Coughlin had a radio show, with more than 35 million listeners, on which he encouraged hatred for bankers, whom he typecast as Jewish. Another popular leader of the time, Governor Huey Long of Louisiana, came up with his own depression plan—$2,000 to $3,000 a year for every American family that earned less than $1,000, to be paid for by taxing the rich. Long had great appeal to voters, but an assassin cut his life short in 1935.

Despite his critics, Roosevelt preserved America's business system and involved the government with the welfare of its average citizens more than ever before. His New Deal did not, however, pull them out of the depression. It took World War II to end the business slowdown and employ all the jobless—suddenly hundreds of thousands were needed to manufacture war supplies and raise food for the troops. But, though the New Deal did not end the depression, it lessened the suffering and showed the government's heartfelt concern for the millions who felt hungry, hopeless, and deserted.

Photographer **Dorothea Lange** captured their hunger and hopelessness in pictures that forever document the period. From photographs of breadlines to street demonstrations to migrant families, her work helped make the president and others aware of the extent of the suffering. So did the novels of **John Steinbeck,** whose characters ranged from Mexican peasants to Oklahoma farm migrants to cannery workers in Monterey, California. Radio and movie artists created fantasy shows that provided relief from the harsh reality of the time and even helped some people deal with that reality. The hit song "Who's Afraid of the Big Bad Wolf?" (from Disney's movie *The Three Little Pigs* [1933]) helped lift spirits as people marshaled their courage to battle the deep, dark depression.

In their desperation, some Americans reached out for help to the president's wife, **Eleanor Roosevelt.** She cared deeply and responded in various ways, from answering fifty letters a day, to writing a book, to approaching her husband on their behalf. The First Lady championed the causes of minority groups and women. With Democrat leader Molley Dewson, she helped see to it that fifty women were appointed to high-level posts. While FDR, concerned for his political survival, would not support an antilynching bill, Eleanor Roosevelt did. (Lynchings—unlawful killings, usually by hanging—increased during the depression.) Along with Harry Hopkins, leader of the Works Progress Administration (WPA), she also helped make sure that New Deal programs reached blacks and took stands to support black Americans in other ways.

There were, to be sure, inequalities in the New Deal. Women earned only 60 percent of men's earnings on WPA projects. The Civilian Conservation Corps hired only men, and it segregated its black and white workers. But, if FDR's New Deal did relatively little for blacks, it was still more than any administration had done since the post–Civil War era. Fifty blacks were appointed to positions in New Deal departments and agencies. Of these fifty, Mary McLeod Bethune had perhaps the greatest effect on jobs for blacks.

In sum, the New Deal tried but did not lift America out of the Great Depression. World War II did. Yet the New Deal restored confidence in America's government and economy and maintained this faith until the war. Furthermore, by beginning to recognize the rights and needs of different groups, the Roosevelt government did, in fact, give America a "new deal."

Some New Deal Agencies

Civilian Conservation Corps (CCC)
1933; employed men aged eighteen to twenty-five on road and park construction, flood control, and other projects. The men lived in work camps, earning $30 a month. They had to send $25 home to their families.

Tennessee Valley Authority (TVA)
1933; constructed nine major dams and many minor ones across seven states and brought electricity to millions of homes, creating thousands of jobs.

Works Progress Administration (WPA)
1935; hired over 8 million Americans to build bridges, airports, schools, hospitals, and roads. Also employed artists on federal theater and writing projects.

National Youth Administration (NYA)
1935; provided young people aged sixteen to twenty-five with part-time jobs on WPA projects, helping them stay in school.

Franklin D. Roosevelt

1882-1945

Personal Background

Early influences. Franklin Delano Roosevelt was born January 30, 1882, on his wealthy family's estate at Hyde Park, New York. He was the only child of Sara Roosevelt, his rather domineering mother, and James Roosevelt, his elderly, ill, and somewhat remote father. His boyhood was sheltered but happy. He did not attend public school but was instead taught at home by a series of governesses and tutors. He accompanied his parents on numerous trips to Europe. At the age of fourteen, he was enrolled in the elite Groton School in Massachusetts, whose founder, Rector Endicott Peabody aimed to educate the sons of the wealthy in their Christian responsibilities to society. Roosevelt's later dedication to public service can be traced to the influence of Reverend Peabody and his good friend (and Franklin's distant cousin) future President Theodore Roosevelt, who thrilled the boys at Groton when he spoke there in 1897.

Harvard. In 1900 Franklin entered Harvard University, where he majored in history and government. He was an undistinguished student there, largely because his outside activities and busy social life took up so much of his time. In his freshman year, his father died and his mother soon after moved to Boston, where she rented an apartment "near enough to the University to be on hand should ... [Franklin] want me and far enough removed not to interfere in his

▲ Franklin D. Roosevelt

Event: New Deal Program.

Role: Franklin D. Roosevelt, the thirty-second president of the United States, led the American people through the Great Depression and history's most terrible conflict, World War II. His New Deal program, designed to reduce the suffering brought on by the depression, resulted in a tremendous expansion of the powers of the federal government.

college life" (Freedman, p. 20). Franklin's greatest disappointment at Harvard was that he "did not receive an invitation from Porcellian, the most exclusive and snobbish of all the clubs that signified social success" (Freedman, p. 22). It was perhaps the first time in his life that he was socially snubbed. This disappointment was partially offset by his greatest success at Harvard, his election as editor in chief of *The Harvard Crimson,* the undergraduate daily newspaper.

Marriage. The most important event of Franklin's Harvard days was his secret engagement to his distant cousin, Eleanor, during his senior year. When he told his mother of his wedding plans, she did her best to change his mind, even taking him on a Caribbean cruise in the hope that he might forget Eleanor. The separation, however, only made him more eager to marry her. The marriage took place on March 17, 1905, with President Theodore Roosevelt giving the bride away and Reverend Peabody presiding over the ceremony. After honeymooning, the newlyweds moved into a house rented and furnished by Sara Roosevelt, who moved into an adjoining house. The Roosevelts would eventually have six children, and Eleanor would become the most active and influential First Lady in American history.

Politics. Franklin Roosevelt followed a political path remarkably similar to that of his cousin Theodore, except that Franklin joined the Democratic Party. He ran for the New York Senate in 1910, becoming the first Democrat elected in his district in more than fifty years. He was a dedicated young Progressive, calling for an end to political corruption and attacking city bosses. He led a successful fight to deny a seat in the U.S. Senate to the Tammany Hall (the political machine dominating New York City politics) candidate. He skirmished often with the Tammany machine over the years but eventually learned to work with its leaders and gained its support when running for governor and president.

Cabinet. FDR supported Woodrow Wilson against his cousin Theodore in the presidential election of 1912. When Wilson became president, he appointed Franklin to the position of assistant secretary of the navy, a post in which he served with great distinction throughout World War I. His wartime service and his famous name led to FDR's nomination by the Democratic Convention in 1920 for vice president of the United States, with James M. Cox as the

▲ The Roosevelt family

party's nominee for president. Though the Democrats lost to Warren G. Harding, Roosevelt learned a great deal from his experience
in the 1920 campaign. He became a skillful campaigner and an
effective public speaker, getting to know the country as only a candidate for public office or a traveling salesperson could.

Polio. Personal disaster struck Roosevelt the year following
his unsuccessful run for vice president. On vacation at the family's
summer home at Campobello Island, off New Brunswick, Canada,
Roosevelt fell into the water while sailing. He became chilled and
extremely tired. Within three days, he was in severe pain and
unable to move his legs. His back, arms, and hands were partially
paralyzed as well. Roosevelt was a victim of polio, or infantile paralysis. He grew depressed, but his natural positive approach to life

helped him fight the disease. He rejected his mother's advice to retire and, encouraged by his loyal campaign aide Louis Howe and his wife, Eleanor, continued his political involvement. Through vigorous exercise, he was able to regain the use of his hands and overcome the paralysis in his back. He tried hard to walk again, falling frequently but refusing to give up. His determination and courage made it possible for him to stand, but he was never able to walk again without braces and crutches and spent most of his time in a wheelchair. (The American public was largely unaware of this; the press, with whom FDR had a warm relationship, did not run photographs of him in his wheelchair.)

Roosevelt never fully recovered from the ravages of polio. Through constant exercise, he did develop powerful arms and upper body strength, but his legs withered badly. Despite years of physical struggle, he won a distinct spiritual victory. His battle against the disease made him more sympathetic to others who had experienced misfortune. Frances Perkins, later appointed by FDR as secretary of labor, wrote of the changes she saw:

> Franklin Roosevelt underwent a spiritual transformation during the years of his illness.... The years of pain and suffering had purged the slightly arrogant attitude he had displayed on occasion before he was stricken.... Having been in the depths of trouble, he understood the problems of people in trouble.... He learned in that period ... that the "only thing to fear is fear itself." (Perkins, p. 29)

Eleanor Roosevelt played a key role in FDR's political recovery. She invited writers and thinkers to visit so that he might broaden his knowledge of important issues. She attended political events for him, serving as his eyes and ears. Triumphing over her natural shyness, she became a highly effective public speaker. Most importantly, she encouraged her husband to reenter politics.

Ironically, Roosevelt's disease turned out to be, in some ways, a political asset. He received a thunderous ovation when he delivered his first speech since the onset of his illness at the Democratic Convention of 1924. He struggled slowly to the podium aided by his sixteen-year-old son, James. His courageous appearance and well-chosen words made him an important Democratic leader as well as a man much admired for overcoming personal tragedy.

▲ **Roosevelt**

In 1928 Roosevelt was elected governor of New York in a very close election. When the stock market crashed the following year, the nation plunged into the Great Depression. FDR responded with a groundbreaking system of relief for the vast number of unemployed workers in New York. His popularity soared and he won reelection to the governorship in 1930. He began to be mentioned as a possible candidate for the presidency.

Roosevelt was nominated for president by the Democratic National Convention in 1932. FDR traveled to the convention by plane and accepted the nomination in person. He promised a "new deal" to lead the American people out of the depression and to set up safeguards to help prevent future depressions. To prove that he was physically fit to be president, FDR conducted a vigorous campaign, making personal appearances in thirty-eight states. He promised direct relief to the unemployed and to poverty-stricken farmers. In November Roosevelt won a decisive victory, receiving 472 electoral votes to only 59 for Hoover.

Roosevelt did not take his oath of office until March 4, 1933. In the long interval between election and inauguration (which would be shortened for later presidents), he survived an assassination attempt and worked with his advisors to prepare a series of dramatic proposals to combat the depression. His aim was to restore the confidence of the American people in their government and economic system. It was an awesome challenge. While he waited to take office, conditions in the country steadily worsened. A desperate people waited to see how their new leader would meet the most severe economic crisis in the nation's history.

Participation: New Deal

The Great Depression. By the time FDR took office, many of the nation's banks had closed and industrial production was only about half of what it had been before the stock market crash. Millions—one-fourth of the work force—were unemployed and in danger of losing their homes. A growing army of homeless people slept outside every night in tents and automobiles or clustered in makeshift shanties called "Hoovervilles." Charity soup kitchens had to turn away many who were on the edge of starvation.

The young. Suffering extended to the middle class as well as the poor. Middle-class Americans also lost their jobs, their savings, and their homes. Young people were severely affected by the economic collapse. Those who graduated from college had little or no hope of finding a job. A great many dropped out before they finished college. Most did not get to college at all. A few lucky young people found marginal jobs, but hundreds of thousands between the ages of sixteen and twenty-one left home and wandered about the country, unemployed, undernourished, and begging for old clothing and food.

Roosevelt rises to the challenge. Roosevelt struck the right note in his first inaugural address to a desperate nation. He reassured people that the great nation would endure, revive, and prosper. He promised bold experimentation, feeling that above all it was time to try something. Roosevelt asserted his belief that the government should act forcefully to guarantee the well-being of the people. Right from the outset, FDR demonstrated two of the qualities that have led historians to rank him as one of the greatest American presidents: his ability to instill confidence in others and his willingness to greatly expand the power of the federal government to meet the crisis brought on by the Great Depression.

Roosevelt brought other important strengths to the presidency: personal warmth, self-confidence, tremendous energy, and an infectious zest for life. He had the skills of a brilliant politician and was perhaps the greatest orator ever to serve as president. He became the most popular of all American political leaders and won the devoted loyalty of the majority of an entire generation. He raised the Democratic Party to the leading position in politics, attracting the support of Midwestern farmers, labor unions, the urban poor and middle class, and liberal intellectuals. Black Americans, who had supported the Republican Party since the days of Lincoln, switched their allegiance to the party of FDR. And he, in turn, appointed more blacks to government posts than all former presidents combined. In four consecutive elections, Roosevelt led a victorious Democratic Party to control of the White House and both houses of Congress.

Fireside chats. Roosevelt was tremendously successful as a communicator. He won support from most of the press by holding frequent press conferences. Twice a week he met with the press in a frank, open atmosphere. His popularity with reporters helped him present his ideas to the public and dominate the news headlines as no previous president had ever done. Perhaps his most effective means of communicating with the American people was his use of the radio. In his famous "fireside chats," which he always began with "My friends," he managed to make listeners feel that the president of the United States was speaking directly to them.

> When he talked on the radio, he saw them gathered in the little parlor, listening with their neighbors. He was conscious of their faces and hands, their clothes and homes.
>
> His voice and his facial expression as he spoke were those of an intimate friend. After he became President, I [Frances Perkins] often was at the White House when he broadcast, and I realized how unconscious he was of the twenty or thirty of us in that room and how clearly his mind was focused on the people listening at the other end. (Perkins, p. 72)

Strategy. Acutely aware of shifts in public opinion, FDR tried a variety of approaches to solve the nation's problems. He relied on a group of college professors, known as his "brain trust," for advice. From the clash of ideas among his advisers, he was able to choose those proposals most likely to win public support and meet the demands of the time.

Banks. Roosevelt launched his first term with a flurry of activity. As soon as he took office, he declared a "bank holiday," closing all of the nation's banks. (Thousands had failed earlier.) He called Congress into a special session and obtained a law permitting officials of the Treasury Department to examine the banks and allow those that were sound to reopen. This action, coupled with a "fireside chat" on the banking crisis, restored public confidence in the banks and the U.S. government almost overnight. With these steps, Roosevelt ended the "runs," panic-stricken rushes by people to withdraw all their funds that had caused so many banks to fail. At the same time, he sent a series of other measures to Congress for immediate action. No less than fifteen different measures were enacted by Congress in the 100 days of the special session. These were aimed at providing immediate relief, and then work, for the jobless and at stimulating the recovery of business activities.

The New Deal can be divided into the three *R*'s that expressed its purposes: Relief, Recovery, and Reform. Relief and Recovery dominated what historians call FDR's "First New Deal," which ended in 1935. The "Second New Deal" focused on reform measures designed to prevent future depressions.

Two New Deals. The first priority of the early New Deal was to provide relief for the hungry and the unemployed. Some programs doled out food and money to the needy, but most tried to create jobs for those out of work. FDR's sensitivity to the feelings of the poor is shown in his decision to provide relief through jobs. Handouts would have been cheaper, but morale and self-respect would be boosted if people could work. Work relief was successful. Millions

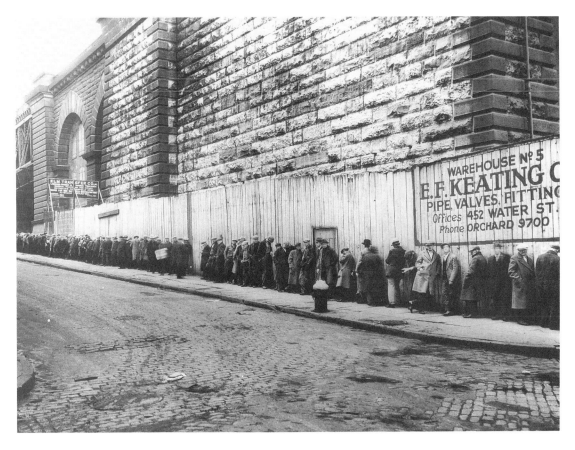

▲ **Men lining up for a job during the depression**

were employed and kept from starving. The government also had something to show for what it spent.

The Civil Conservation Corps (CCC), which employed young men between the ages of seventeen and twenty-eight in U.S. parks and forests, created many recreational areas and wildlife sanctuaries (2.5 million young men served in the CCC before it was disbanded during World War II). The National Youth Administration (NYA) provided part-time work to 2 million high school and college students, making it possible for them to complete their educations. The largest work relief program, the Works Progress Administration (WPA), put people to work building roads, airports, hospitals, schools, parks and dams across the nation. The WPA was criticized for wasting money on useless projects, but it gave jobs to 8 million people, built valuable public works, and, just as FDR hoped, raised the morale of desperate workers.

Two Agricultural Adjustment Acts (1933, 1938) were designed to help farmers recover lost income by reducing surpluses and raising prices for farm products. The first act paid farmers to limit production, and the second act provided loans to farmers who, in times of surplus, agreed to store their extra crops instead of selling them. Farmers in the depressed Tennessee Valley were aided by the Tennessee Valley Authority (TVA), which built dams to control floods and produce low-cost electricity.

Roosevelt versus the Supreme Court. Roosevelt's major effort to encourage business recovery through cooperation among government, business, and labor was the National Recovery Administration. The law establishing this agency (and a number of other pieces of New Deal legislation) was at first declared unconstitutional by the Supreme Court. The Court struck down these laws in language that seemed to threaten any New Deal measures that expanded government authority in economic affairs.

These rulings by the Supreme Court were handed down just prior to the presidential election of 1936, which FDR won in a landslide victory. He received 61 percent of the popular vote and 523 electoral votes, which showed the people's support for his New Deal.

Angered by the Supreme Court's opposition to so much of the New Deal, FDR proposed a Court reorganization plan that would have allowed him to appoint one more Supreme Court justice for each member of the Court who had reached the age of seventy with at least ten years' service. The plan was labeled "Court-packing" and drew severe criticism even from Roosevelt supporters. FDR was perceived to be upsetting the separation of powers among the branches of the federal government. In the midst of the controversy, the Court upheld a state minimum wage law and upheld two of the most far-reaching reforms of the "Second New Deal," the National Labor Relations (Wagner) Act and the Social Security Act. Soon thereafter one of the old justices resigned, and FDR appointed a New Dealer to the Court. FDR could claim that although he had lost the battle to enlarge the Court, he had won the war to uphold New Deal laws.

The Court fight, growing opposition from business leaders, labor violence, and a recession brought on by FDR's decision to reduce government spending made his second term far less successful than his first.

Effect of the New Deal. Roosevelt and his New Deal programs remain controversial to this day. His admirers praise him and the New Deal for restoring faith in our political and economic systems. His program of work relief helped the unemployed regain their self-respect while building valuable public works. Massive spending programs helped stimulate economic recovery. At a time when dictatorships were created in many parts of the world to deal with the chaos brought on by the depression, the United States, led by FDR, maintained its democratic society and individual freedoms.

The New Deal produced laws and agencies of lasting value. The Securities and Exchange Commission still serves as a watchdog over the stock market. The Federal Deposit Insurance Corporation (FDIC) protects our bank deposits and shields us from "runs" and bank failures. The National Labor Relations Board guarantees our right to join unions, bargain collectively, and use weapons such as the strike. The Tennessee Valley Authority continues to control floods and bring low-cost electricity to people. And our Social Security System provides old-age pension, survivors' benefits, assistance for the handicapped, and unemployment insurance when needed. These institutions, along with the other measures of the New Deal, illustrate perhaps the most profound effect of the "Roosevelt Revolution": the tremendous expansion of the role of the federal government in American society.

Critics. FDR was hated by many. He was accused of being a dictator and of destroying the Constitution. The New Deal was condemned for its wastefulness, for increasing the national debt, for destroying the free enterprise system, for introducing socialism, and for creating a vast government bureaucracy that has become too involved in the economy and in the lives of American people.

It is true that the New Deal did not restore anything near full employment or end the depression. It took World War II for the economy to recover, but the New Deal did improve conditions significantly. Moreover, the New Deal lessened the appeal of communism by demonstrating that democracy and capitalism could survive times of crisis. His admirers see FDR as the savior of American capitalism and democratic government:

> At a time when economic difficulties elsewhere were causing other people to give up liberty, democracy, and capitalism for totalitarianism, whether Communist or Fascist, America had its New Deal. This movement provided enough welfare and security to keep the country from turning to more drastic solutions, and therefore enabled the United States to retain its capitalist system of economy and its democratic form of government. (Davies, p. 86)

Aftermath

World War II. FDR led the United States through another great crisis: World War II. He recognized the threat posed by German leader Adolf Hitler, Italian dictator Benito Mussolini, and Japanese militarism long before most statesmen. Strong isolationist sentiment in the country made it difficult for him to take forceful measures before war broke out on September 1, 1939. Congress had passed Neutrality Acts, which seemed designed to avoid war at all costs.

The outbreak of war in Europe and Japanese aggression in Asia prompted FDR to take strong action. After winning an unmatched third term as president, he persuaded Congress to pass a peacetime draft law. He gave Great Britain fifty destroyers in exchange for naval bases in British-controlled areas of the Americas. And he led Congress to enact Lend Lease, a law that allowed him to send supplies and weapons to nations resisting Axis aggression.

War leader. When FDR announced an embargo on the trade of war materials with Japan and froze Japanese assets in the United States, he was trying to force Japan to pull back from her attack on China and against British and French colonies. Militants in Japan decided to attack the United States rather than pull back, an outcome, according to some historians, that Roosevelt prompted by his actions. The surprise Japanese attack on American naval forces at Pearl Harbor, Hawaii, led to an American declaration of war.

FDR proved to be a powerful war leader. He made the crucial decision to concentrate on defeating Germany first. He oversaw total mobilization of the American economy for war. He authorized the Manhattan Project, which resulted in the creation of the atomic bomb, and he made the crucial decisions that led to the founding of the United Nations.

More criticism. Roosevelt has received much criticism about his role as commander in chief. Among these criticisms are:

1. He deliberately permitted the attack on Pearl Harbor in order to unite the American people behind the effort to fight the Axis powers.

2. He lied about U.S. naval activities against Nazi submarines, claiming that U.S. ships were innocent victims when in fact our forces were helping to locate and destroy enemy U-boats.

3. He authorized the "relocation" of Japanese Americans to concentration camps.

4. He did not order the desegregation of the U.S. armed forces during the war.

5. He took no steps to help Jewish refugees escape the Holocaust and failed to authorize bombing of the railroads transporting victims to Hitler's death camps or the camps themselves.

6. He consented to Russian domination of Eastern Europe at the peace conference.

Roosevelt's defenders have dismissed some of these charges. The Pearl Harbor accusation is rejected by many historians. The United States had broken the Japanese code and knew an attack was coming somewhere but did not know the exact location. All military bases in the Pacific were alerted. FDR did mislead the public about American actions against German submarines before the United States entered the war, but the actions were within his authority and deemed necessary by him. The failure to protect the civil rights of Japanese Americans and to desegregate the armed forces cannot be defended except as practical submission to public prejudices. The American failure to take action on behalf of Jewish refugees is also real. State Department officials downplayed evidence of Hitler's mass killing of Jews at death camps, and military commanders argued that diverting planes and people from bombing military targets "would only delay a military victory—the Jews' best chance to

▲ U.S.S. *Shaw* exploding during the Japanese raid on Pearl Harbor, December 7, 1941

survive" (Freedman, p. 152). When Roosevelt learned that officials in the State Department had actually blocked the rescue of Jews, he finally took action, creating a War Refugee Board, condemning on radio the Nazi mass murders, and promising to punish those responsible for these crimes. The War Refugee Board managed to save only 200,000 Jews and 20,000 non-Jews.

Yalta Conference. Roosevelt journeyed to Yalta in southern Russia shortly after he was reelected to a fourth term. The conference plotted the strategy of concluding the war and rearranging postwar Europe. Though he appeared frail and sick to British prime minister Winston Churchill, Roosevelt was strong enough for eight days of hard bargaining.

FDR returned home and reported on the Yalta Conference to Congress. He showed his fatigue by speaking from his wheelchair.

Shortly thereafter, he left for a rest at Warm Springs, Georgia, where he had been going since the onset of polio in 1921. He died there of a massive cerebral hemorrhage on April 12, 1945.

For More Information

Davies, Wallace E. *The New Deal Interpretations.* New York: Macmillan, 1964.

Freedman, Russell. *Franklin Delano Roosevelt.* New York: Clarion Books, 1990.

Freidel, Frank Burt. *Franklin Delano Roosevelt: A Rendezvous with Destiny.* Boston: Little, Brown, 1972.

Morgan, Ted. *FDR: A Biography.* New York: Simon & Schuster, 1985.

Nevins, Allan. "The Place of Franklin D. Roosevelt in History," *American Heritage* (June, 1966): 12-15, 101-104.

Perkins, Frances. *The Roosevelt I Knew.* New York: The Viking Press, 1946.

John Steinbeck

1902-1968

Personal Background

John Ernst Steinbeck was born on February 27, 1902, in Northern California's picturesque Salinas Valley. The third of four children and the only son of Olive Hamilton and John Ernst Steinbeck II, John grew up amidst the rolling hills and valleys of California's agricultural heartland.

Adventurous youth. John was from the first an imaginative child, full of curiosity and energy. Even as a small boy, he loved to hunt, fish, and ride horseback through the woods and fertile farmland. Dubbed the "Salinas Tom Sawyer," John had a thirst for adventure and spent much of his time roaming and exploring, learning about the land and its people (Valjean, p. 24). Each summer he accompanied his family to the Pacific Ocean, where he developed a fascination for sea life and the Monterey coast.

Growing up just east of Monterey and west of the Sierra Nevada mountains, John had a deep appreciation for his surroundings and the rugged assortment of farmers, fishermen, and tradespeople among whom he lived.

Exposed to the classics. Early on, John developed a strong love for books and storytelling. While his father, a sugar mill operator, encouraged John's outdoor activities, his mother introduced him to literature and the arts. A retired kindergarten teacher, Mrs. Stein-

▲ John Steinbeck

Event: The Great Depression, 1929–40.

Role: A Nobel Prize–winning novelist, John Steinbeck wrote stories about the Great Depression of the 1930s. His fiction, most notably his novel *The Grapes of Wrath,* captured both the depression's disastrous effects on Americans and the triumph of the human spirit in overcoming such hardship.

beck taught John how to read at age three and read to him nightly. John heard such literary classics as John Milton's *Paradise Lost,* Sir Walter Scott's *Ivanhoe,* and Robert Louis Stevenson's *Treasure Island,* and most of William Shakespeare's plays. Though weighty material for such a young child, the stories thrilled John and sent his mind racing with ideas. The sitting room, where the Steinbecks' rich library was housed, quickly became his favorite retreat.

Influence of the Pacific

Steinbeck learned a great deal from watching animals survive in nature. As he observed schools of fish hunting and eluding predators by working together, he realized it was their unity that preserved them from death. John began to think that if human beings worked together, as the fish did, they too could overcome difficulties. This observation made a lasting impact on Steinbeck. He conveyed it in much of his writing, especially when he wrote about how people overcame the odds of the Great Depression.

Arthurian legend. The book that most influenced John in his development as a writer was Sir Thomas Malory's *Le Morte d'Arthur* (The Death of Arthur). Given to him on his ninth birthday by his Aunt Molly Martin, *Le Morte d'Arthur* thoroughly enchanted John and showed him the power of great storytelling. He was so captivated by Malory's tale of King Arthur and the Knights of the Round Table that he began carrying a homemade sword with him everywhere he went.

Power of storytelling. But as an allegory (a story in which the characters or events symbolize a deeper meaning), Malory's Arthurian tale was more than just a fine story to John. It also seemed to convey some general truths about honor, friendship, and dignity. The tale showed John that stories could do more than entertain: they could also teach. Thoroughly inspired by Malory, John began to invent stories of his own, based on childhood observations and experiences.

Rebellious and shy. By age ten, John had a well-developed imagination that he constantly exercised through storytelling. The habit was of little use to him in school. Often bored in class, John generally preferred daydreaming or telling stories to his classmates to doing his homework. Such behavior would lead to his being punished for disrupting class. It wasn't until his senior year in high school that John excelled in school.

Despite his reputation as a gifted storyteller, the boy was rather introverted (kept his thoughts to himself) and shy. He never felt comfortable being the center of attention and liked to think of himself as a loner. Often lost in his thoughts, John was more of an observer than a participant in many school and social activities. He had only a few close friends and never felt he was "a part of things" in his childhood (Valjean, p. 19).

The writer. By high school, John knew he wanted to pursue a career in writing. He read often, especially his favorite authors—Thomas Malory, William Shakespeare, Fyodor Dostoyevsky, and Geoffrey Chaucer—and tried his hand at writing poems, essays, and short stories. He served as the associate editor of his high school yearbook and even attempted to get some of his work published. But thoughts of success or failure seemed to terrify him. John always signed his stories with a false or "pen" name and never included a return address on his manuscripts so that he was never notified about whether his work was accepted or rejected.

Stanford. Steinbeck graduated from high school in 1919 and was accepted to Stanford University as an English major in 1920. Though not thrilled with their son's desire to become a writer (they did not think it a stable profession), his parents gladly raised the money necessary to pay for Steinbeck's schooling. Stanford was very expensive, though, so he had to work during the summers to help meet costs.

Work education. Steinbeck took on different jobs but worked mostly as a hard laborer. He dug irrigation canals for local farmers, cleared brush for the paving of the Pacific Coast Highway, and milled sugar beets with his father at the Spreckels sugar refinery. He worked with migrant laborers, many of whom were Mexican and Chinese. Watching employers take advantage of these workers, Steinbeck soon realized how mistreated and misunderstood they were. The migrants, who had a bad reputation as a rough bunch of drinkers and smokers, were paid less than survival wages to perform backbreaking labor. After spending summers working alongside these men and listening to their stories around the campfire at night, Steinbeck developed a deep admiration for them. He realized he was uniquely positioned to tell their story, and he began outlining some ideas. Steinbeck did not yet know it, but he had found the general subject matter that he would write about during his entire career.

Rebellion resurfaces. Though Steinbeck was learning a great deal outside of school, he was not doing well at Stanford. He made a few lasting friendships and was encouraged by a creative writing instructor, but, as in his younger years, most of his classes bored him. Instead of following the English Department curriculum, Steinbeck invented his own. He spent hour after hour in the library, reading what interested him rather than the books that were assigned. He worked on his own stories instead of his homework, rarely attended class, and was repeatedly expelled through 1924. Finally, to his parents' disapproval, he quit school altogether in 1925 to pursue a career in writing.

Participation: The Great Depression

Steinbeck spent the next several years traveling and working. In November 1925, he went to New York City, where he found employment first as a construction worker and then as a reporter for the *New York American.* However, the twenty-three-year-old Steinbeck was more interested in meeting women and exploring the city than covering his beat and was soon fired by the newspaper. He attempted to meet publishers while in New York, but after little success and no signs of interest in his short stories, Steinbeck returned to California in August 1926.

Cup of Gold. Discouraged by the rejection of his short stories, Steinbeck decided to focus his attention on writing a novel. He found a job as the caretaker of a Lake Tahoe resort and for the first time in his life concentrated most of his time on his writing. He had an idea for a novel about pirates chasing after a pot of gold, loosely based on Malory's story of King Arthur and the Knights of the Round Table searching for the Holy Grail. Steinbeck's idea was to show the futility of placing value in material things—a theme he often used in his books—and he worked on the story for two years.

Steinbeck finished the book in 1928 but lamented to his good friend from Stanford, Carlton "Duke" Sheffield:

> I finished my novel ... and it was no good. I thought it was going to be good. And it is not.... Isn't it a shame, Duke, that a thing which has as many fine things in it as my *Cup of Gold,* should be, as a

whole, utterly worthless. It is a sorrowful matter to me. (Steinbeck in Valjean, p. 109)

However, Sheffield did not agree with Steinbeck and convinced him to send the manuscript to a publisher. To the young writer's utter amazement, the manuscript was purchased by Robert H. McBride. Steinbeck was paid a $250 advance, and the novel was published in 1929.

Stock market crash. Just as Steinbeck's first novel reached bookstores, the stock market crashed and America plunged into the Great Depression. Literally overnight, millions lost their jobs and life savings when American banks collapsed and closed their doors. With the nation out of work and money, *Cup of Gold* sold only 1,533 copies, and McBride earned less than the $250 he paid Steinbeck. However, Steinbeck made great strides with the novel on another front. Though not a financial success and not Steinbeck's proudest achievement, *Cup of Gold* was solid gold in his parents' eyes. The Steinbecks, who had been deeply disappointed in their son for dropping out of Stanford, were filled with pride over his accomplishment. The novel proved to them that he was a gifted writer and, more importantly, that he was serious about his career. From that point on, the Steinbecks supported their son wholeheartedly in his effort to make a living as a writer.

Monterey. The next decade was as turbulent for Steinbeck as it was for the nation. In 1930 he married Carol Henning, who had been working as his typist and copy editor, and the same year met the man whom he would model many of his most memorable characters after. Ed Ricketts, a marine biologist from Monterey (the positive-minded Doc character in a host of novels, including *Cannery Row*), became Steinbeck's best friend and renewed his interest in nature and the Monterey coast. The newlyweds moved to the Steinbecks' beach cottage in Pacific Grove, on the Monterey Peninsula, and Steinbeck set a goal of writing a novel a year.

Depression years. Though Steinbeck was able to write three novels and several short stories during the next few years, he made little money for his efforts. Income from his books totaled less than $900 after four years of work, and John had to rely on help from his father to keep up his writing. The elder Steinbeck gave the couple

▲ A family on the road during the Great Depression

$25 a month along with free rent at the cottage, his wife worked as a typist, and Steinbeck fished when not writing. But times were tough, and the young Steinbecks struggled to keep food on the table. For Thanksgiving, Steinbeck made a papier-mâché turkey and filled it with sandwiches. Though they could not afford the real thing, the Steinbecks settled for what they had and joked about their feast of "stuffed turkey." They were poor but happy.

Tortilla Flat. The depression made more than a personal impact on Steinbeck's life; it strongly influenced his writing. He felt deep compassion for those less fortunate than he, especially the migrant farm workers who were reduced to hopeless poverty, and began writing about them in his novels. John believed that "when human beings starve, democracy squanders its greatest asset, creative energy," and he wanted to illustrate the talent and human potential he thought America was wasting by not helping ease the depression (Gray, p. 32).

In 1934 he visited Tortilla Flat, a community of Mexican *paisanos* or peasant workers, just outside of Monterey and saw the miserable squalor in which the workers lived. Men, women, and children were crowded into run-down shacks with no plumbing or heating and were forced to work for pennies an hour on nearby farms. Like the migrant workers he had known, the paisanos were proud, hard-working people who were terribly mistreated by their employers. Steinbeck was so moved by their plight that he wrote a novel about them. Published in 1935, it was simply titled *Tortilla Flat*.

Bittersweet success. "Imagine a situation in which employers think 20 cents an hour is over-pay and try to get the standard lower," Steinbeck said in a rare public interview regarding the farm workers. It was his objective through the book to illustrate how damaging that kind of thinking was and to sway popular opinion against the farm owners. To a great extent, Steinbeck accomplished his goal. Though he did not expect the book to be well received because of its controversial subject matter, the novel became a huge success. He was paid $4,000 for the film rights alone—more than he had made in his entire life to date—and won a gold medal from the Commonwealth Club of California as the best native writer. However, Steinbeck cared little for awards, and the success of the book was bittersweet because just five days before it was published, his father died. His mother had died a few years earlier, and now neither parent would ever know their son's achievement.

While the publishing of *Tortilla Flat* changed the Steinbecks' financial situation, it did not alter the writer's beliefs or personality.

▲ A depression–era work camp

He was as convinced as ever that man owed something to his fellow man, as well as to the planet, and he set out to write books to illustrate his convictions.

Hates fame. As in his youth, Steinbeck hated publicity. He shunned fame and would not grant interviews or allow his photograph to be taken. In a revealing moment, he confessed to his publisher: "I am scared to death of popularity. It has ruined everyone I know" (Steinbeck in Fensch, p. 33).

To counteract his newfound fame, Steinbeck purposely set out to write an unpopular book that would expand on the mistreatment of land and workers. Ironically, however, it ended up being his most popular work to date and earned him a Pulitzer Prize.

Grapes of Wrath. Inspired by a series of articles titled *The Harvest Gypsies* that he had written for a San Francisco newspaper, John wrote *The Grapes of Wrath* over a period of four years. The novel, published in 1939, described the struggle of displaced Oklahoma farm workers who migrated to California in droves during the 1930s to escape poverty and search for work. John researched the book for three years, visiting the squatters camps or "Hoovervilles" where the "Okies" lived. There he witnessed the same kind of horrifying conditions he had seen in Tortilla Flat.

> ### Steinbeck on Fame
>
> "Nobody is going to exploit me ... I don't want my face to be known.... As soon as I get over this condition [a sore throat] I'll be out on the road again, sleeping in a ditch somewhere, getting material for another yarn." (Steinbeck in Fensch, p. 20)

But *The Grapes of Wrath* did more than portray the plight of displaced farm workers. It celebrated the human instinct for survival that he saw so clearly during the depression. Through his main character, Okie farmer Tom Joad, Steinbeck expressed his belief that the human spirit would not die, even in the face of the Great Depression, and would ultimately triumph in the end. Joad concludes the book:

> I'll be around in the dark. I'll be everywhere—wherever you look. Wherever there's a fight so hungry people can eat, I'll be there.... An' when our folks eat the stuff they raise an' live in the houses they build—why, I'll be there. (French, p. 98)

The novel was also a plea from Steinbeck for man to help his fellow man and to take care of the planet.

Cannery Row. Steinbeck wrote one more book concerning the depression. Published in 1945, five years after the era ended,

Cannery Row was widely considered one of his finest works. The novel shares the adventures and misadventures of California cannery workers and their friends. In creating it, Steinbeck took a nostalgic journey back to his days as a struggling writer in Monterey during the early 1930s. *Cannery Row* ultimately celebrates life and expresses his belief in the human potential for good. Yet it also illustrates mankind's skewed set of values. As the character Doc puts it:

> It has always seemed strange to me. The things we admire in men, kindness and generosity, openness, honesty, understanding and feeling are the concomitants [companions] of failure in our system. And those traits we detest, sharpness, greed, acquisitiveness, meanness, egotism and self-interest are the traits of success. And while men admire the quality of the first, they love the produce of the second. (Steinbeck, p. 89)

Aftermath

Personal and professional changes. Steinbeck continued to write after the Great Depression, publishing fourteen novels and a host of screenplays, short stories, and theatrical plays until his death on November 20, 1968. He meanwhile embarked on new personal and professional relationships. Steinbeck divorced his first wife in 1942, married twice more, and had two sons, John and Thom. During World War II, he served as a war correspondent, and in the 1950s he wrote speeches for presidential candidate Adlai Stevenson. In 1962 he finally received the Nobel Prize for his lifetime of literary achievement.

Though he wrote on a variety of topics, Steinbeck is perhaps best remembered for his portrayal of the depression in California. With sympathy, humor, and understanding, he illustrated for the world the consequences of human mistreatment and the ability of individuals to overcome oppression. When asked why he wrote about these subjects and what his guiding life philosophy was, Steinbeck answered frankly, "I don't like people to be hurt or hungry or unnecessarily sad. It's just about as simple as that" (Steinbeck in Fensch, p. 27).

Fensch, Thomas. *Conversations with John Steinbeck.* Jackson, Miss.: University Press of Mississippi, 1988.

French, Warren. *John Steinbeck.* Boston: Twayne Publishers, 1975.

Gray, James. *John Steinbeck.* Minneapolis: University of Minnesota Press, 1971.

Steinbeck, John. *Cannery Row.* New York: Viking Press, 1945.

Valjean, Nelson. *John Steinbeck, The Errant Knight.* San Francisco: Chronicle Books, 1975.

Dorothea Lange

1895-1965

Roots. Fighting battles and excelling at her craft were two activities that came naturally to Dorothea Lange. All her life she overcame odds, with her childhood serving as a training ground for her role as one of the nation's first and finest documentary photographers.

Dorothea Margaretta Nutzhorn was born in Hoboken, New Jersey, on May 25, 1895. Her parents, Heinrick "Henry" Martin and Joanna "Joan" Lange Nutzhorn, were children of German immigrants who made their home in the Hoboken shipping port situated across the Hudson River from New York City. Her father ran a thriving law practice in Hoboken while her mother, a former librarian, raised Dorothea and her younger brother, Henry Martin.

Keen eye early on. By age six, Dorothea's maternal grandmother, Sophie Lange, was convinced her granddaughter "had a line in her head" (Meltzer, p, 5). That is, she thought Dorothea highly intelligent and a good judge of quality and character. Grandma Sophie—"Grossmutter"—speaking in her heavy German accent would often show Dorothea the simple perfection of an egg or an orange, saying "of all the things that were beautiful in the world, there was nothing finer than an orange, as a thing" (Meltzer, p, 5). Dorothea knew just what she meant. She too had a strong appreciation of nature and humanity. Like her grandmother, she strove for perfection and appreciated the natural beauty of life.

▲ **Dorothea Lange**

Event: Photographing the Great Depression, 1929–1940.

Role: Photographer Dorothea Lange opened the eyes of a government and a generation to the terrible effects of the Great Depression. Using a camera as her weapon, she waged a successful war for federal aid for victims of the economic disaster and, in the process, produced some of the most highly regarded and moving photographs ever taken.

Polio. When Dorothea turned seven, the family moved upriver to Weehawken, New Jersey. Shortly after their relocation, Dorothea was stricken with polio. With no cure for the disease at the time, Dorothea suffered permanent damage to her right leg, which resulted in a lifelong limp.

The crippling effect of polio on young Dorothea was both a blessing and a curse. Because of her noticeable limp, she was often ridiculed by schoolmates and stared at on the streets. But she also developed deep feelings for fellow disabled persons. As an innocent victim of circumstance herself, Dorothea could sympathize with victims of oppression, and her bout with polio proved to open doors for her as an adult. When she became a photographer, her limp made her nonthreatening to her subjects, and the deep sympathy she developed shone through in the pictures she took.

Father flees. At age twelve, Dorothea suffered a second major blow. Her father, charged with embezzling, or cheating his clients of money, left town and abandoned his family. Dorothea, Henry, and their mother were left to fend for themselves. Hurt and ashamed, Dorothea never spoke of her father again.

Lower East Side. The fragmented family returned to Hoboken to live with Grandma Sophie, and Dorothea's mother went back to work as a librarian. She landed a job at the Lower East Side branch of the New York Public Library and enrolled Dorothea in school in the same neighborhood. The school (P. S. 62) was dominated by Jews, as was the neighborhood. Dorothea had never been to the Lower East Side before, and the crowded noisy streets, sweatshops, and miserable living and working conditions had a profound impact on her. It opened her eyes to the tragic reality of life for many Americans.

Being the only non-Jew among 3,000 Jewish classmates, Dorothea felt like an outsider and observed rather than participated in the activities that went on around her. She greatly admired the Jewish childrens' clear hunger for knowledge and drive to excel in school. But she never felt she quite fit in and found school at P. S. 62 very difficult, both scholastically and socially.

Always the observer. Dorothea's role as an outside observer was further enhanced by daily walks through New York City and visits to her mother's library. She and her mother took the ferry from New Jersey to New York every day, and when Mrs. Nutzhorn worked nights, Dorothea had to make the return trip alone. These solo excursions afforded her the opportunity to see New York's colorful inhabitants and scenery up close. Though parts of the city were very dangerous, Dorothea soon developed the ability to look at others without drawing attention to herself. Because she was "never obviously there," she could watch them without attracting harm to herself. This ability, as well as her lack of fear, would later enable Dorothea to become one of the world's finest documentary photographers.

During visits to her mother's library, Dorothea realized her love of pictures. She spent hours poring through books of photography and art and hung copies of her favorite pictures on the walls of her bedroom.

Dorothea was enchanted by art of all types and recalled having a religious-like experience seeing dancer Isadora Duncan perform in 1908. Duncan's ability to "electrify thousands of people at once" showed Dorothea that great art had the capacity to evoke strong emotional responses and move people to action (Meltzer, p. 14).

Photography begins. Dorothea graduated from high school in 1913 and knew instinctively that she wanted to be a photographer, even though she had never before taken a picture and did not own a camera. However, her mother insisted she enroll in a teacher training college to have an occupation to fall back on should the need arise. As a compromise, Dorothea enrolled in the New York Training School for Teachers and worked in photography studios at night and on weekends.

Arnold Genthe. As luck would have it, Dorothea's first job made her an assistant to famous photographer Arnold Genthe (renowned for his photographs of the San Francisco earthquake of 1906). Genthe encouraged Dorothea's ambitions and taught her everything from lighting to printing to posing subjects. He also told her that in his life as a photographer he never had a dull moment, which was enough to cement Dorothea's determination to enter the occupation. Within a year, she dropped out of the teacher's college and found a job as a portrait photographer for an upscale studio on Third Avenue.

Participation:
Photographing the Great Depression

Call of the West. Happy in her new occupation but bored with her surroundings, Dorothea decided in 1918 to leave home. Along with a childhood friend, she traveled west, stopping in New Orleans, Louisiana; El Paso, Texas; and Los Angeles, California. She finally settled in San Francisco, California. There, Dorothea not only took on a new name—adopting her mother's maiden name "Lange" and dropping Nutzhorn—but began a new life.

Living at the YWCA (Young Women's Christian Association), Lange found a job at a photofinishing shop her second day in San Francisco. She made friends with the shop's customers and with members of the San Francisco Camera Club, which she joined to gain use of their darkroom. A gifted budding photographer and personable young woman, Lange was soon offered the opportunity to start her own portrait studio by one of the camera club's wealthy members.

Sutter studio. Lange opened her studio at 540 Sutter Street, behind an established photofinishing shop, and moved into the room below. Displaying her work in the shop's picture windows, Lange attracted customers who wished to have portraits made of themselves and their families. After meeting and photographing a prominent Jewish woman, Lange became the photographer of choice for the local Jewish community. As in New York, Lange had great admiration for the Jews in San Francisco, whom she felt "were great helpers in building an interesting city" because of their support of education and the arts (Meltzer, p. 47). But this time, she felt part of the community rather than an outsider.

Though her studio became a gathering place for local artists, Lange considered herself a tradeswoman, not an artist. She did not think her work was extraordinary, just useful, and for that she was proud. Lange ran her studio very efficiently and became known for her keen business sense as well as for her afternoon tea parties.

Marriage. By 1920 Lange had met the man she would marry. A painter who frequented her studio, Maynard Dixon was twenty years Lange's senior and a very popular Bay Area artist. They were

▲ Lange's "Migrant Mother," Nipomo, California, 1936

married in Lange's studio on March 21, 1920, she at age twenty-five and he at forty-five. Despite their age difference, the two had much in common, sharing an interest in nature and politics. The first eight years of their marriage saw the birth of two sons: Daniel Rhodes and John Eaglefeather.

The marriage was turbulent and unusual. Dixon traveled often to sketch in the wilderness while Lange continued to work in the city and care for the boys. When Lange joined her husband on trips, the boys were sent to boarding school, and the separation proved difficult for all concerned. But the trips were not all negative for Lange. During a visit to a Hopi Indian reservation in Arizona in 1929, she had a revelation, similar to her earlier religious-like experience of seeing Isadora Duncan. As Lange sat on a rock amidst a thunderstorm in the picturesque Arizona landscape, she realized she must "take pictures and concentrate upon people ... all kinds of people," whether they paid her or not (Meltzer, p. 63). Though she wasn't sure exactly what this meant yet, Lange knew that her life was about to change. She returned to San Francisco to begin the second—and most important—stage of her career.

Stock market crash. Lange reentered the city during the stock market crash of October 1929, which sent the nation into its worst economic depression in history. Like others all around her, she was directly affected by the Great Depression. Customers had no money for portraits, and payment on previously commissioned work was stopped. But most of all, it was the suffering of others that affected Lange. Seeing the thousands of city residents—men, women, and children—standing in breadlines, unemployed, homeless, and hopeless, Lange felt compelled to do something to help. As the crisis worsened, she sprang into action.

Documentary photography begins. Lange took to the streets with her camera and began photographing those hardest hit by the depression. She photographed labor strikes at Fisherman's Wharf, displaced farm workers' camps outside the city, and breadlines set up by the few humanitarians willing and able to provide aid to the needy. She captured the sad and angry faces of the unem-

Lange's "Demonstration Signs," San Francisco, California, 1934 ▶

▲ Lange's "White Angel Breadline," San Francisco, California, 1933

ployed and mistreated; the dirty clothes and desperate smiles of mothers and their children; the sense of longing and lost pride apparent in the families fleeing to California for refuge from the Dust Bowl crisis of the plains states. On these early excursions, Lange took two of her most famous photographs, "White Angel Breadline, 1933" and "Street Demonstration, 1933." She displayed her work in her studio, and soon art critics began to praise her photographs as "art for life's sake" (Meltzer, p. 72). Though Lange did not fully realize it yet, she had embarked on the career she would become most noted for, documentary photographer.

From photos to politics. More than taking great photographs that displayed the human toll of the depression, Lange set out to effect change with her work. Since Franklin Delano Roosevelt had been elected President in 1933, Lange was hopeful that federal aid would be granted to the millions who desperately needed it. Specifically, Lange wanted the government to provide housing for the hundreds of thousands of homeless who lived in squatters camps throughout California and to help the unemployed establish farming and trading

> ### Favorite Quote
>
> Dorothea Lange's favorite quote, which she hung on her darkroom door, was by Francis Bacon. It expresses the goal of her photography, as well as her life's philosophy: "The contemplation of things as they are, without error or confusion, without substitution or imposture, is in itself a nobler thing than a whole harvest of invention." (Time-Life, p. 184)

cooperatives. Such cooperatives would allow them to pool their resources to buy and sell goods, thereby making it easier for them to survive. In 1934, at the first exhibit of Lange's depression photographs, she met a man who would greatly aid her in her effort to influence change.

Paul Taylor. A sociology professor at the University of California at Berkeley, Paul Schuster Taylor saw Lange's photographs and immediately sought to team up with her. Taylor was writing articles to publicize the terrible effects of the depression but felt he needed photographs to accompany his essays. Lange agreed to work with him, and their first effort was published in *Survey Graphic* in September 1934.

The publication of this first article caused an immediate sensation and thrust Lange into national prominence as the first so-called documentary photographer of the depression. She was unimpressed by her newly won fame but hoped to use it to influence the government and win public support for Roosevelt's "New Deal" policies aimed at easing the depression. Together with Taylor, Lange continued to photograph victims of the economic crisis and to compile reports for state and federal relief agencies. The reports, which included dozens of Lange's photographs, were sent everywhere, from magazine offices to the White House. Greatly impressing others with their work, Lange and Taylor were hired first by the State Emergency Relief Administration (SERA) and then by the Federal Emergency Relief Administration (FERA) to produce more reports and suggest remedies to the situation. For the next six years, the two canvassed California and the Southwest documenting the depression.

Hoovervilles

Through her photographs, Lange raised public awareness of squatters camps, or "Hoovervilles," and the homeless and unemployed families that filled them. Hoovervilles were named after President Herbert Hoover, in office during the great stock market crash of 1929. The Hoovervilles consisted of makeshift shacks clustered on rural land, privately and publicly owned. Overcrowded slums, they had no plumbing and were generally unsanitary.

To further her understanding of their situation, Lange both photographed and interviewed her subjects. She felt deeply for their plight and did her best to meet her subjects on common ground without belittling them. She recognized how difficult it was to photograph a proud person against the background of utter poverty, proclaiming that her primary duty was to "register the things about those people that were more important than how poor they were—their pride, their strength, their spirit" (Meltzer, p. 97).

Lange and Taylor's years of effort paid off when President Roosevelt created the first federally funded public housing project in Marysville, California. It was one of Lange's photographs entitled "Migrant Mother" (Time-Life, p. 133) that is credited with convincing the president to rush the migrant farmworkers an additional 20,000 pounds of food.

Aftermath

Partners in work and marriage. Lange continued to work for the federal government until it turned its attention away from the depression and onto World War II in 1940. Her marriage to Dixon broke up in 1935 and shortly thereafter she married her partner,

Paul Taylor. Lange retained custody of her sons and raised them along with Taylor's children. She continued to work as a photographer until her death from cancer on October 11, 1965, at age seventy.

Impact. Lange's haunting photographs of the unemployed and downtrodden not only influenced change in American domestic policy, they remain as visual documents of a tragic chapter in U.S. history. Lange "achieved impact not because she used tricks or unusual techniques but because the depth of her compassion guided her camera. She got people at moments that told about their lives and their feelings" (Time-Life, p. 184).

For More Information

Meltzer, Milton. *Dorothea Lange: A Photographer's Life.* New York: Farrar, Straus, Giroux, 1978.

Schuneman, R. Smith. *Photographic Communication.* London: Focal Press, 1972.

Time-Life. *Great Photographers.* Alexandria, Va.: Time-Life Books, 1983.

Lange's Description of Good Documentary Photography

"A documentary photograph is not a factual photograph per se. It carries with it another thing, a quality [in the subject] that the artist responds to. It is a photograph which carries the full meaning of the episode or the circumstance or the situation that can only be revealed ... by this other quality [of the subject]. There is no war between the artist and the documentary photographer. He has to be both." (Lange in Meltzer, p. 83)

Eleanor Roosevelt

1884–1962

Personal Background

Anna Eleanor Roosevelt was born in New York City on October 11, 1884, to Anna Hall and Elliott Roosevelt. Her parents, attractive and socially prominent, descended from families of considerable wealth and influence in America. Elliott's brother, Teddy, would later become president of the United States, and Anna's relatives were one of the original "400" aristocratic families of the United States (Cook, p. 22).

A difficult childhood. Though Eleanor grew up surrounded by wealth and privilege, she had a lonely and sad childhood. Her mother has been described as a very beautiful but cold and physically weak woman, while her father was an alcoholic who spent most of his time away from the family. With her mother often bedridden and her father routinely in Europe, Eleanor was left alone or shipped off to relatives much of the time. She had few friends because her parents insisted she not attend school and be tutored at home. Given this background, Eleanor developed a very real fear of abandonment and became a serious, lonely, and self-reliant young girl.

Competition. Tall but not traditionally beautiful, Eleanor was continually reminded by her mother of her awkward appearance. She felt shut out and unloved by Mrs. Roosevelt, who called her

▲ **Eleanor Roosevelt**

Event: The Great Depression, 1929–1940.

Role: Eleanor Roosevelt redefined the role of First Lady by using her position to help create and promote government-sponsored programs during the Great Depression and beyond. She became the "conscience of the New Deal," pushing for aid and employment for women and minorities.

"Granny" because of her somber and "old-fashioned" nature (Cook, p. 39). Aloof and seemingly critical of Eleanor, her mother appeared to be an enemy to the child.

Inventing a father. Probably because she felt so distant from her mother, Eleanor romanticized her father and the memories she had of him. She created elaborate fantasies about his life on the road and expressed the belief that "he dominated my life as long as he lived, and was the love of my life" (Roosevelt, *The Autobiography*, p. 5). But, though he showered fondness on his daughter when he was home and sent her many loving letters, his parenting, like her mother's, proved to be quite weak. The perfect father that Eleanor spoke of did not reflect the real person who seldom even spent Christmas at home.

Charity work. Whatever problems the Roosevelts may have had as parents, they did teach their daughter the value of charity. Eleanor's mother regularly hosted charity balls, and her father contributed food to homeless "newsboys" from the streets of New York and money to one of the earliest orthopedic surgeons working to help crippled children. Eleanor was often sent to soup kitchens to feed the poor. She learned to help those unable to help themselves, a habit that Eleanor would practice for the remainder of her life.

Tragedy and abandonment continue. Tragedy and abandonment seemed to mark Eleanor's entire childhood. When she turned six, her father was sent to a sanitarium because of his alcoholism and a "nervous breakdown." Shortly thereafter, Mrs. Roosevelt became very ill, experiencing such severe headaches that she could not get out of bed. With her father permanently away, Eleanor for the first time felt that her mother needed her. She cared for Mrs. Roosevelt daily, spending long hours rubbing her forehead and sleeping at the foot of her bed. For Eleanor, this time with her mother was invaluable. She recalled, "the feeling I was useful was perhaps the greatest joy I experienced" (Cook, p. 69). However, the "joy" did not last long. When Eleanor was eight, both Mrs. Roosevelt and Eleanor's younger brother, Elliott, died of diphtheria. Two years later, Mr. Roosevelt died, and Eleanor was sent to live with her grandmother in Tivoli, New York.

School. From age fifteen to eighteen (1899–1902), Eleanor attended boarding school outside of London, England. She recalled the period as "the happiest years of my life" (Cook, p. 4). Finally surrounded by friends and supportive authority figures, Eleanor blossomed at school. One particularly influential person was an instructor named Marie Souvestre, who taught Eleanor to be bold, assertive, and independent. Souvestre was active and encouraged Eleanor to be the same, stating flatly "Never be bored; and you will never be boring" (Cook, p. 4). It was advice Eleanor took to heart. Returning to New York for her coming-out party, she was a changed, highly confident, independent young woman.

Society, marriage, and family. A "coming out" was a way of preparing young women for what was considered a proper entrance into society. Dressed in a short dress, which accentuated her thin, graceful figure, Eleanor attended several parties and met eligible young men. This almost sent her into "a state of nervous collapse" (Roosevelt, *The Autobiography,* p. 37). Clearly the life of a society belle was not for her.

During this time, Eleanor began dating her future husband, Franklin Delano Roosevelt (FDR). He was a distant cousin whom she had met a few times before. In 1903 FDR proposed, and two years later they were married. Their St. Patrick's Day wedding was widely publicized because President Theodore Roosevelt gave the bride away. Reporters swarmed around the president and newlyweds, the new Mrs. Roosevelt receiving a quick education on being in the public eye.

During the next decade, Roosevelt had six children, one of whom died of influenza after only a few months. Besides learning how to be a mother, she learned to be a public figure. With FDR being a career politician, she was constantly in the limelight. "Politics does not excite me. It never did. I take things as they come" (Roosevelt in Lash, p. 336). In keeping with this attitude, Roosevelt would over the years take all the attention in stride. She in fact came to enjoy it and learned to make the most of her position.

War and Washington. During World War I, Roosevelt became an active charity organizer. She set up a Red Cross canteen that served food to soldiers passing through Washington, D.C., by train. Roosevelt stayed busy during and after the war years. While her husband was preoccupied with his job change from senator to

▲ Roosevelt and three of her children

assistant secretary of the navy, she visited hospitals for wounded and insane soldiers. Noticing that a hospital was overcrowded and understaffed, Roosevelt used her influence to improve conditions there. She meanwhile gazed at dead and dying soldiers, who brought home to her how much she hated war. Roosevelt often said, "There are only two unacceptable four-letter words: Hate and Wars" (Roosevelt in Cook, p.2).

Turbulence continues. Like her childhood, Roosevelt's marriage was filled with drama. In 1918 she discovered that FDR was having an affair with his social secretary, Lucy Mercer. Deeply hurt, Roosevelt offered her husband a divorce, but the two decided to stay together. A few years later, a second tragedy occurred when FDR was struck by polio and lost the use of his legs. Though devastating, both events served to make his wife tough and assertive and opened her life to new adventure. At age thirty-seven, Roosevelt began a new chapter in her life. She set out to make a difference in society, becoming more active than ever in social reform.

FDR worked on his recovery, encouraged by his wife. Meanwhile, Roosevelt focused on her own political agenda. She joined the League of Women Voters and the New York Women's City Club, and became the leading woman politician of the New York State Democratic Party. She raised money, organized events, and brought her groups' concerns to her husband, who helped enact policies in their favor when possible. His wife especially pushed for child labor laws, a forty-eight hour work week for women, legalized birth control, and government-subsidized housing for the urban working classes. No group was to be left out if she had any say in the matter.

Fast friends. During the 1920s, Roosevelt became closely associated with Nancy Cook and Marion Dickerman. The three became co-owners of Todhunter School for Girls in New York City, and Roosevelt taught there several days a week. She also became editor of the *Women's Democratic News.* During most of her years in the Governor's Mansion and the White House, Roosevelt would remain close friends with these women. She would also develop other extremely close friendships over the years—with bodyguard Earl Miller, with newswoman Lorena Hickok, and later with her physician David Gurewitsch.

Participation: The Great Depression

New Deal. In 1928 Roosevelt helped FDR become governor of New York, and the following year the couple faced their greatest challenge yet: the onset of the Great Depression. First as governor in New York, and by 1932 as president in the White House, FDR enacted far-reaching programs to ease the depression. His wife supported him all along the way, carving out an active role for herself. The package of programs, called the New Deal, aimed to provide immediate relief for millions of homeless and out-of-work Americans. New Deal programs were developed to employ the unemployed, increase government spending in order to stimulate the economy, and enact changes that would prevent bank collapses like the ones that had led to the depression. Here, said the First Lady, was "an opportunity for government to render a permanent service to the general happiness of the working man and woman and their families. This is what we mean as I see it by the "new deal" (Roosevelt in Lash, p. 390).

Eleanor to the rescue. While FDR concentrated on pushing his plans through the courts and Congress, the First Lady made sure the New Deal included aid for *all* Americans. Her primary concerns were employment for women and youth and programs that would help all the people who were not well represented in the government. Having lost free use of his legs, FDR had fortunately married a woman who happily served as his "eyes and ears": Roosevelt traveled, lectured, met with leaders, and spoke her mind to groups throughout the country. She served as a liaison, or go-between, speaking to the president on behalf of interest groups such as the NAACP, the American Youth Congress, and the Tenant Farmers Union. Roosevelt tended to go further than her husband on issues. For example, FDR felt that in starting work projects for unemployed writers, actors, and musicians, the government might be acting too dangerously for his own political survival. His wife, however, fully supported such government-sponsored projects.

Roosevelt breaks ground for women. The most active First Lady to that date, Roosevelt served as a role model for other women. She was also largely responsible for bringing women to positions of power in her husband's administration. She used her influence to get more than fifty women appointed to federal and state government offices and encouraged women to increase their presence within political parties. With her help, more than 100,000 women had been hired by 1933 to fill positions in her husband's new government organizations.

Roosevelt was almost single-handedly responsible for the

acceptance of women as serious political journalists. She created the White House Women's Press Corps and made herself available only to them. If a publication was to cover the activities of the First Lady or wanted to attend one of her press conferences, they had to send a female reporter. Roosevelt later remarked on her activities during the 1930s: "I became a much more ardent citizen and feminist than anyone ... would have dreamed possible" (Roosevelt in Flemion and O'Conner, p. 87).

It's Up to the Women. In 1933 Roosevelt wrote her first book, *It's Up to the Women.* It combined advice on menus and household budgeting with calls for women to lead the way in social reform. For the United States to survive the depression, the book argued, women had to become the crusaders in society. Roosevelt put her own advice into practice. Under the Agricultural Adjustment Act, for example, the government intended to pay farmers to plow under cotton and to slaughter piglets so that there would be less of a supply and farm prices would rise. Roosevelt objected, pointing to another, more useful solution to the problem.

> "While it may be necessary to raise farm prices," said the First Lady, "I do think some way should be found to take things which are not needed and give them to people who, in any case, will not be able to buy them. Why do you dump all these little pigs into the Mississippi when there are thousands of people in the country starving? Why not give the meat away to them?" (Roosevelt in Lash, pp. 383–84)

After her questions, the extra farm products were fed to the hungry instead of being thrown away. She talked to others in office about work projects for the unemployed, especially women and young people. Her speeches were addressed largely to these groups, whom she saw as more willing to accept drastic change than men. Americans, said Roosevelt, were going through a nonviolent revolution. To succeed, they would have to accept higher taxes and other changes. These were unpopular views, yet she shared and won support for them.

A typical day at the White House. In the daily goings-on at the White House, Roosevelt engaged in activities that helped build and sustain confidence in her husband's administration. Her suite lay next to Franklin's. Her day began at 7:30 A.M. with exercise of some sort, typically a horseback ride. After breakfast, she worked with her secretary on the volumes of mail addressed to her. About fifty letters a day were selected for her immediate attention. Loving all the mail, Roosevelt either made a note of how she wanted her secretary to reply to each letter or else dictated or wrote the reply herself. She worked on various projects as the day wore on, from writing newspaper articles, to giving afternoon teas for dignitaries, to dealing with the children. At dinner there were almost always guests whom she was in charge of entertaining. She afterwards went to her desk to deal with her mail again, then took her dogs for a walk around the White House circle before turning in for the evening. The First Lady next stopped in her husband's room to say good night. She would sit on his bed and chat for a time, this often being her only chance to tell him what was on her mind. So busy was she that she "would gladly have seen the days so arranged that one never had to sleep" (Roosevelt in Lash, p. 377). By the end of the first 100 days, she, as well as her husband, had captured the imagination and the hearts of many citizens in America.

> ## Fortune in Misfortune
>
> If the depression taught Americans any one thing, the First Lady hoped it was the lesson that in their complicated world to survive "they must survive together.... If we can get back to the feeling that we are responsible for each other, these years of depression would have been worth while." (Roosevelt in Lash, p. 383)

Arthurdale. The First Couple had a dream and a scheme to put into effect. They believed that life in America would be vastly improved if industry could be brought to rural areas so farmers had work to occupy them in wintertime. This would relieve both rural poverty and congested cities.

Miners in West Virginia were desperate. Out of work, they lived in hovels and slums without hope. The president decided the government should sponsor the building of a planned community, which put into practice the idea of bringing industry to rural areas. Some poverty-stricken miners in West Virginia would be resettled in the first planned community, called Arthurdale. Arthurdale became the First Lady's pet project. The government would buy the land, build the houses, and purchase the livestock and farm machinery, and the settlers would have thirty years in which to repay their share of the cost. Wholeheartedly behind the project, the First Lady visited the miners in their hovels and slums and held their babies in her lap. She interested herself in every detail of Arthurdale, from selecting the 200 families to be resettled (the first ones arrived in June 1934) to shopping for refrigerators.

The industry first suggested was a furniture factory that made post-office equipment. Roosevelt herself knew something about furniture factories. She already owned one with her two partners, Cook and Dickerman, on her husband's family estate in Hyde Park, New York. Removed from the main house was an area called Val-Kill, where Roosevelt, with FDR's consent, built a retreat of her own. She lived there from Memorial Day until September 30, and the furniture factory, which was run mainly by Cook, was located nearby.

In Roosevelt's eyes, the miners were casualties of the depression and deserved to have the government resettle them and bring industry into Arthurdale. Congress, however, objected to the government's involving itself in the furniture factory and refused to advance money for it. In the end, Roosevelt's attention to Arthurdale in the 1930s proved to poor Americans that the government really did care about their misfortunes, but with the coming of World War II, Congress withdrew support for planned communities altogether. There were by then ninety-nine of them in the country.

Radio, lectures, and the newspapers. While her husband was president, Roosevelt earned money that she poured into pet projects. In 1934 she returned to radio, giving talks for $500 a minute. She kept none of the money for herself, having it paid to the American Friends Service Committee (Quakers) to spend at her direction. She also signed a speaking contract in 1935, hiring a manager who arranged lectures for her at the rate of $1,000 per lecture.

In 1935 Roosevelt began a daily newspaper column. Called "My Day," it was a diary of 400 to 500 words on the small human happenings of her life. She mostly stayed away from the subject of politics for her husband's sake, yet the column contributed greatly to the public's confidence in their president. Once, for example, after the Supreme Court made a series of judgments cutting down New Deal measures, she wrote a "My Day" article about a family swim in the White House pool, showing the nation a president who was not angry at the Supreme Court but took defeats calmly in stride and moved on.

> Washington, January 8—Needless to say, the big thing in the past twenty-four hours has been the Supreme Court decision....
>
> It seemed to me ... we would have a rather quiet and subdued swim at 6 o'clock.... I dropped my wrapper, plunged into the water and, swimming about very quietly, I inquired hesitatingly how they all were feeling.
>
> To my complete surprise, instead of either discouragement or even annoyance, I was told that everyone was feeling fine, and on that note we finished our swim. Then we went up to dress for dinner and the family met again at the dinner table.
>
> I prepared for some candid opinions.... Instead I found that we were discussing ... the history of the past....
>
> [Later] my husband plunged into work on a speech and I went off to work on an article. Midnight came and bed for all, and all that was said was "Good night, sleep well, pleasant dreams."
>
> With the new day comes new strength and new thoughts. (Roosevelt, *My Day,* pp. 6–7)

The First Lady's Lectures

Roosevelt restricted her lectures to five main topics:

   Relationship of the Individual to the Community

   Problems of Youth

   The Mail of a President's Wife

   Peace

   A Typical Day at the White House

Roosevelt would go on writing "My Day" for twenty-six years, beyond the depression, World War II, and her husband's death.

Civil rights. Roosevelt helped arrange a meeting at the White House of black leaders in 1934, at which it was agreed that extending aid programs of the New Deal to black Americans should have a higher priority than the problem of segregation. Lynch mobs reappeared in the depression, and an antilynching bill was brought before Congress. The First Lady supported the bill, though her husband, worried about losing the backing of Southern congressmen, withheld his support.

As the 1930s were coming to a close, the First Lady's stand against segregation became bolder. While attending a conference in

Atlanta, Georgia, she moved her chair to the middle of an aisle that separated the blacks from the whites. In perhaps her most famous public statement, Roosevelt resigned from the Daughters of the American Revolution (DAR) women's group after it refused to let African American contralto Marian Anderson sing at Constitution Hall in 1939. Roosevelt afterward supported a free concert at the Lincoln Memorial in which Anderson sang for over 75,000 people.

World War II and beyond. Throughout World War II and beyond, Roosevelt continued to voice her hatred of war. When FDR was elected to his fourth term in 1944, she worried about his health. Her worst fear became a reality in April 1945. While in a meeting, she received an urgent call to return to the White House immediately. There, she received the news that her husband had died in Warm Springs, Georgia. She told Harry Truman that he was now president and began the long journey by train to Warm Springs. While accompanying his body on the funeral train from Georgia back to Washington, D.C., Roosevelt sat at a window and observed the thousands of people gathered near the tracks and at the passing stations. Her time in the White House had ended, but she was to remain powerful and active in the country and the world.

No Time for Self-Pity

"It is a wonderful thing to keep your mind always full of something that is worth while doing. If you can get hold of something that you feel is going to help the people around you, you'll find that you're so busy trying to add one more thing to it that you won't have time to be sorry for yourself." (Roosevelt in Lash, p. 420)

Roosevelt went to work as a U.S. delegate at the United Nations in 1946, after which President Truman called her "First Lady of the World." Writing into the last year of her life, she also continued to turn out books and articles. Roosevelt suffered a stroke and died on November 7, 1962. She was laid to rest next to her husband in Hyde Park, New York.

For More Information

Cook, Blanche Weisen. *Eleanor Roosevelt.* New York: Viking Press, 1992.

Flemion, Jesse, and Colleen M. O'Conner, eds. *Eleanor Roosevelt: An American Journey.* San Diego: San Diego State University Press, 1987.

Lash, Joseph P. *Eleanor: The Years Alone.* New York: Norton, 1972.

Roosevelt, Eleanor. *The Autobiography of Eleanor Roosevelt.* New York: Harper & Brothers Publishers, 1937.

Roosevelt, Eleanor. *Eleanor Roosevelt's My Day.* Vol. 1. New York: Pharos Books, 1989.

World War II

1933
Adolf Hitler comes to power in Germany.

1938
Dorothy Thompson comments about events in prewar Europe on weekly American radio broadcasts.

1941
Japan bombs Pearl Harbor. The United States declares war on Japan, Germany, and Italy. **Dwight D. Eisenhower** plans war strategy.

1940
Congress passes the Selective Service and Training Act, beginning the first peacetime draft in U.S. history.

1939
Germany invades Poland. **Felix Frankfurter** is nominated to the U.S. Supreme Court.

1941
A. Philip Randolph threatens a civil rights march on Washington; Executive Order 8802 bans racial discrimination in U.S. defense factories.

1942
J. Robert Oppenheimer takes charge of laboratory at Los Alamos, New Mexico, to create the atomic bomb.

1942
President Franklin D. Roosevelt issues Executive Order 9066, confining Japanese Americans in concentration camps.

1942
News of Nazi extermination of Jews reaches President Roosevelt.

1945
Japanese are released from U.S. concentration camps. Atomic bombs are dropped on Hiroshima and Nagasaki. War ends.

1944
Eisenhower directs Allied forces in Normandy Invasion.

1943
Minoru Yasui's case against the U.S. government reaches the Supreme Court. Race riot erupts in Detroit, Michigan; zoot-suit riots in Los Angeles, California.

WORLD WAR II

World War II began September 1, 1939, with Germany's invasion of Poland, and lasted until August 14, 1945, with Japan's surrender to American forces. Involved in nonmilitary ways from the beginning, the United States was a latecomer to the fighting. It entered the conflict two years into the war, on December 8, 1941, the day after Japan bombed Pearl Harbor, Hawaii. At first the Americans declared war only on Japan, but on December 11 Germany declared war on the United States. The United States then joined with the Allies (mainly Great Britain, France, and the Soviet Union) against the Axis powers (mainly Germany, Italy, and Japan).

The immediate cause of the war was territorial expansion by Germany and Japan. And there were multiple effects. The war had a huge impact on all parts of U.S. society, from the economy, to radio, to relations between ethnic groups. It lifted the United States out of the Great Depression, putting everyone back to work until American industry was producing 50 percent of all the world's goods.

At the same time, there was an enormous price to pay for this recovery from the depression. Beside the billions each nation spent on the war, it cost around 30 million lives.

Close to 300,000 Americans died in the fighting, yet the United States fared better than other nations. Bombing civil-

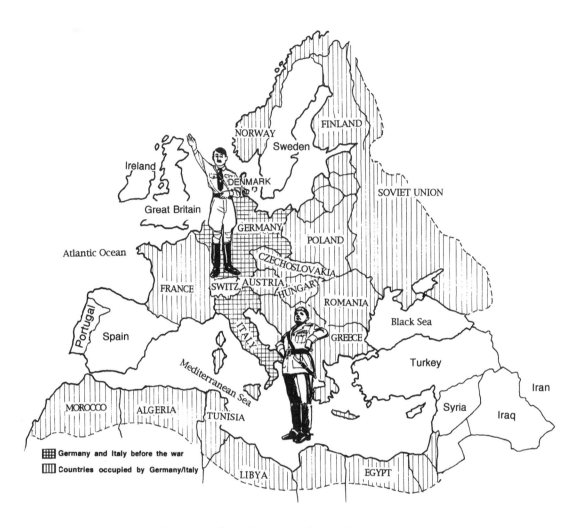

▲ Conquest of the German-Italian Axis

ians became an accepted policy in this war. But, fought oceans away from the United States, all the bombs (except for the ones dropped on Pearl Harbor) landed on foreign soil.

The war effort united Americans as never before. The enemy, Germany under Adolf Hitler, represented evil. It stood for violence, the idea of a superior, racially pure German people and total authority in government. In contrast, U.S. President Franklin Roosevelt declared that the Americans were fighting for four freedoms: freedom of speech, freedom of worship, freedom from want, and freedom from fear. This was a battle against racism (the idea that one race is superior) abroad, which would precipitate the battle against racism at home.

Roosevelt set out to end the war as quickly as possible, a goal that depended largely on his generals. Supreme among them was **Dwight D. Eisenhower,** who commanded first the campaign against the Axis powers in Northern Africa and later the invasion of Normandy, France, that led to Allied victory in Europe. It was the first time an American general would lead world forces in military campaigns. Able to get different people to cooperate with one another, Eisenhower cared deeply about the troops and showed it. Assisting him on the battlefield were U.S. generals such as George Patton and enlisted men, or GIs (which stands for "government issues"), from all American ethnic groups.

The U.S. Army unit whose men received the most awards was the 442nd Infantry Combat Team, made up entirely of Japanese Americans. Mexican Americans joined the military in great numbers, and many Native Americans were recruited for special service in the Marine Corps. Black soldiers were segregated into all-black units, with whites serving as the high-ranking officers. Altogether their contributions gave the lie to racist policies that existed in the United States.

African Americans took action to combat racism at home. **A. Philip Randolph,** a black leader, threatened to lead 100,000 African Americans on a march on Washing-

Comparison Chart– World War II Losses		
Nation Total Forces	**Military Deaths**	**Civilian Deaths**
United States 14,900,000	292,100	68*
Great Britain 6,200,000	397,760	65,000
France 6,000,000	210,670	108,000
Soviet Union 25,000,000	7,500,000	10,000,000+
Germany 12,500,000	2,850,000	500,000
Italy 4,500,000	77,500	40,000+
Japan 7,000,000	1,506,000	300,000

*At Pearl Harbor. Other totals are estimates adapted from R. Ernest Dupuy and Trevor N. Dupuy, eds., *The Harper Encyclopedia of Military History* (New York: HarperCollins, 1993).

▲ Conquest of Japan

ton during wartime to protest inequalities in America. Though alarmed, Roosevelt refused to desegregate the armed forces. He did, however, make a bargain. In return for the march's being called off, he issued Executive Order 8802, which banned discrimination in U.S. government offices and all factories that supplied war goods to the government.

Fearful of the Japanese in America, who looked like the enemy, the U.S. government violated their rights. Roosevelt, responding in 1942 to public pressure, issued Executive Order 9066, which would send about 110,000 Japanese to U.S. concentration camps. Protesting that the order was unconstitutional, a Japanese American lawyer, **Minoru Yasui** appealed his case to the Supreme Court. The camps, isolated in dry inland spots and surrounded by barbed wire, were grim centers with communal toilets, dining, bathing, and sleeping facilities. After issuing the order that confined the Japanese, the Roosevelt administration granted camp leaves to 35,000, mostly to serve in the U.S. army. Public opinion kept the camps in existence, however, until 1945.

There were other ethnic shifts in location during the war. Taking jobs in war industries and on farms, blacks and Mexicans moved to different areas. Race riots broke out in Detroit, Michigan; Mobile, Alabama; Los Angeles, California; Beaumont, Texas; and New York City. In Detroit, twenty-five blacks were killed in a riot, and property valued at over $2 million was destroyed. Young Mexicans of the time wore "zoot suits"—long loose coats with padded shoulders, ballooned pants, a wide-brimmed hat and a watch chain. Contact with whites brought the "zoot suit" riots, in which, for the most part, U.S. sailors and marines beat up young Mexicans.

Meanwhile, few Jews marked for Hitler's death camps were admitted to the United States. As early as 1933, **Felix Frankfurter** appealed to Secretary of State Cordell Hull to relax immigration laws, which kept out Jewish refugees. During the war, Frankfurter, a Supreme Court justice, became involved with some key cases and had great behind-the-scenes influence with Roosevelt. But his early appeal to relax immigration laws remained unsatisfied. The policy toward admitting Jews reflected prejudices in American society, just as segregated troops and concentration camps for the Japanese did. Prejudice against Jews had mounted in the Great Depression before the war, and there was widespread fear of a mass of Jews immigrating to the United States.

By November 1942, information had reached the United

▲ A wartime factory

States that the Nazis were systematically murdering the Jews. Still, the official position was that the best way to help save them from the Holocaust—that is, the Nazi attempt to wipe out Europe's Jews—was to win the war as quickly as possible. So rescue schemes were turned down, although later the official position was greatly criticized. After the war, details of the Nazis' anti-Jewish policy became more fully known. And the belief spread that the United States could have acted sooner and done more for victims of the Holocaust.

Americans tuned in to about 4.5 hours of radio a day during the war, listening to news commentators such as

Dorothy Thompson. Thompson, who battled Nazism abroad and in the United States, became one of many American women who participated more fully than ever before in war. For the first time, in World War II, women formed branches of the army and the navy, and they took jobs by the thousands in industry. "Rosie the Riveter," a character in a popular song, came to stand for the woman who rolled up her shirt sleeves and went to work for the war. Inequalities between men and women would continue to exist, however. They earned less than men in the factories, and they would be sent home after the war and again restricted to the roles of wife and mother.

Realizing America could not fight a full-scale war against both Germany and Japan, Roosevelt and his advisers had concentrated first on victory in Europe. Russia's leader, Joseph Stalin, pressured him to invade Western Europe and deflect some of the destruction being laid on Eastern Europe. After two years of delays by Roosevelt and British leader Winston Churchill, this was done. The invasion, a victory for the Allies, led to the end of the war in Europe. But the Americans and Japanese continued to do battle in the Pacific. Roosevelt pressed Stalin for Russia's help there. If Japan could be defeated without the United States invading its mainland, a great number of American lives would be saved.

Meanwhile, a secret team of scientists under **J. Robert Oppenheimer** worked at using forces in the atom to create a bomb with enormous destructive power. In 1945 the United States used two of these atomic bombs on the Japanese cities of Hiroshima (August 6—75,000 killed) and Nagasaki (August 9—39,000 killed). On August 14, three months after Germany, Japan surrendered and World War II came to an end.

Dwight D. Eisenhower

1890-1969

Personal Background

Tough kids. The six Eisenhower boys in Dwight's family had a reputation in Abilene, Kansas, as tough kids from the poor section in the south of the town. They were quick to defend themselves against any slurs or challenges from the more well-to-do boys to the north. And they were called to this defense often, for the family was poor, exceedingly poor.

Family. The Eisenhowers belonged to a fundamentalist Christian group called the River Brethren. The Brethren had lived in Pennsylvania and earned their livelihood mostly as farmers. Jacob Eisenhower, Dwight's grandfather, moved to Kansas and bought farmland in Dickinson County. He was so successful that he planned to give each of his children 160 acres and $2,000 at marriage. He wanted each child, including David (Dwight's father), to have an opportunity to be a successful farmer.

Not interested in farming, however, David was allowed to enter the small campus of Lane University where he met Ida Elizabeth Stover. Ida's family, like the Eisenhowers, had come to America from Germany and belonged to a fundamentalist Christian group, this one in Virginia. Also like the Eisenhowers, the Stovers were successful farmers, but at age twelve, Ida became an orphan. Two brothers took their inheritances and moved to Kansas, and when

▲ **Dwight D. Eisenhower**

Event: The Allied invasion of Europe in World War II.

Role: Dwight D. Eisenhower was called to Washington as a war planner on the staff of Commander in Chief George Marshall shortly after the bombing of Pearl Harbor in Hawaii. He played a major role in planning the attack on German positions in Europe and was then assigned to command the troops charged with carrying out the plans.

Ida was twenty-one, she followed them. In 1883 she enrolled in Lane University, where she met David. The two were married in 1885.

Jacob gave the newlyweds 160 acres of land and $2,000, as planned, but David was not swayed to farming by the wedding present. Instead he mortgaged the land to raise another $2,000 and joined Milton Good in opening a general store in Hope, not far from Abilene.

David Dwight Eisenhower. For three years, the store seemed to be succeeding. The couple had their first son, Arthur, in 1884, and two years later, Ida was about to bear a second child when the store went bankrupt. With no money or land left, David decided to start over far from Abilene. Leaving Ida and Arthur, he moved to Denison, Texas, and found work with a railroad for $40 a month. By 1889, David had enough money put aside to bring Ida, Arthur, and the second son, Edgar, to Denison. The family was together again, but far from their religious group and struggling to survive on David's earnings. Conditions became even more difficult when, on October 14, 1890, a third son was born. He was named David Dwight Eisenhower but his mother called him Dwight and he would later reverse his given names. (Ida called him Dwight because she hated nicknames and Dwight could not be shortened as David could to Dave. However, Dwight's classmates still found a way to nickname him, shortening his last name to Ike. Dwight was "Little Ike"; Edgar was "Big Ike.")

Back in Abilene, the River Brethren were about to open a new creamery. The foreman was to be Chris Musser, David's brother-in-law. When Musser invited David to come home to Abilene and work in the creamery, the five Eisenhowers moved again. David started at the creamery for "less than fifty dollars a month" (Lyon, p. 36). On this meager salary, the family, soon to include six boys, barely scratched out a living.

Ida was at least as strong an influence on her boys as was their father and easily as devout in her religion. She taught them that the only way to get what they wanted in life was to work for it. When Dwight was ten, she advised him, "If you want an education, go out and get it" (Gunther, p. 52). The boys attended public school, filling up the rest of their hours with work. They raised vegetables for the family meals and took outside jobs to help support the household.

Their poverty sometimes led the boys to dress differently from others in school. Dwight was the only boy in the fifth grade to show up for the class picture wearing overalls. For a short time, he even had to wear his mother's shoes to school because the family could not afford new shoes for everyone. Their lack of money made the Eisenhower boys the subjects of childhood teasing, and Dwight gained a reputation for his ability to fight.

Education. Otherwise, Dwight Eisenhower's early life was not much different from that of a typical farm boy in Kansas. He found time to engage in sports and to play pranks on the neighbors, meanwhile earning average or better grades in school, working on the family's small farm plot, and selling some of the vegetables to more well-to-do neighbors. The routine of hard work and the strong guidance from his mother led to success for Dwight and his brothers in later life.

In high school, Little Ike's great interest was sports. His football coaches considered the six-foot, 160-pound running back just an average player. But he loved the game and was popular with his teammates. Along with football, Dwight played baseball and was head of a new "athletic association" formed by the high school students to gain community support for the athletic program.

The Eisenhower boys all had hopes of improving their lot. Edgar (who would become a lawyer) and Dwight wanted to go on to college, but there was not enough money for this. Their solution to the problem was cooperation among the brothers. Edgar and Dwight planned to take turns; each would work one year and attend school the next. Edgar went to school first and Dwight took a job working with his father at the Belle Springs Creamery. For a while, his hours were 6:00 P.M. to 6:00 A.M. seven days a week—an eighty-four-hour work week.

One of Dwight's friends at this time was Everett Hazlett, Jr., the son of a doctor. Hazlett had decided to become a naval officer and encouraged Dwight to join him in taking the exams. In those days, examinations for the naval academy at Annapolis and the military academy at West Point were given at the same time. Dwight's parents were very much opposed to war, so it was a difficult decision for him. On the one hand, he needed the financial help that would come from passing the exams to get through college; on the other hand, he knew his parents would not approve. In the end, financial need won out. Dwight took not just one exam but the examinations for both Annapolis and West Point. He had decided that he really wanted a career in the navy.

West Point. The year off from school had, however, made him too old to start at Annapolis. Instead, after passing both exams, Dwight Eisenhower was admitted to West Point. He enrolled there as a freshman in 1911. In those days, West Point cadets were very sternly disciplined. They were not allowed to have any money and were confined to the campus. Cadets received only one leave in four years, a two-week furlough after the second year. It was a tense atmosphere in which his ability to get along with nearly everyone helped a great deal. Benefiting from the stern discipline at home, Eisenhower adjusted to West Point more easily than most of the other freshman.

There was always football to occupy his attention. By this time, Eisenhower had put on muscle and carried a strong and agile 175 pounds on his six-foot frame. Ike became an outstanding, slashing running back for West Point while managing to maintain above-average grades. Sometime in his second year, the Army played a game against the powerful Carlisle Indians (whose star player was Jim Thorpe) and Ike hurt his knee. Not fully healed by the next game, he broke the same knee and his football career ended abruptly.

Without football, Eisenhower began to lose interest in West Point. He maintained his slightly above-average grades due mostly to his interest in history and English, but now he began to fill his hours playing cards and smoking—both forbidden by the academy. As a result, his last three years were spotted with demerits. He also reentered sports, first as a cheerleader, then as assistant coach of the freshman football players. His achievement at West Point was, like his achievements earlier, not spectacular except that in his last year he managed to earn 100 demerits. Of the 212 students in his beginning class, 168 graduated from West Point in 1915. Eisenhower ranked sixty-first in his class, his placement lowered because of his conduct.

Marriage. His ranking at West Point did not merit any choice assignments in the regular army. After graduating, Second Lieutenant Eisenhower was assigned to the infantry and sent to Fort Sam Houston in Texas. Meanwhile, the pretty and lively Mamie Doud was visiting San Antonio, where her father, a wealthy cattleman, had rented a house for the winter. Ike and Mamie met at a party and soon fell in love. They were wed July 1, 1916 and would remain married until Eisenhower's death. Their family would grow with the births of two sons, David Dwight and John Sheldon. David died early, at the age of four, while John followed in his father's footsteps, advancing to West Point and a military career.

Military trainer. By 1917, when the United States was about to enter World War I, Eisenhower had risen to the rank of captain, mostly on his ability as an instructor. He knew how to discipline his men and gain their friendship. He was assigned during the war to Camp Colt near Gettysburg, Pennsylvania, a training camp for the infantry. After the war, he was promoted to major (1920) and sent back to school to learn about the new tank warfare. Two years later, still without a real career goal, he was assigned to Panama in Central America to serve under General Fox Conner. It was one of the most fortunate turns of his military career.

Fox Conner. Conner was a dedicated military officer. Taking a liking to Ike, he spent the time they had together teaching him the ways of the career officer. Eisenhower greatly respected the general and paid attention. For the first time, he began to take a real interest in his career. General Conner managed by 1925 to secure an assignment for Eisenhower at the staff training school at Leavenworth. Conner also pointed out a young colonel whom he guessed would be the next army leader and advised Eisenhower to seek the man out. The colonel was George Marshall, who would later become commander in chief of the army in World War II.

Eisenhower's change of attitude due to Conner's instructions showed in his record at staff training school. He finished first in a class of 215, yet attracted little attention among the army's ranking officers. From 1929 to 1933, he was just an aide in the office of the assistant secretary of war. Then in 1933 he became an aide to Douglas MacArthur, then chief of staff of the army. Two years later,

MacArthur accepted an assignment as field marshall of a new Philippine army, and Major Eisenhower went along as his aide.

Drifting career. In the first twenty years of his career, Eisenhower never was considered a top commander but served often as chief of staff to a commanding general. He rose slowly to the rank of colonel, meanwhile displaying another interest and skill. Eisenhower excelled at bridge and poker—sometimes winning almost as much as his salary at cards.

Planning talent. Eisenhower was serving as a colonel under General Walter Krueger with the Third Army when it joined in one of the army's most massive practice wars. Eisenhower devised the Third Army's plan of attack; it worked so well in the practice that he finally won recognition as a military planner. Army leaders found that Eisenhower could listen to others, then make sound judgments about what to do.

The day after these practice maneuvers, Japanese aircraft bombed Pearl Harbor in Hawaii. Eisenhower became a brigadier general and was assigned to the War Plans Division in Washington, D.C. His first task was to plan the strategy for the Far East, but he was soon put in charge of the army's operations division. His task changed, in 1942, to planning for a war to defeat Germany and Japan.

The Lackluster Early Career of Dwight Eisenhower

Being older when he entered West Point than the other beginning cadets and lacking real interest in the army made progress difficult for Eisenhower. He moved up rapidly only during World War II. In 1920 he was promoted to major, a rank he held for sixteen years.

1916	First lieutenant
1917	Captain
1918	Temporary major; temporary lieutenant colonel
1920	Captain; major
1936	Lieutenant colonel
1941	Temporary colonel; temporary brigadier general
1942	Temporary major general; temporary lieutenant general
1943	Temporary general
1944	Temporary general of the army (five-star)
1946	General of the Army

Participation: The Allied Landing in Europe

Planning the invasion of Europe. Eisenhower and his staff planned strategy to defeat Germany, Italy, and Japan. Once its enemies were divided, the U.S. military reasoned, they would be easier

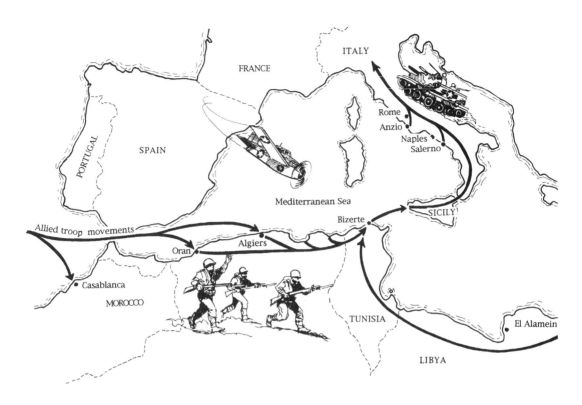

▲ **The Allied troops in Africa and Italy**

to defeat. Ike had been in the Far East and knew something about Japan. To attack Japan first, as General Douglas MacArthur preferred, would require long lines of communication and, Eisenhower felt, consume too much in the way of U.S. energy and resources. Germany would meanwhile be left free to romp around Europe. The Operations Department decided to tackle Germany first.

Eisenhower liked to get the facts, make sense of them, and then take direct action. His plan to attack the Germans called for assembling some 3,500 ships to transport more than 150,000 troops, land these forces on beaches in France, and push the German army back until it submitted. At the same time, Russia would attack German holdings in Eastern Europe and move west toward Germany. As head of operations, Eisenhower presented the plan to Chief of Staff George Marshall. Marshall studied the plan and asked Eisenhower if he was satisfied with it. He was. Marshall then

decided that Ike was the man to take the first step in carrying out the plan. It required gaining the cooperation of Britain and Russia, and Eisenhower's ability to get along with nearly everyone made him the logical choice. He headed for London to meet with the British leaders Winston Churchill and Field Marshall Sir Alan Brooke, and a still unnamed Russian representative. With charm and modesty, the American general soon won both governments' cooperation. Eisenhower returned to Washington to prepare. President Franklin Roosevelt and Marshall chose Dwight Eisenhower to direct the invasion.

Africa. There were immediate differences between the British ideas of invasion and those planned by Eisenhower. Bringing these opinions together was made more difficult because of Eisenhower's rank, which was lower than that of the British leaders who had to take direction from him. Then, too, the British had been fighting this war far longer than the Americans. Some British first wanted to drive out the German tank armies that were rapidly occupying Egypt and north Africa. Eisenhower felt that the allies needed all their resources for Europe. But President Roosevelt agreed with the British, so General Eisenhower soon found himself directing attacks in Africa. Operation Torch began in November 1942. After an initial failure, the Allied forces finally captured the German supply port at Tunis. By May 1943 all of Africa was controlled by the Allied forces. Now Eisenhower could turn toward Italy.

Sicily and Italy. German soldiers had occupied northern Italy and established a strong line there. These would be the first targets for the Allied armies. From his headquarters on the island of Malta, Eisenhower directed troops that drove toward the German lines. Sicily was taken in July and August 1943 and Italy was immediately invaded, but it was June 1944 before the Allies took Rome. The major assault on Germany was yet to come, although American and British bombers had already begun heavy bombing throughout Europe.

Normandy. In 1944, with Italy and Africa now under Allied control, there was another difference of opinion between Eisen-

◀
American troops storm a North African beach, c. 1943

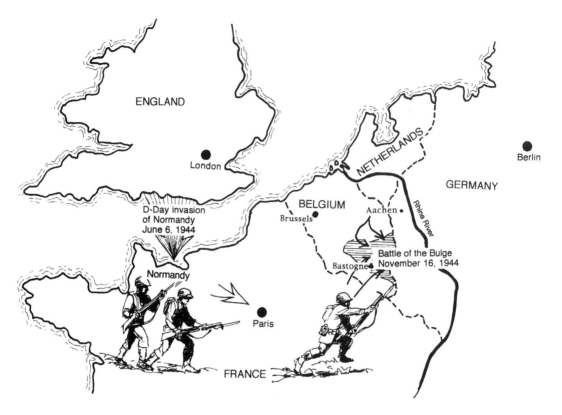

ENGLAND

London

D-Day invasion
of Normandy
June 6, 1944

Normandy

Paris

FRANCE

NETHERLANDS

BELGIUM

Brussels

Aachen

Rhine River

GERMANY

Berlin

Battle of the Bulge
November 16, 1944

Bastogne

▲ Major European World War II battles

hower and the British. They wanted to attack German forces through southern France. But Eisenhower again thought the long supply lines would be a problem, as would keeping Allied plans a secret. He preferred the shorter route from England across the channel to Normandy. This time Eisenhower persuaded the others to go along with his strategy.

The invasion of France was planned for June 5, 1944. The week before, weather conditions had been very poor, and Eisenhower had begun watching them carefully. On the appointed day, the weather remained poor but was supposed to clear. General Eisenhower believed the weather forecasters and set the invasion for June 6. Hundreds of aircraft joined navy ships in bombarding the enemy as 156,000 Allied soldiers stormed the shores of Normandy. Eisenhower and his staff had planned the invasion in detail. So complete were the plans that Eisenhower even wrote a press report to

▲ **Eisenhower talks to the troops**

be issued if the invasion failed. True to his decisive character, the
release took all the blame for the imagined failure on the general:

> Our landings in the Cherbourg-Havre area have failed to gain a sat-
> isfactory foothold and I have withdrawn the troops. My decision to
> attack at this time and place was based upon the best information
> available. The troops, the air, and the Navy did all that bravery and
> devotion to duty could do. If any blame or fault attaches to the
> attempt it is mine alone. (Eisenhower in Gunther, p. 41)

After heavy fighting, the Allies established themselves on
European land and this press release became unnecessary. General
Eisenhower took an active interest in the soldiers, as he had in

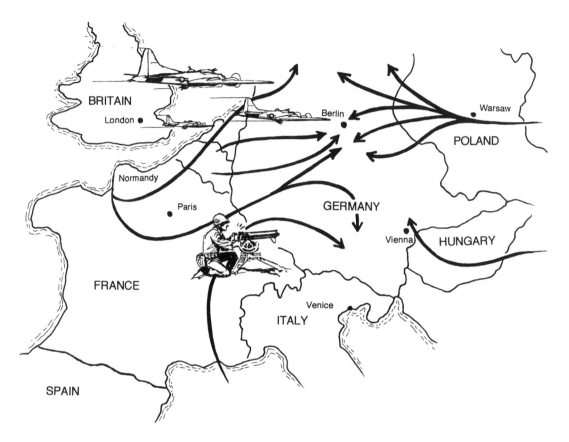

▲ **The final Allied thrusts of the war**

Sicily. Within forty hours after the invasion of Sicily, he had made a secret visit to the island and stopped to thank Canadian troops for their help there. After the Normandy landing, he made frequent trips over the battlegrounds to see for himself how the war was progressing. As the troops moved through France, he joined them often to talk with the leaders of the armies or just walk with the troops. His broad smile helped win people to his side even in battle conditions.

By the end of the war, Eisenhower had commanded 3 million soldiers, airmen, and sailors and had succeeded in defeating the Germans. Along the way, he had witnessed the horrors of war. One grisly sight was a German concentration camp at Ohrdruf piled with the bones of victims. He called Washington to send reporters to the

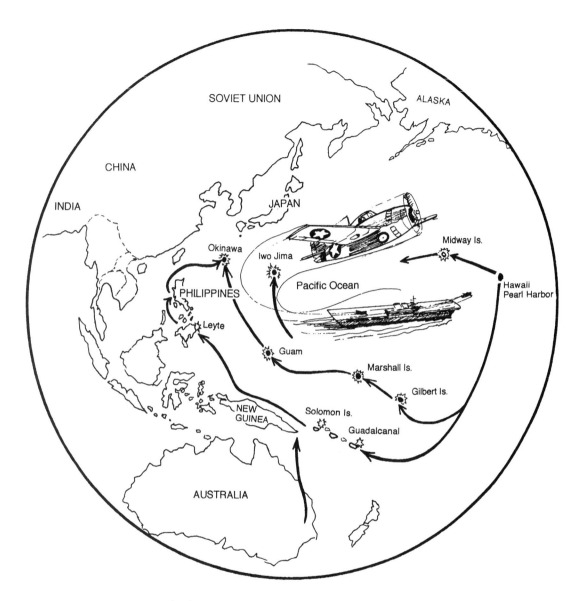

▲ Major battles in the Pacific theater

scene, then made German civilians aware of the sight by requiring a nearby town to clean up the mess. The town mayor and his wife were so overwhelmed that they committed suicide. Not every German was fully aware of the Nazi war crimes, but Eisenhower set out to make them aware.

These experiences turned him against war and against friend-liness with the German soldiers. He refused to talk with German officers except to remind the German general who signed the peace agreement that he would be held personally responsible for carrying out the conditions of surrender.

Aftermath

NATO. Eisenhower returned home a hero, not only in America but throughout the Allied nations. He became chief of staff of the army when George Marshall left that office.

In 1948 he retired from the active army to become president of Columbia University. Two years later, he returned to Europe as Supreme Commander of the forces of NATO—the North Atlantic Treaty Organization set up to defend Europe from possible Soviet occupation.

President Eisenhower. In 1952 Eisenhower was nominated to be the Republican candidate for president. People throughout the nation campaigned wearing buttons reading "I Like Ike." As president, Eisenhower led the country steadily on the path to peace.

He had become president while the United States was at war again in Korea. But Ike declared that total war would be suicide for an American generation. "There is no glory in battle worth the blood it costs," he declared (Eisenhower in Gunther, p. 42). President Eisenhower directed the country toward a stalemate and peace in Korea and several important changes at home, including tax reform. Although he suffered a mild heart attack during his first term in office, he was reelected in 1956.

In 1960 Eisenhower was once again a civilian. He continued to speak about public issues but finally found the time to return to his first love—sports. He became an avid golfer. When reporters asked if mild arthritis in one hand was serious, he announced that of course it was. It interfered with his golf.

Former president Dwight Eisenhower died in 1969 at the age of seventy-eight. He was still one of America's most famous citizens, known for his success as a general and as an immensely popular president.

For More Information

Gunther, John. *Eisenhower, The Man and the Symbol.* New York: Harper & Brothers, 1952.

Lyon, Peter. *Eisenhower, Portrait of the Hero.* Boston: Little, Brown, 1974.

Miller, Frances Trevelyan. *Eisenhower: Man and Soldier.* New York: Winston Press, 1944.

A. Philip Randolph

1889-1979

Personal Background

Father's influence. Asa Philip Randolph was born in Crescent City, Florida, on April 15, 1889. His father, James Randolph, was a minister in the African Methodist Episcopal (AME) Church; his mother, Elizabeth Robinson Randolph, one of her husband's former Sunday School students, came from a family of strong church supporters. The AME Church, often called the earliest black rights institution in the United States, preached racial equality, and James Randolph, though poor and untrained, had a reputation for especially fiery sermons. Asa never "got religion" the way his father would have liked, but he did inherit from his father a strong sense of racial pride and dignity of spirit.

Jacksonville and Cookman. When Asa was two, his parents took him and his older brother James, four, to Jacksonville, where their father had been invited to preach in a small congregation. The boys, close friends and constant companions, grew up in the segregated city. In 1903 they both entered the Cookman Institute, Florida's first black high school. There the brothers soon became two of Cookman's most popular and successful students. James, always a brilliant scholar, established one of the best records in Latin and mathematics in the school's history. Often under his brother's shadow in earlier years, Asa now blossomed into a school

▲ A. Philip Randolph

Event: The Brotherhood of Sleeping Car Porters and March on Washington Movement.

Role: In 1925 A. Philip Randolph, a pioneer of black labor rights, organized the Brotherhood of Sleeping Car Porters, an all-black union of railroad workers. In 1937 the powerful Pullman Company signed a contract with his union. From this early black labor victory grew Randolph's March on Washington Movement, which in 1941 forced President Franlin D. Roosevelt to issue Executive Order 8802, banning racial discrimination in companies with war-related government contracts.

leader in his own right, excelling in literature, drama, public speaking, singing, and baseball.

Lasting impression. Much later, a friend remembered qualities in Asa, the boy, that others would notice in the man as well:

> The biggest crowds came out to watch baseball at Cookman when Asa Randolph was playing. I would guess he could have made a career as a baseball player, if he had wanted. With that voice of his, he could also have made a career as a singer. He was very artistic; he had no interest in the trivial aspects of life. He was retiring [quiet], he spoke impeccable [perfect] English, but he wouldn't open his mouth unless asked. (Anderson, p. 46)

Quiet, serious, and dignified, with a remarkable ability to attract a crowd—these were qualities that would mark Randolph for the rest of his life.

Washington versus Du Bois. The Randolphs could not afford college, so after his glory days at Cookman, Asa held a series of low-level manual labor jobs. In the meantime, he bought as many books as he could afford and continued his education on his own. The book that impressed him most was *The Souls of Black Folk,* by W.E.B. Du Bois, who in the early 1900s was challenging Booker T. Washington for leadership of American blacks. Whereas Washington called for blacks to forget about struggling for equality and to work their way up from the bottom of society, Du Bois demanded political and social rights equal to those of whites. His arguments appealed to Randolph, who was unhappy with the lowly jobs that were the only ones open to most blacks.

Radical in Harlem. Randolph spent several summers working in New York City, and in 1911, at twenty-two, he moved there with a friend. Again he took a series of low-paying jobs, waiting tables, carrying bags, and operating an elevator to support himself. He lived in Harlem, which at that time was becoming the center of black city culture. Randolph, in fact, was part of a great migration of rural, southern blacks to northern industrial cities. Between 1910 and 1920, over 1 million blacks came north in search of work and freedom.

It was an exciting time, and Randolph soon became involved in politics. There was a growing number of socialists at the time, who believed in public or government ownership of industries. Randolph listened to street-corner "soapbox" speakers such as the black socialist Hubert Harrison or the white leader Eugene Debs, who won nearly a million votes as the socialist candidate in the 1912 presidential election. He also took classes at the City College of New York, having learned that it was free. Both on street corners and in the classroom, he encountered new and daring ideas calling for social change. The set of ideas that made the most sense to him was socialism, which demanded equal rights for all and government ownership of industry.

Marriage. In 1914 Randolph married Lucille Campbell Green, a young widow and businesswoman, who had made a small fortune with a successful beauty salon on 135th Street in Harlem. Asa and Lucille shared two important interests: Shakespeare and socialism, both of which Asa had been devoting time to in Harlem. He had participated in performances of Shakespeare's plays for several theater groups. Already, though, politics was taking up more and more of his time.

Randolph up to this time never thought much about money. He held a job only until he had enough to live on for a few weeks. Then he went out and worked for a candidate whose views he supported or gave his time to some other worthy cause. Now, however, he suddenly found himself with a rich wife who admired his abilities and shared his opinions. She agreed to support him in his political efforts and ended up doing so for years. Randolph never would make much money on his own, nor would he ever really try to.

Soapbox. Lucille introduced Asa to a young man who would become his partner over the next decade or so, Chandler Owen. By 1916 both had joined the Socialist Party and were frequent soapbox speakers in Harlem. (The term comes from the old soap boxes that the speakers would stand on.) For several years, they were regulars at "bug house" corner, Lenox Avenue and 135th Street, where they spoke in favor of socialism and labor rights most weekday evenings. One Harlem resident later remembered the soapbox era and Randolph's part in it:

> Randolph attracted large numbers of young people. He got us thinking in social and economic terms.... His delivery was so impeccable [perfect] and his culture so attractive. Instead of rab-

ble rousing, he just talked.... And if other soapboxers wanted to hold on to their audience, they had to be careful not to hold their meeting too close to where Randolph was preaching (Anderson, p. 77-78).

Messenger. In 1917, using funds provided by his wife, Randolph started his own magazine, the *Messenger.* Known as Asa or Philip in the past, he now signed the articles A. Philip Randolph. For over a decade, the *Messenger* published articles and editorials—many written by Randolph himself, others by leading black writers—that called for social change. Like other socialists, Randolph and Owen opposed American participation in World War I and argued that blacks should refuse to fight for a country that denied them the most basic rights. While one reviewer described it as one of the most brilliantly edited magazines in the history of African American journalism, the Justice Department saw it as by far the best and the most dangerous of all the publications put out by blacks.

Participation: Creating the Brotherhood of Sleeping Car Porters and the March on Washington Movement

Pullman and the porters. The Pullman Company was founded in 1867 by George Pullman, who had seen a need for comfortable sleeping cars on long train journeys. To take care of passenger needs—bedding, baggage and customer service in general—Pullman hired black ex-slaves to act as porters in his sleeping cars. He chose blacks because he thought they were used to serving whites cheerfully and would be grateful for the work. This racist attitude to employees shaped the company's policy. Despite low pay ($60 a month in 1925), heavy expenses and long hours, anyone not happy with the job could look elsewhere as far as the company was concerned. Whenever the porters tried to organize a union to press for better conditions, the company simply fired those involved. Jobs for blacks were scarce enough that replacements could always be found. By 1925 every attempt to unionize had been crushed in this way, and many porters had grown desperate.

A new mission. Meanwhile, Randolph and the *Messenger* had fallen on hard times. The socialism that Randolph preached had failed to become popular among blacks, and the magazine's quality had slipped. Jazz and art had replaced politics as the center of Harlem's cultural life. Fewer people bought the *Messenger,* and financial collapse appeared to be just around the corner. Randolph, now thirty-six, remained dignified and hopeful, but it seemed his days as a major black voice were over.

In 1925 several porters asked Randolph if he would be interested in trying to organize a porters' union. At first he refused. He had tried labor organizing before and had been unsuccessful. He did write two articles about the porters for the *Messenger,* however. The articles stirred such enthusiasm among New York porters that he finally agreed to try.

Brotherhood. While it may seem odd for the union to be headed by someone who was not himself a porter, it gave Randolph one great advantage: he could not be fired. The Brotherhood of Sleeping Car Porters slowly grew in membership as Randolph and his aides traveled to cities like Chicago and St. Louis to enlist new members. Hundreds were fired when the company learned they were members, and company spies—"stool pigeons," or porters who gave information to the company—attended most meetings. Randolph warned members to keep quiet at the meetings, conducting them himself, and warned porters not to discuss the union among themselves.

New Deal. Yet, despite strong membership, Randolph could not force the company managers to deal with the Brotherhood. The threat of a strike was just that, a mere threat, because Randolph knew that the company could always replace the strikers. After several defeats in the late 1920s, porters began dropping out of the union because they felt the whole situation was hopeless.

Hope, however, was not lost. As Brotherhood officer C. L. Dellums pointed out, Franklin D. Roosevelt came along, started the New Deal, and Congress began passing laws. Elected as a pro-labor president in 1932, Franklin Roosevelt pushed through Congress a revolutionary package of laws known as the New Deal. What most unions had lacked in the past was legal support, laws that would force companies to recognize the elected union leaders as the employees' representatives, and that would prevent employees from being fired just because they had joined a union. Such laws were included in the New Deal, and suddenly union members found themselves in a much more powerful position. Randolph's was only one of many unions that benefited from the new laws.

Blank Check

Whether true or merely part of Randolph's legend, the story of how he refused a blank check from the Pullman Company made him into a hero to the porters. As the story goes, the check could be made out in any amount up to six figures, if Randolph would quit the Brotherhood. Brotherhood Secretary-Treasurer William Bowe recalls the incident: "I was present at the attempt to purchase Randolph.... The stool pigeon ... gave Randolph the check and told him all he had to do was fill in the amount. And Randolph, with his poker face, said, 'Take this blank check back to where you got it and tell them I'm not for sale.'" (Anderson, p. 224)

Victory. The Pullman Company still fought tooth and nail, claiming that the law applying to railroads did not apply to them because they were not a railroad. Firmly, Randolph led the fight to have the laws changed to include sleeping-car companies. This time, he was supported by other, white, railroad unions. Then the Pullman Company tried to organize its own union and claim that it, not the Brotherhood, was the porters' true representative. A vote was held among the porters to decide the issue. The company's union received 1,422 votes to the Brotherhood's 8,316. No longer able to deny Randolph's right to speak for the porters, in 1935 the company finally agreed to meet with him.

Contract. It was an incomplete victory, however, for the parties still had to work out the actual contract. For two years the company stalled, waiting to see if Roosevelt's laws would stay in effect. During this time, an incident occurred that would become legendary. The company reportedly tried to bribe Randolph to resign by handing him a blank check.

The Supreme Court upheld the laws in 1937, and the company got serious about working out a contract. In August a contract was finally signed, improving pay and reducing the porters' standard work month from 400 hours to 240. It was the first time a large company had ever signed a contract with a black union.

Wartime issues. All along, Randolph had viewed his work for the Brotherhood as part of a larger struggle for black rights in general. He had always tied social equality to economic equality, to the rights of the black worker. In his view, without one, there could not be the other. After the outbreak of war in 1939, America's economy began to recover from the depression, spurred by growth in defense industries. American factories geared up to turn out tanks, planes, guns, and ammunition. Other industries, especially steel, benefited from the new orders for their goods. Yet black workers were left out of this economic recovery. As one aircraft company president insisted, regardless of their skill or training, he simply would not employ blacks in his plant. It was against his company policy. Similarly, blacks joining the army found themselves in all-black units, or assigned as laborers and cooks.

Randolph's victory over the Pullman Company had suddenly made him America's most powerful black political figure. Along with other black leaders, such as Walter White of the National Association for the Advancement of Colored People (NAACP), Randolph met with President Roosevelt in September 1940 to discuss job discrimination and army segregation, or separation of the races. The meeting, however, produced no results. Segregation, the White House announced two weeks later, would remain army policy. The announcement did not even mention the leaders' other main concern, job discrimination.

March on Washington. Not only had Randolph's victory with the Brotherhood made him a national leader, it had also supplied him with an effective and organized staff. Milton Webster, big, strong and tough, was head of the Chicago, Illinois, division and Randolph's right-hand man. Bennie Smith from Detroit, Michigan, and C. L. Dellums from Oakland, California, were other former porters who contributed local leadership as well as organizing skills on the national level.

Soon after the White House meeting, Randolph remarked to Webster that he did not think such meetings were going to get them anywhere. "We are going to have to do something about it," Randolph continued. There was a pause. The Brotherhood officers were not always happy about Randolph spending time on "outside business." Randolph went on, "I think we ought to get 10,000 Negroes to march on Washington in protest, march down Pennsylvania Avenue. What do you think of that?" (Randolph in Anderson, p. 248). The two men were on a train journey south to visit Brotherhood divisions. When they hit each stop, they announced the new

▲ Randolph (center) and Whitney Young, executive secretary of the Negro
Urban League, meet with President Lyndon Johnson in the mid-1960s

plan to march on Washington for jobs in the defense factories. Word
spread fast as newspapers picked up the story, and the March on
Washington Movement was born.

"Let the Negro masses march!" By early 1941, other black
organizations, such as the NAACP, had joined the Brotherhood in
planning the march, set for July 1. As more and more support was
gathered, the goal of 10,000 grew to 100,000. "When 100,000
Negroes march on Washington," Randolph said, "it will wake up
Negro as well as white America.... Let the Negro masses march! Let
the Negro masses speak!" (Randolph in Anderson, p. 251).

Mrs. Roosevelt. Randolph's earlier White House meeting had been arranged by the president's wife, Eleanor Roosevelt, who was very active in the cause of civil rights. She supported the black struggle for equality, she wrote to Randolph, but believed the march was a mistake that might "create in Congress even stronger opposition from certain groups than we have had in the past" (Anderson, p. 252). She was also afraid of violence, she told Randolph on June 13. Randolph remembered the meeting:

> I replied that there would be no violence unless her husband ordered the police to crack black heads. I told her I was sorry, but the march would not be called off unless the President issued an executive order banning discrimination in the defense industry. (Randolph in Anderson, p. 255)

Executive Order 8802. On June 18, President Roosevelt and several cabinet members met at the White House with Randolph and Walter White. Roosevelt offered personally to ask the heads of the factories to hire blacks. Randolph politely told the President that was not good enough. "We want you to do more than that," he said. "We want you to issue an executive order making it mandatory that Negroes be permitted to work in these plants" (Randolph in Anderson, p. 257). Impossible, Roosevelt responded. How many people did they plan to bring to the march? There would be 100,000 was Randolph's quiet but firm answer.

On June 25, six days before the march was scheduled to take place, President Roosevelt signed Executive Order 8802, banning racial discrimination in any factory that supplied goods to the government. Despite some anger from younger black leaders, Randolph called off the march. He had achieved his goal. He and the other march leaders decided not to press the issue of segregation in the armed forces, preferring to wait until after the war.

Joseph Rauh, the aide assigned to write the Executive Order, had to rewrite it many times before Randolph was satisfied. Annoyed, Rauh wondered what was so special about Randolph and why the President of the United States cared so much about satisfying him. After Rauh had met and worked with Randolph, however, he had a different reaction. "I don't know that I've met a greater man in my life," he said (Anderson, p. 259).

Executive Order 9981. The opportunity to try to integrate the army came in 1948, after President Truman ordered a peacetime draft. Again using the threat of mass protest, Randolph called for blacks to resist the draft. They had fought for their country in two world wars, he told Truman, but would never take up arms again in a segregated army. He asked Truman to issue an executive order banning segregation in the armed forces. Truman refused, ending the meeting.

Randolph and other protesters marched that summer with signs outside the Democratic National Convention. Inside at the convention, a young future senator and vice-president named Hubert Humphrey was fighting southern Democrats to include a strong civil rights plank in the party platform. Polls showed that over 70 percent of young black men were prepared to resist the draft. Facing strong pressure from Randolph and his supporters, President Truman signed Executive Order 9981, banning segregation in the armed forces.

> ## Randolph and the AFL
>
> Randolph carried out a long struggle to integrate the labor movement. Not until 1936, when it was clear that the Brotherhood would win against Pullman, did the American Federation of Labor (AFL) accept the porters' union as a full member. But some powerful unions continued to exclude blacks. From before 1936 to his own membership on the AFL's executive council in 1955, Randolph gave hundreds of speeches attacking discrimination in the unions. After one such speech, union president George Meany supposedly asked who had appointed Randolph the guardian of all the blacks in America? In response, virtually every black organization backed Randolph in his right to speak for them.

March for jobs and freedom. Randolph continued his civil rights leadership and his work for the Brotherhood through the 1950s and 1960s. During the 1950s, he worked with younger civil rights leaders like Reverend Martin Luther King, Jr. Such younger leaders gradually came to the forefront as Randolph grew older. Randolph and King together organized a small example of peaceful protest, the Pilgrimage of Prayer, in 1957. In August 1963 came the crowning moment of his career, the March on Washington for Jobs and Freedom, organized by Randolph and his assistant, Bayard Rustin. It brought over 250,000 people to Washington to protest racial discrimination. Randolph made the first speech, then introduced Martin Luther

King, whose "I have a dream" address became one of history's most famous speeches.

Randolph resigned from the Brotherhood in 1968, at the age of seventy-nine. He continued to live in New York, where he died on May 16, 1979.

For More Information

Anderson, Jervis. *A. Philip Randolph: A Biographical Portrait.* New York: Harcourt Brace Jovanovich, 1973.

Pfeffer, Paula F. *A. Philip Randolph: Pioneer of the Civil Rights Movement.* Baton Rouge: Louisiana State University Press, 1990.

Minoru Yasui

1917-1987

Personal Background

Parents. During the early 1900s, many Japanese people moved to the United States because of better opportunity for advancement. Due to historical racism against Asians, however, they often found only backbreaking labor open to them. Many of the Japanese labored in the lumber mills and fruit orchards. Employers doubted that these slender laborers could endure hard work, and so the Japanese worked twice as hard to prove their abilities. For example, logging companies cut down thousands of acres of forest, leaving only stumps and brush behind. Up to 600 Japanese laborers were hired each season to clear the stumps with hoes and dynamite. There might be as many as 100 stumps per acre, and often it took several days to clear one stump.

Many of the Japanese immigrants came to America intending to earn their fortune and return home to Japan. Minoru's father, Masuo Yasui, however, intended to settle in America. In Japan, Masuo learned English and converted to Christianity, following his father and brothers to America in 1903. In 1908, when he was twenty-one years old, he moved to Hood River, Oregon, a town with a large Japanese population. With the help of his brother Renichi, Masuo established a merchandising business called the "Yasui Brothers Company." The store sold Japanese goods such as soy

▲ Minoru Yasui

Event: The confinement of naturalized and U.S. born Japanese in concentration camps during World War II.

Role: Minoru Yasui, a Japanese American attorney, brought his own case to court to protest U.S. government policies against Japanese American citizens during World War II. Heard first in Oregon, his case eventually reached the Supreme Court.

sauce, imported rice, and toys. Renichi worked the counter, talking to customers and running the register, while Masuo kept track of the accounts and the bills. Together they built a small and successful business. Masuo gained recognition in Hood River as a key businessman and leader, eventually expanding his business to include contract labor and selling insurance.

Minoru's mother, Shidzuyo Miyake, finished college in Japan and worked as a teacher before coming to America. This was unusual because at that time, most Japanese women were uneducated. She and Masuo met briefly as children and exchanged letters and photographs while Masuo lived in Hood River. When Masuo proposed marriage in a letter, Shidzuyo accepted and moved to America to live with her new husband.

Shidzuyo traveled by ship to the United States to marry Masuo, breathing stale air, eating hard rice and sleeping in bunk beds. Ship toilets consisted of mere holes in the floor; the women could see the sea water rushing below. After three long weeks, Shidzuyo arrived in Hood River in 1912.

Childhood. In time, Shidzuyo and Masuo had eight children—Minoru was the third son in a wealthy family. His parents encouraged their children to become Americanized and expected them to succeed in church and school. Minoru, a small, wiry boy with a quick wit and love for challenge, excelled. Independent and confident, Min, as he was called, set high academic goals for himself and performed well. He and his older brothers, Kay and Chop, were the first Japanese Americans to attend school in Hood River and the first to enroll in the Methodist Sunday school and Boy Scouts.

Children born in America to Japanese immigrants were called *nisei,* meaning "second generation." The *nisei* acquired both Japanese and American identities. Parents expected their *nisei* children to respect customary Japanese values such as authority, yet at the same time, the *nisei,* born and raised in the United States, displayed American characteristics such as independence. But *nisei* children were not totally accepted by others. The community viewed them as foreigners because they looked Japanese and spoke both languages.

Despite their success in school, Kay, Chop, and Min found childhood difficult as *nisei.* Due to their Japanese background, they made few friends during their school years. Isolated, Kay, Chop, and Min played with one another, fishing, hunting, and exploring the Oregon countryside.

Tragedy. As the oldest son, Kay held considerable power and authority within the family. His parents, however, expected Kay not only to be a role model for the younger children but also to represent the family within the community. Despite Kay's excellence in school and status as a budding poet, Masuo, a very strict father, disciplined Kay more harshly than the other children. On February 27, 1931, Shidzuyo told Kay to wake Minoru. Instead, Kay played a joke on Minoru by painting his face black. When Minoru awoke, both Minoru and his father yelled at Kay, shaming him tremendously. When a person is shamed in Japanese culture, they bring shame not only upon themselves but upon the entire family. Perhaps the combination of shame and pressure from his school and family grew too much for Kay to endure. Nobody knows exactly why, but Kay poisoned himself that evening, drinking water mixed with strychnine, a rat poison. He died that night.

Stricken with grief by the suicide, the family spoke little about the circumstances, simply informing the community that Kay died. Few people, including Minoru's younger bothers and sisters, knew that Kay had killed himself. The loss affected both Minoru and his father immensely, and Masuo blamed them both. He wrote Minoru:

> Yourself and father are directly responsible for the loss of our dearest one. Your feeling and thought of the 27 of February meet exactly mine. You will surely feel very keenly toward your responsibility.... There lies our common sorrow and great point which we must suffer for the rest of our lives. (Kessler, p. 152)

School. In 1933, at the age of sixteen, Minoru left Hood River to attend the University of Oregon in Eugene. He continued scoring high marks, rising quickly to the top of his class by making the honor role every quarter and performing well in debates. Participating in the Reserve Officers Training Corps (ROTC), he was promoted to commanding officer by the end of his junior year. Minoru's classmates also elected him as secretary/treasurer of the dormitory and president of the school's international organization.

Despite his obvious talents, Minoru continued to experience prejudice due to his Japanese background. The fraternity clubs excluded him, for example, because membership was reserved for white males only.

After graduating, Minoru entered the University of Oregon's law school. He found his studies uninteresting but worked hard and at the end of his first year became the first Japanese American member of the Phi Beta Kappa honor society. In 1941 Minoru Yasui became the first *nisei* to graduate this law school. He passed the Oregon bar exam that summer.

Career move. Yasui tried to set up a law practice in Portland, but few people had money due to the Great Depression. So he took a job with the Japanese Consulate in Chicago. Meanwhile, prejudice against the Japanese grew. Other Americans believed that the Japanese filled jobs that did not belong to them, noting that the Japanese worked hard and became successful businessmen who competed with whites. Some whites, afraid the Japanese would take over the country if they could buy land, sought to limit land ownership to U.S. citizens only. In California, angry whites passed a 1913 act forbidding aliens to own land. The following commentary, made in 1935, illustrates the prejudice behind such acts:

> Wherever the Japanese have settled, their nests pollute the communities like the running sores of leprosy. They exist like the yellowed, smoldering discarded butts in an over-full ashtray, vilifying the air with their loathsome smells, filling all who have misfortune to look upon them with a wholesome disgust and a desire to wash. (Leathers, p. 38)

▲ Yasui

Participation:
Japanese American Concentration Camps

World War II and Pearl Harbor. By 1941 the Allied powers of Great Britain, France and Russia had fought for several years against Germany and the Axis powers. The United States, however, refrained from entering the war until December 7, 1941, when Japan bombed Pearl Harbor in Hawaii. The decision to declare war against Japan, Germany, Italy, and the other Axis powers greatly affected the Japanese Americans. Most Japanese immigrants lived on the West Coast, and the U.S. government began to fear that Japan had spies among the immigrant and *nisei* populations. Encouraged by anti-Asian groups, the government questioned the loyalty of the Japanese and Japanese Americans, assuming that they would side with Japan because of their ethnic background. The government, in fact, accused Japanese Americans of disloyalty to the United States and arrested many people on suspicion of spying or conspiracy. The frightened victims went to great lengths to prove that they were loyal Americans. In California, for example, a Japanese group bought the U.S. government a $50,000 antiaircraft weapon to show their support for the war.

Effects of prejudice. Yasui resigned his position at the Japanese Consulate the day of the Pearl Harbor attack. Later that week, the government informed Yasui that his father had been taken into custody on suspicion of spying. Yasui, it said, had to report to Fort Vancouver in Washington to fulfill his duty as a commanding officer in the U.S. Army.

When Yasui arrived at Fort Vancouver on January 19, 1942, the army would not let him report for duty. They turned him away because they did not understand how somebody who looked Japanese could fight for the United States in a war against Japan. Yasui repeatedly tried to report for duty, but the army refused each time and, after some debate, eventually classified him as not eligible for service.

Yasui traveled to Fort Missoula to attend his father's trial. At the trial, Yasui saw his father, a man who gave up his homeland to work and raise his children in the United States, accused as a spy and a traitor. Helpless, Yasui returned to Portland and set up a small office to help Japanese immigrants and their children deal with new legal problems caused by the war, such as the mounds of paperwork the government required of all people with Japanese ancestry.

Minoru's arrest. On February 19, 1942, President Franklin Delano Roosevelt signed Executive Order 9066, designating some areas as sensitive military zones from which any or all persons might be removed as the military saw fit. Yasui realized that this was directed at the Japanese.

The U.S. Constitution states that all citizens are equal under the law, and Yasui, recognizing the order as a violation of this ideal, prepared to fight a legal battle. "It is my belief that no military authority has the right to subject any United States citizen to any requirement that does not equally apply to all other U.S. citizens," Yasui declared (Yasui in Kessler, p. 177).

In order to test the constitutionality of a law, the law must first be broken. Yasui decided to fight the first discriminatory order against the Japanese that resulted from Executive Order 9066. On March 24, 1942, General John L. DeWitt issued a curfew for all German, Italian, and Japanese nationals, as well as for citizens of Japanese descent. Yasui believed this violated his basic constitutional right as a citizen to equal and fair treatment. He aimed to challenge "special treatment" of persons based on race alone.

On March 28, 1942, at 6:00 P.M., Yasui calmly told his secretary to inform the police that a Japanese man was illegally out after curfew. He walked out the front door, down the street and waited for the police to come. They never showed. He kept walking and eventually found a policeman standing on the street. Yasui told the policeman to arrest him since he was obviously of Japanese ancestry and was therefore breaking the law by walking around after dark. The policeman told Yasui to run along because he would only get himself into trouble. Finally, about 11:00 P.M., Yasui walked into the police station and demanded to be arrested. The police sergeant threw him into the drunk tank, where he stayed until Monday morning when his bond was posted.

The fight begins. After his arrest, Yasui began an intense letter-writing campaign to Japanese associations and to General DeWitt. To drum up support, he circulated petitions protesting the discriminatory treatment of the Japanese. Yasui contacted various Japanese organizations, including the Japanese American Citizens League (JACL). But the JACL chose not to support Yasui because it did not want to support a constitutional challenge. Eager to demonstrate loyalty to the United States, many Japanese believed it was best to comply with governmental requests. The JACL supported this philosophy and actually tried to put a stop to Minoru's case. Still, Yasui held fast to the idea that loyalty to the United States meant abiding by its Constitution. If the nation strayed from the basic rights outlined in the Constitution, Yasui believed that it was his duty as a citizen of the nation to correct the error.

The war increased hostility against the Japanese. The attack on Pearl Harbor had created an atmosphere of fear and suspicion. Many citizens, including some military persons, feared a Japanese attack on the West Coast. Japanese submarines sank several American ships in the Pacific in late December 1941, causing an uproar among the nation's leaders. They were positive that Japan had spies in the United States and suspected all Japanese Americans as capable of betrayal. From February to March 1942, people of Japanese descent were encouraged to move from the West Coast to other areas of the country. But it was difficult to find any other area where they were welcome. And often relocation was not possible because the Japanese had no money or connections.

On March 26, 1942, the military posted a notice in West Coast newspapers stating, "All Japanese and Japanese Americans residing in military area number One, comprising the western parts of Washington, Oregon, California and southern Arizona will be forbidden to leave the area after Sunday, the Western Defense Command announced tonight." (Hopkinson, p. 67). It was the last chance to leave voluntarily. In May 1942, the military posted a final order forcing the Japanese to evacuate. They had to leave their homes and relocate to special centers designed to keep them in one place and under control. Yasui notified the army that he would evacuate only if they arrested him. On May 12, the military arrested and escorted him to the Portland detainment center, which he dubbed the "North Portland Pigpen."

Minoru's case and constitutional debate. In June 1942, the case *United States of America* v. *Minoru Yasui* was brought before the U.S. District Court in Portland. The case was important to the government because the outcome could confirm that its wartime policies towards the Japanese were legal. The government argued that Japanese characteristics naturally prompted these people to betray the United States, and therefore all Japanese were potential spies for Japan. The government realized, however, that this would be difficult to prove and intended to use "judicial notice." Under "judicial notice," lawyers do not have to prove facts that are deemed self-evident. The government wanted to establish the genetic tendency of Japanese towards treachery as self-evident.

Yasui and his lawyer Earl Bernard argued that it was unconstitutional for the government to single out one group of citizens based on ancestry. The Fourteenth and Fifth Amendments guaranteed the civil rights of citizens to equal protection and due process of law. Everybody agreed that these rights were absolute during times of peace and that internment constituted a violation of these rights. During wartime, however, the government has special authority. At stake was whether General DeWitt had the power, during a time of war, to single out U.S. citizens based on their race and strip them of these rights.

The verdict was not reached until November. Judge Alger Fee referred to a decision set in 1866 called *Ex Parte Milligan*. In this case, the courts ruled that while Congress could authorize the president to suspend *habeas corpus* (which protects citizens from illegal or unjust imprisonment) and declare martial or military law, martial law could not exist unless civil courts ceased to function. Judge Fee noted that in Minoru's case, the president and Congress had not declared martial law, nor suspended *habeas corpus*. He declared that holding citizens was undeclared martial law and was not constitutional due to the Fifth and Fourteenth Amendments. Aliens, however, could be detained. Judge Fee then ruled that because Yasui had worked with the Japanese Consulate, he had renounced his desire to be a U.S. citizen. He stripped Yasui of his citizenship and pronounced Yasui guilty, as an alien, sentencing him to one year in jail. Although Yasui immediately instructed his attorney to begin the appeals process, he spent nine months in solitary confinement. He was allowed neither to exercise nor shower.

In May 1943, Minoru's appeal reached the Supreme Court, the highest body of law in the country. The government restated its position that the Constitution allowed the government special "war pow-

Fifth Amendment

No person shall ... be deprived of life, liberty or property, without due process of law; nor shall private property be taken for public use without just compensation.

Fourteenth Amendment

Section 1 ... No State shall make or enforce any law which shall abridge the privileges or immunities of citizens of the United States; nor shall any State deprive any person of life, liberty, or property without due process of law; nor deny to any person within its jurisdiction the equal protection of the laws.

▲ A Japanese-American family waits to be evacuated to an internment camp

ers" for the protection of the people and that the Japanese were dangerous. The Fifth and Fourteenth Amendments, it said, must give way to the decision-making of the military during wartime. The government argued that the order was a military necessity and proceeded to describe the supposedly forthcoming Japanese invasion on the West Coast as reason enough to detain the Japanese Americans.

The justices considered the case for months, finally reversing Judge Fee's decision. They referred to the recent case of *United States* v. *Hirabayashi*. In this case, the Court determined that special governmental powers, outlined in Articles I and II of the Constitution, such as "provide for the Common Defense" and "make all Laws which shall be necessary and proper," override individual rights during wartime. General DeWitt's actions were, in fact, constitutional during a time of war. Also, the Supreme Court ruled that Minoru's citizenship had nothing to do with the issues at hand. It returned his citizenship, and Yasui, as a Japanese American, was sent to the Minidoka Relocation Center in southern Idaho.

Life in the internment camps. When the Japanese received their orders to evacuate, many were given less than forty-eight hours to leave their homes. Two-thirds of these people were United States citizens by birth. They left their homes, their possessions and their businesses, often selling them for less money than they were worth. The government froze Japanese bank accounts, and bandits either stole or destroyed most of the possessions left behind. People sometimes threatened the Japanese physically.

Most of the internment or concentration camps contained numerous barracks with no furniture. Located in remote desert regions, the camps were filled with dusty air. Inmates lacked hot water and privacy. People ate together, slept together and bathed together. Camp life shattered family solidarity, an important characteristic in Japanese culture. Fathers had little power over their family, and mothers lost control over their children. Parents ate in huge mess halls, often separated from children and relatives. Some Japanese died in the camps, while many found the conditions hard to bear:

> The thing that really hit most of us was the lack of privacy. There was no privacy whatsoever.... No closets. Just a potbelly stove for each family in one room. I really felt sorry for some of the teenagers, especially the shy ones. Some couldn't take it. I recall one girl that lost her mind. (Fukei, p. 55)

Months passed, and the internment camps slowly came to resemble life in the outside world. Some developed recreation facilities, libraries, social halls, and playing fields. Each center housed several

▲ Manzzanar, a Japanese internment camp, 1942

thousand children, so schools opened in 1942. They were woefully lacking in desks, chairs, and most importantly, teachers. To pass the time, women organized arts and crafts classes, such as flower arranging and gardening. Cut off from the outside world, the interns lived a ghostlike existence. One intern expressed a feeling of being forgotten:

> It seems that since evacuation, I have gradually lost contact with my friends outside. You see, when one is enclosed in the narrow con-fines of a camp, strange things happen. Time and the life of the world outside simply pass by without touching us. (Hopkinson, p. 94)

By November 1, 1942, almost 112,000 evacuees were in temporary or permanent centers, even though during this time there was not one proven case of spying or sabotage by a Japanese American. Italian and German Americans, whose families came from other Axis countries, were not bothered.

Aftermath

Postwar life. Japanese internment officially ended on December 17, 1944, towards the end of World War II. Many people spent as long as two years in the camps and afterward faced new problems. A great number did not have anything to return to, having lost their homes and businesses due to the move to the camps. Yet Japanese Americans continued to face fear and prejudice. There were instances of racial terrorism and refusals to let them buy supplies or apply for desperately needed jobs. Movie theaters refused to sell them tickets, and barbers would not cut their hair. In many towns, businesses posted signs stating, "NO JAPS ALLOWED."

Released from Minidoka in 1944, Yasui moved to Colorado, passed the state bar exam, and set up a law practice. In 1946 he married True Shibata, with whom he had three daughters. Despite Minoru's talents, the family remained poor for many years. Yasui did a great deal of volunteer work, founding a City League and the first interracial Boy Scout Troop. During the 1950s he quit law. Yasui labored for the next twenty-four years on Denver's Commission on Community Relations to set up programs for the city's minorities. In time, the city recognized him as an outstanding citizen, established a monthly service award in his honor, and proclaimed Minoru Yasui Recognition Day.

Yasui continued his protests against the federal government for the rest of his life. In the 1970s, he led the JACL in a fight to right the wrongs done to the Japanese during WWII. He believed the government should admit its mistake by publicly apologizing to the Japanese Americans and paying compensation to those who suffered internment. In 1980 Congress funded a committee to report on the internment camp situation, and in 1983 the committee recommended that the government apologize. The committee also suggested $1.5 billion (about $20,000 per person interned) as compensation. Yasui meanwhile fought the government to clear his name, as his 1942 conviction still held. The government refused to reverse its decision, and when he died of cancer in 1986, the Supreme Court closed the case. Minoru Yasui died fighting.

On August 10, 1988, President Ronald Reagan signed the Civil Liberties Act of 1988, which provided each survivor of internment with the proposed $20,000. He also issued a formal apology, admitting the United States had wronged its citizens:

> What is important in this bill has less to do with property than with honor, for here we admit to wrong. Here, we reaffirm our commitment as a nation to equal justice under the law. (Kessler, p. 276)

Although Minoru Yasui was no longer alive, his children heard the message. It had taken over forty years for the United States to formally recognize its mistake. But, in the end, the government had reaffirmed the constitutional right of all of its citizens to be treated as equals. Minoru Yasui, in his long series of legal battles, played an important role in launching the struggle that led to this just verdict.

For More Information

Fukei, Budd. *The Japanese American Story.* Minneapolis: Dillon Press, Inc., 1976.

Hopkinson, Lynall. *Nothing to Forgive.* Trafalgar: Chatto and Windus, 1990.

Kessler, Lauren. *Stubborn Twig.* New York: Random House, 1993.

Leathers, Noel L. *The Japanese in America.* Minneapolis: Lerner Publications Company, 1967.

Felix Frankfurter

1882-1965

Personal Background

Felix Frankfurter was born in Vienna, Austria, on November 15, 1882. German Jews, the Frankfurters came from a long line of rabbis and scholars. Felix's parents, Leopold and Emma Winter Frankfurter, brought their six children from the Jewish ghetto in Vienna to New York in 1894, when Felix was twelve. Like most immigrants, they traveled steerage, crowded into the cheapest section of the ship with other families. The family settled in a German neighborhood on New York's Lower East Side. Leopold Frankfurter worked as a fur merchant and later set up a shop at home from which he sold linens. Though poor, he found his greatest satisfaction helping poorer neighbors, contributing money and food whenever he saw a need.

"Believing unbeliever." Though Leopold Frankfurter had studied to be a rabbi as a young man, the household was not highly religious. Later Felix would call himself a "believing unbeliever" (Baker, *Felix Frankfurter,* p. 18). He meant that, while not a religious person by nature or upbringing, he identified strongly with his Jewish cultural heritage.

Library attractions. Like many poor immigrants, Felix saw education as his best chance to improve his place in life. When he failed to win a scholarship to a private school, he attended P. S. 25 and later the City College of New York. But much of his education

▲ **Felix Frankfurter**

Event: Supreme Court civil liberties decisions; behind-the-scenes wartime advice to President Franklin D. Roosevelt.

Role: Appointed to the Supreme Court in 1939, Felix Frankfurter applied "judicial restraint" to his work, believing that the Court should hold back as much as possible from overturning laws passed by state legislatures or Congress. Alongside his position as Supreme Court justice, he served as one of President Franklin Roosevelt's closest advisors both before and during World War II.

came from reading on his own. As a boy and then as a college student, he spent long hours in the New York Public Library. He later claimed (only half-jokingly) to have read every newspaper there and said he could tell just by glancing at a few lines of type which paper it was. He also spent three or four late afternoons each week reading at the Cooper Union, a free library in lower Manhattan. He read constantly and widely and was always on the lookout for new books. In winter, aside from the fun of reading, he was also attracted to the libraries for another reason: free warmth.

Harvard Law School. While at City College, where he enjoyed success at debating and graduated third in his class, Felix decided on a career in the law. In 1903 he enrolled at Harvard Law School. His Jewishness was not the only obstacle he faced at that traditionally Anglo-Protestant institution. At five-feet-five-inches tall, he was shorter than his classmates. "The first day I was there," he later recalled, "I had one of the most intense frights of my life. I looked about me. Everybody was taller" (Frankfurter in Lash, p. 4). At the top of his class all three years, he left Harvard in 1906 with strong letters of recommendation from his professors, especially from James Barr Ames, dean of the law school. Yet law firms at the time were still dominated by Anglo-Protestant, upper-class members of old English colonial families. Despite his brilliant performance in law school, job offers did not flow in for the penniless young Jewish immigrant.

Henry L. Stimson. After a short while assisting John Chipman Gray, an old professor of his at Harvard, he did find a job at a fine New York law firm, Hornblower, Byrne, Miller and Potter. He was the first Jew the firm ever hired—and he only stayed a few months. For soon after, Dean Ames gave Frankfurter's name to the new United States Attorney for the Southern District of New York, Henry L. Stimson, who needed young lawyers on his staff. Appointed by President Theodore Roosevelt, Stimson wanted to clean up the office of shady dealings; previous officials had used it to line their own pockets with profits from big money cases. Stimson, by contrast, would be paid a regular government salary and take no percentage from the settlement of cases. At the time, Frankfurter made $1,000 per year at Hornblower. Stimson only offered him $750, but the idea of public service was such a strong temptation that he accepted Stimson's offer.

War Department. Stimson came from the upper-class background that had given Frankfurter so much trouble in his earlier job search, but the two got along very well. In 1910 President William Taft selected Stimson to be Secretary of War, and Stimson soon offered Frankfurter a job in the War Department. The following year, the young lawyer arrived in Washington, D.C.

While growing up in a poor New York neighborhood, Frankfurter heard coffee-shop discussions about ideas like socialism (public ownership of industry) and the troubles of the working man. He believed strongly in the government's taking action to control the power of the wealthy over the poor. In his work for the War Department, he represented the government in court, often against big corporations.

Oliver Wendell Holmes. Frankfurter had arrived in Washington with a letter of introduction from John Chipman Gray to Oliver Wendell Holmes, the famous Supreme Court justice (and Harvard Law School graduate). The two immediately liked each other. Like Stimson, Holmes came from the old upper class, in this case one of Boston's colonial Puritan families. Also like Stimson, he offered his younger friend an example of deep commitment to public service. But Holmes offered more: a view of the law that fit in closely with Frankfurter's own developing ideas.

As a younger man, Holmes had written a book, *The Common Law,* that had changed the way lawyers thought of the law. Instead of something handed down unchanged over centuries, the law was seen by Holmes as alive and constantly changing to suit the changing needs of society. He had brought this interpretation to his Supreme Court work, seeing the legislature, not the courts, as the proper channel through which to put society's desires into law. The courts, not being democratically elected, should not interfere with the laws unless the laws were clearly against the Constitution. Seventy when Frankfurter met him, Holmes had served on the Supreme Court for nine years. Tall and handsome, with distinguished features and a long white mustache, he would often be spotted on walks with the short stocky Frankfurter, who almost had to run to keep up. Both men specialized in witty, bubbling conversation, and they had long discussions on life and the law at Holmes's Washington apartment.

Return to Harvard. In 1914, after three years at the War Department, Harvard Law School offered Frankfurter a teaching job as a professor of law. Most of his friends, including Holmes and Stimson (both of whom thought his talents were best used in Washington), advised him to refuse the offer.

The only one who urged him to accept was Louis D. Brandeis, like Frankfurter a brilliant Jewish immigrant who had managed to open the normally locked doors of the Anglo-Protestant legal circle. Some twenty-five years older than Frankfurter, Brandeis in the 1870s had forced Harvard Law School to change its rules so that he could graduate under the age of twenty-one. He did so with the best record in the school's history. Famous for supporting causes such as labor unions and regulation of large corporations, Brandeis was also a close friend of Holmes and would join Holmes on the Supreme Court in 1916. Brandeis believed that Frankfurter could make his greatest contribution to society by helping to shape future generations of lawyers and leaders. Frankfurter agreed and left Washington for Massachusetts in the summer of 1914.

Teacher. It was a happy choice: Frankfurter loved teaching, and Harvard created a new professorship specially for him. For the next twenty-five years, he was the first Byrne Professor of Administrative Law. They were busy years. For one thing, Frankfurter did not cut off his Washington connections. During World War I, for example, he returned briefly to Washington (in 1917) as special assistant to Secretary of War Newton Baker. And in 1918 he served as chairman of the War Labor Policies Board, overseeing the channeling of four million workers from their regular jobs into defense industries. He also helped many law graduates find jobs in law firms, and each year he selected students to work as clerks (assistants) for friends such as Holmes and Brandeis.

Marriage. In 1919 Frankfurter married Marion Denman, whom he had met six years earlier and courted ever since. The two rounded out each other's personalities. His outgoing, talkative humor was balanced by her quiet wit, and his thinking side found its match in her sensing of right from wrong. He almost always sought her opinion on important things, valuing the difference in their approaches. Childless, their marriage was happy and lasting.

Activist. While at Harvard, Frankfurter won a growing reputation as a liberal activist, especially for his support of civil liberties causes. In 1920 he was a founding member of the American Civil Liberties Union (ACLU), an organization devoted to protecting the rights and liberties guaranteed in the Constitution. He also led the way in protesting the conviction and execution of Nicola Sacco and Bartolomeo Vanzetti, Italian immigrants who were charged with killing two people during an armed robbery. Such activities made Frankfurter highly unpopular with certain Bostonians, especially with Harvard president A. Lawrence Lowell, who publicly feuded with Frankfurter over the Sacco and Vanzetti case.

Participation: Civil Liberties Decisions and Wartime Advice to President Roosevelt

New Deal. In 1906 a mutual friend had introduced Frankfurter to another young lawyer named Franklin Delano Roosevelt, a cousin of then-president Theodore Roosevelt. The two had become friends, and after Franklin Roosevelt was elected president in 1932, he often turned to Frankfurter for advice and assistance. Still teaching at Harvard, Frankfurter played a major role in shaping much of the social program Roosevelt called "the New Deal." He helped write several pieces of legislation for it, including the Securities Act of 1933 and the Securities Exchange Act of 1934.

Supreme Court. In 1939 President Roosevelt appointed Frankfurter to the United States Supreme Court. Liberals applauded the choice at first, but many soon had second thoughts. Frankfurter, the activist law professor, proved to be anything but an activist as a judge. In his years teaching, Frankfurter had developed his own philosophy of the law, one that owed much to the ideas of his friend Oliver Wendell Holmes. Like Holmes, he thought that the courts should be slow to overturn the laws passed by Congress or state legislatures. The legislatures, he reasoned, not the courts, were the elected representatives of the people.

In more than two decades on the Court, Frankfurter's main concern was always to avoid putting his personal views over the aims of the legislatures, unless the laws clearly went against the Constitution. This policy of "judicial restraint" disappointed many liberals but was the cornerstone of Frankfurter's method of operation.

Nazi threat. Like many immigrants, the Austrian-born Frankfurter was fiercely patriotic towards his adopted country. He witnessed the rise of Hitler during the 1930s, regarding it as a terrible threat that must be met with unity and strength. As a Jew, he was horrified at the brutal policies of Nazi anti-Semitism (hatred and persecution of Jews). But to Frankfurter, the danger presented by Hitler went beyond his persecution of the Jews. Frankfurter saw the forces of Nazism as a threat to Western civilization itself.

When war broke out in Europe in 1939, Roosevelt, knowing that the public wished to stay out of the war, declared America's neutrality. Frankfurter, however, continually urged the president to support the democracies of Europe against the Nazi threat. In the months leading up to the German invasion of Poland, which started the war, Frankfurter sent his friend almost 300 notes arguing for U.S. opposition to Germany. There was much the United States could do, he urged, even without declaring war. Roosevelt held a "fireside chat" to the nation a few days after the outbreak of war. In the chat, the president declared that the United States would remain neutral but added that he would not ask his listeners to stay neutral in their minds. Roosevelt knew that there was a strong sympathy in America for Hitler's victims. Following the chat, Frankfurter sent the president a telegram: "MANY THANKS AND ESPECIALLY FOR NOT REQUIRING US TO BE NEUTRAL IN OUR THOUGHTS" (Frankfurter in Lash, p. 74).

The Gobitis case. The first civil liberties case that came up after Frankfurter's appointment to the Court showed how seriously he took the possibility of war. The Gobitis case turned out to be one of the most controversial decisions of his Supreme Court career. In November 1935, Lillian and William Gobitis had been expelled from their public school in Minersville, Pennsylvania, because they refused to salute the flag. Their family belonged to a religious sect, the Jehovah's Witnesses, that prohibited flag saluting. Their father took the case to court. He won on the grounds that making the children salute the flag violated their constitutional right to freedom of religion. After an appeals court upheld the decision, the school board appealed to the Supreme Court in June 1940.

"National unity." Although he personally did not approve of forcing children to salute the flag, Frankfurter wrote the Court's opinion overturning the lower court decision. In a time of peril, he argued, the country had the right to demand a show of patriotism from its citizens. "National unity," he wrote, "is the basis of national security.... The flag is the symbol of our national unity, transcending [rising above] all internal differences, however large" (Baker, *Felix Frankfurter,* p. 245). Frankfurter might also have had in mind his old friend Oliver Wendell Holmes's famous decision in a similar case that arose during World War I. In that case, concerning freedom of speech, Holmes had written that circumstances, such as war, affect the rights of people in society. For example, Holmes wrote, the First Amendment "would not protect a man falsely shouting fire in a theater and causing a panic" (Baker, *The Justice From Beacon Hill,* pp. 523-24).

Reversal. A second flag-saluting case came up in 1943. This time the Court reversed its earlier stand and decided that flag-saluting laws did in fact violate freedom of religion. Three justices, earlier persuaded by Frankfurter's arguments, changed their minds and publicly said that they had been wrong to vote as they had in *Gobitis.* Frankfurter stuck to his guns, but this time he was on the losing side. His liberal friends could not understand why he would seemingly support flag-saluting laws, but they could not shake him in his beliefs.

Behind the scenes. When selected for the Supreme Court, Frankfurter had resigned from the many liberal associations to which he belonged, including the ACLU and the National Association for the Advancement of Colored People (NAACP). Despite getting out of these official commitments, though, he remained one of Washington's most influential insiders through his friendship with President Roosevelt. As war drew nearer in 1940, for example, Roosevelt began looking for a new secretary of war, having little confidence in Harry Woodring, the man currently filling the position. It was Frankfurter who suggested his old friend Henry Stimson, now seventy-two but tough and experienced. Stimson held this highly important position right through the war, until 1945. Like Roosevelt, he often turned to Frankfurter for advice.

Preparation for war. One reason Frankfurter pushed Stimson for war secretary was that Stimson, like Frankfurter, believed in doing everything possible to oppose the Nazis, despite America's official neutrality. From the early 1930s, Frankfurter had encouraged Roosevelt to favor Britain and the Allies. By 1941, it had become clear that America would join the war, and Frankfurter spent much of that year helping the government prepare. In January, for example, he helped write the Lend-Lease Act, which provided the Allies with over $50 billion worth of military supplies by 1945. Using his international connections, he also helped Roosevelt's advisor Harry Hopkins establish a warm relationship with British leader Winston Churchill. Hopkins's successful visit to England paved the way for close relations between Churchill and Roosevelt himself.

A scientist's concerns. Frankfurter's British friendships had been cemented in 1933, when he had spent a year as a visiting professor at Oxford University in England. During that year, he had met the Danish scientist Niels Bohr, pioneer nuclear physicist and Nobel Prize winner. The two had become friends when Bohr looked up Frankfurter during a visit to Washington, D.C., in 1939. When the Germans occupied Denmark, Bohr stayed there, despite British offers to help him escape. But by late 1943 the Nazis planned to arrest Bohr, who publicly opposed them, and make him work on their own atom bomb project. He allowed the British to smuggle him and his family out of Denmark.

Soon called on to help Allied scientists already working on the atomic bomb in America, Bohr realized for the first time how close they were to success (see **J. Robert Oppenheimer**). At lunch one day, Bohr confided to Frankfurter his worries over the bomb's international consequences. His major fear was of a dangerous international nuclear arms race after the war. Because his theories had been central to the bomb's development, he felt a heavy burden of responsibility.

Approach to Roosevelt. Frankfurter approached the president, who admitted that he had worries similar to Bohr's about a postwar nuclear arms race. For almost a year, Frankfurter acted as a go-between, helping Bohr write notes and suggestions, then presenting them to Roosevelt. Bohr's main point was that the United States should share its nuclear technology with the Soviet Union. The technology could never remain secret, and the Soviet Union had its own scientists who would eventually develop the bomb on their own, Bohr argued. By sharing the technology before that happened, Bohr thought, the two nations might develop an attitude of friendly cooperation rather than hostile competition. In August 1944, after a long meeting with Bohr, Roosevelt agreed that the information should be shared with the Soviet Union.

Objections. Soon after, however, Roosevelt met with Winston Churchill, and the iron-willed British prime minister voiced strong objections to Bohr's idea. Churchill distrusted Bohr and viewed him as a security risk. He persuaded Roosevelt to keep the bomb a secret from the Soviets, and even to keep a close eye on Bohr as a possible spy. After Roosevelt's death in early 1945, Frankfurter and Bohr lost any chance to influence American policy. With the new president, Harry S Truman, Frankfurter lacked the old and lasting friendship that had made him one of Roosevelt's most trusted advisors.

Aftermath

Further career. Though no longer quite the insider he had been with a close friend in the White House, Frankfurter continued his influential career on the Supreme Court. He also kept challenging other liberal judges on the Court with his philosophy of judicial restraint, especially in cases involving civil liberties.

Illness. By the early 1950s, Marion Frankfurter began suffering from arthritis that soon kept her in bed. Felix spent hours nearby, reading to her or just talking. He would often rush in quickly to share something interesting he had just heard from one of the household's many visitors. In 1962, he himself suffered a severe stroke and retired after twenty-three years on the nation's highest court. Confined to a wheelchair, he continued to enjoy the lively conversations that had become his trademark. Frankfurter died on February 22, 1965, after suffering a heart attack the previous day. He was eighty-two years old.

For More Information

Baker, Liva. *Felix Frankfurter.* New York: Coward-McCann, 1969.

Baker, Liva. *The Justice from Beacon Hill: The Life and Times of Oliver Wendell Holmes.* New York: HarperCollins, 1991.

Lash, Joseph. *From the Diaries of Felix Frankfurter.* New York: Norton, 1975.

J. Robert Oppenheimer

1904-1967

Personal Background

J. Robert Oppenheimer was born in New York City on April 22, 1904. His father, Julius, a German Jew from the town of Hanau, had immigrated in 1888. In 1903 Julius Oppenheimer, a successful exporter of cloth, married Ella Friedman, a young painter. They called their first child Robert, later adding Julius's first initial "J." at the front because it seemed to sound better.

"Ask me a question." Because of his father's success, Robert grew up in the comfortable surroundings of New York's upper-middle class, spending his childhood in the family's elegant apartment on fashionable Riverside Drive. Though Jewish by blood, his parents had for the most part separated themselves from Jewish culture and religion. They sent Robert and later his younger brother Frank to the Ethical Culture School, which rejected religion, teaching that moral values come from independent thought instead of religious beliefs. Robert spent ten years at the school. He loved learning and excelled in a wide range of subjects, from science to poetry and ancient Greek. "Ask me a question," he boasted to a cousin at age eleven, "and I will answer you in Greek" (Oppenheimer in Goodchild, p. 12).

Mountains. Graduating from the Ethical Culture School with ten straight A's in his last year, he spent a restless year at home. An

▲ J. Robert Oppenheimer

Event: The Manhattan Project.

Role: As head of the weapons lab at Los Alamos, New Mexico, physicist J. Robert Oppenheimer led the U.S. effort, called the Manhattan Project, to build the first atomic bomb. Racing against the Germans to complete it, Oppenheimer's team of scientists and engineers tested the bomb in July 1945. In August the United States dropped two atomic bombs on the Japanese cities of Hiroshima and Nagasaki, thereby ending World War II.

intestinal illness prevented him from enrolling in college as planned. Earlier in life seen by friends as somewhat of a "mama's boy," he now shut himself away in his room and ignored her attempts to pamper him.

In the spring, his father asked one of his teachers to take Robert on a trip west, to the Rockies, to see if a change would help his obvious depression. The trip worked. The two rode horseback through the mountains of Colorado and New Mexico, camping at guest ranches. At one ranch, young Robert had his first crush, on the pretty older woman who ran it. For the rest of his life, Oppenheimer would return to those mountains when his spirit needed refreshing.

Harvard. In 1922, at eighteen, Oppenheimer enrolled in Harvard University. He decided to major in chemistry, after considering other choices such as poetry, Greek and Latin classics, painting and architecture. Working intensely, he finished the chemistry major in just three years. But near the middle of his stay, his interest was captured by a physics class he took with the well-known physicist Percy Bridgman. In his last year, he conducted a research project with Bridgman. When Oppenheimer decided to go on to do graduate work in physics, Bridgman wrote him a letter of recommendation to the renowned Cavendish Laboratory in Cambridge, England.

England and Germany. Oppenheimer stayed only a few months at Cavendish, however. It was the leading center of experimental physics, and Oppenheimer soon realized that he was simply not good at doing experiments. He suffered another bout of depression. Once more, a camping trip with friends was called for, this time to the Italian islands of Corsica (where another romantic crush helped lift his spirits) and Sardinia.

On returning to England, Oppenheimer accepted an offer from Max Born, a leading theoretical physicist, to finish his graduate degree at the University of Göttingen in Germany. Just as Cavendish led the way in experimental physics, Göttingen dominated theoretical physics. (The two branches of physics work together. Theoretical physicists come up with theories or ideas that the experimenters can check; experimental physicists come up with results that the theorists try to explain.) Oppenheimer turned out to be much better at this type of physics and earned his doctorate at Göttingen in 1927.

Cal Tech and Berkeley. In 1928 Oppenheimer went to the California Institute of Technology (Cal Tech) to teach and to continue his research. No sooner had he begun work there than his success in Germany brought him job offers from ten American universities and two foreign institutions. He accepted the offer from the University of California at Berkeley for two reasons. First, in his words, Berkeley was "a desert. There was no theoretical physics and I thought it would be nice to try and start something" (Oppenheimer in Goodchild, p. 22). Also, Berkeley, in northern California, agreed to let him go south each spring to teach at Cal Tech.

Building American physics. Over the next thirteen years, Oppenheimer did more than any other person to bring American physics up to the standards of Europe. He did indeed "start something," attracting the brightest young students to both Berkeley and Cal Tech, many of whom went on to distinguished careers of their own. Crucial also to Berkeley's excitement in the 1930s was the presence of Ernest Lawrence, a brilliant experimental physicist whose work challenged Oppenheimer's theoretical skills. Lawrence pioneered the use of the particle accelerator, which uses powerful magnets to speed up some atomic particles and smash them into other ones. The results of these high-energy collisions allow scientists to draw conclusions about the structure of atoms themselves. The accelerator remains the modern physicist's basic tool.

> ## Birth of the Quantum
>
> Oppenheimer came to Göttingen at a remarkable time, just as European physicists were developing the theory of atomic structure known as "quantum mechanics." Quantum mechanics is the description in mathematical terms of how matter works on the smallest possible scales. It describes the behavior of electrons, protons, and neutrons, which make up atoms. Finding a way to describe these tiny particles turned out to be one of the most important events in the history of the twentieth century. Not only did quantum theory lead to the atomic bomb, but it made possible lasers, computers, and other devices that have transformed modern life.

Spell of excitement. Using Lawrence's results, Oppenheimer made important contributions to the theory of the atomic nucleus, the new theory of antimatter, and the understanding of cosmic rays. With his student Hartland Snyder, he provided the first theory to explain the gravitational collapse of stars and the possibility of resulting black holes. Despite such contributions, however, his greatest importance was in his ability to inspire others. Tall, skinny, with unruly dark hair and an intense way of making his points while teaching, Oppenheimer held his students under a spell of excitement. Many of them copied his style of speaking or walking. He took them to dinner and led discussions on literature or poetry as well as the latest physics discoveries. By the late 1930s, he and Lawrence had made Berkeley the equal of any European physics center. Students flocked there, rather than having to go abroad as he had done, to finish their educations.

Participation: The Manhattan Project

Splitting the atom. In 1934 Enrico Fermi succeeded in bombarding a type of uranium with neutrons, particles from the nucleus of an atom. Fermi reported the reaction, which in 1938 was called "nuclear fission" by German scientists.

The scientists recognized the importance of nuclear fission. Uranium is itself a source of free neutrons. When one uranium atom gives off a neutron, the neutron might split the nucleus of a nearby atom. When that nucleus is split, it releases some of its neutrons and large amounts of heat energy are produced. Some of the released neutrons bombard other nuclei, splitting them as well. If enough of the right kind of pure uranium (U-235) is present, a quantity called "critical mass," the process will continue by itself.

This chain reaction, the scientists realized, could result in a vast, instant outpouring of energy—in other words, an explosion stronger than anyone had ever imagined. But enough active material had to be brought together to sustain the chain reaction for there to be an explosion.

First involvement. The German scientists, men with whom Oppenheimer had worked closely in the 1920s, made their discovery in December 1938. By this time, Hitler and the Nazis had been in power in Germany for five years. World War II would break out the following year. Learning that the Germans might construct such a terrible weapon, Roosevelt created a U.S. atomic research program.

For two years, however, the program made little serious progress. By September 1941, its senior scientist, James Conant, had begun to grow impatient with the delays. Many U.S. scientists had also become increasingly alarmed. One of them was Oppenheimer's old friend Ernest Lawrence, who approached Conant. When Conant asked Lawrence to devote himself to the project, Lawrence agreed. He could use his particle accelerators in Berkeley to help make the special uranium needed for the bomb. But how much would be needed? To answer that question, Lawrence turned to Oppenheimer. For several weeks, Oppenheimer worked on the calculations. On October 21, he presented his results. Critical mass, he concluded, was about 220 pounds.

Rapid Rupture. From that point on, Oppenheimer was closely involved in meetings held by Lawrence, Conant, and others. In May 1942, with the United States now at war, Oppenheimer was appointed chairman of the "Rapid Rupture" group of physicists who were investigating possible designs for the bomb. The name (which Oppenheimer found hilarious) referred to the central problem of how to bring the critical mass together quickly enough so that it would explode violently.

Army control. It soon grew clear that much more money would be needed than had been spent on the project so far. Purifying enough U-235 would require not only research but also massive plants, which would have to be built. Similarly, putting together the bomb itself would require special facilities as well as physicists and other experts to do the work. During wartime, only one organization could undertake such a large and complex task: the army. So far, a number of different institutions had been working pretty much on their own. Now, under army control, the entire project would be centralized into one effort.

The German Bomb

European scientists led the world in physics in the early 1900s, and many of them—men such as Albert Einstein, Max Born, and Werner Heisenberg—were German. A number of these European scientists, especially Jews like Einstein, fled Nazi persecution in the 1930s. Most came to America—Hans Bethe, Edward Teller, Leo Szilard, and many others—contributing to the American war effort with their work on the Manhattan Project. Others, like Werner Heisenberg, stayed in Germany. Heisenberg was in charge of developing an atomic bomb for Germany. In 1941 the Germans were far ahead of anyone else in their research, yet Heisenberg discouraged his countrymen from making such a weapon during wartime. In early 1942, he advised Hitler that it would be too expensive even to try making an atomic bomb. After Heisenberg's advice, the German effort pretty much ground to a halt.

In September 1942, the project was assigned to Colonel Leslie R. Groves, the military engineer who had been in charge of building the U.S. military headquarters, the Pentagon. Groves, tough and ruthless, had a reputation as a man who got things done.

Wives, girlfriends, and communists. Aside from the huge problems of organization, Groves also faced the issue of security. Though Germany was the enemy, many in the army were more concerned about the Soviet Union, whose communist government was also fighting the Germans. A major army concern was to keep the work on the atom from falling into Soviet hands.

To many Americans, it seemed that communism was the best hope of fighting fascist governments like that of Hitler, and of improving life for workers in industrial nations. Oppenheimer and many of his friends had connections to the American Communist Party. Oppenheimer's younger brother, Frank, had joined the Communist Party, as had Frank's wife, Jackie. Oppenheimer himself had a girlfriend in the 1930s who was a member of the party, and he had supported causes, like organized labor, with communist-like aims.

Pronto. In November 1940, Oppenheimer married Kitty Puening, who was also once a communist. Her first husband, with whom she had joined the party, had died (like many other American volunteers) fighting the fascist armies of Spanish dictator Francisco Franco during the Spanish Civil War. The marriage to Oppenheimer was Kitty's fourth. A son, Peter, was born in May 1941. They called him Pronto, because he had been born so soon after their wedding date. Kitty, in fact, had divorced her fourth husband the same day she married Oppenheimer, with whom she had become involved while still married. Most of Oppenheimer's friends disliked her strongly, viewing her as a schemer who took advantage of his lack of experience.

Clearance. By late 1942, as meetings on Rapid Rupture continued, the head engineer, Groves, had come to value Oppenheimer highly. Oppenheimer suggested to Groves that it might be best to create a single laboratory where all the scientists could work together. That way, they could discuss their ideas freely, without worrying so much about security, because the laboratory itself could be protected from the outside world. Groves liked the idea.

But who should head the lab? Groves considered Lawrence, but Lawrence was needed to work on purifying the uranium. He quickly settled on Oppenheimer, impressed by his enthusiasm.

When questioned about his past by security agents, Oppenheimer openly admitted to having been "a member of just about every Communist front organization on the West Coast" (Oppenheimer in Goodchild, p. 51), though he had never joined the party itself. Against FBI recommendations, Groves decided to give Oppenheimer full security clearance to do top secret work.

Los Alamos. After Groves had considered and rejected a number of sites for the lab, Oppenheimer suggested a distant spot in his beloved New Mexico. He had been through the area many times on horseback. Near the rugged Sangre de Cristo range, remote Los Alamos lay at 7,000 feet in the mountains west of Santa Fe. A boys' school already existed there, which the government could take over, so buildings, electricity and water would be available. Groves approved immediately.

Eggheads. Oppenheimer spent Christmas of 1942 planning the layout of the laboratory complex, figuring on perhaps 100 scientists and technicians living and working there. As construction began, though, he began to realize that he had seriously underestimated the task before him. By March, he had increased the lab's personnel to 1,500 and had begun the difficult job of finding and recruiting the workers. He could not tell them what they would be working on until after they had agreed to join the top secret project. Also, he had to warn them that they would be completely cut off from the outside world until the war ended. Yet by concentrating first on recruiting a few famous physicists to head various divisions of the lab, he managed to make the project attractive to others.

It was a clever solution to a challenging problem, but there would be many other such problems. The physicists were high-powered men, many—like Enrico Fermi, Hans Bethe, and Edward Teller, for example—with great scientific reputations. They did not always take kindly to being told what to do by the army, especially when it came to security, since the scientists were in the habit of freely exchanging ideas. For their part, the army people saw the physicists as spoiled and out-of-touch with reality. As Groves himself was reputed to have complained, "at great expense we have assembled the greatest collection of eggheads ever" (Goodchild, p. 79). By the end, there would be over 3,000 physicists and technicians, men who did not fit into the army mold. It was Oppenheimer's job to make this uneasy partnership work.

Critical mass. In early 1943, Oppenheimer's main problem was still how to assemble critical mass—that is, how to bring together two pieces of U-235 quickly enough to create a chain reaction that would produce the explosion. Earlier work with the Rapid Rupture group had settled on the "gun method," in which one piece of uranium would be fired like a bullet into another, sphere-shaped uranium target.

A young scientist named Seth Neddermeyer had a different idea, called implosion. Neddermeyer pictured a hollow ball of uranium, surrounded by explosive. When the explosive went off, the hollow center would collapse, and the now compacted sphere would become critical. Most rejected the idea—the explosion would have to be perfectly even all around the sphere, which seemed impossible—but Oppenheimer told Neddermeyer to go ahead with research on his own.

Material for fission. Oppenheimer worked under very difficult conditions. He had to develop an atomic weapon without enough radioactive material to properly test possible designs. (Radioactive material is material made up of atoms with the type of nucleus that gives off neutrons on its own.)

By early 1944, under Groves's supervision, huge factories with tens of thousands of employees had been built at Oak Ridge, Tennessee, and Hanford, Washington. Some were based on Lawrence's accelerators; others used different methods to refine the uranium to the high level of purity needed. One of the Hanford plant's missions was to produce plutonium, a man-made radioactive material thought to be possible for a bomb. But production was slower than expected. None of the methods for refining uranium seemed to work well, and the plants kept breaking down. As for plutonium, Oppenheimer and his team were not even sure it would be useful.

Time of crisis. By the summer of 1944, both problems— material and assembly—had become connected. Uranium would work with the gun method, but production had become so slow that only enough material for one bomb would be ready by mid-1945. This meant if Oppenheimer wanted to test a bomb, there would not be one available for use in war. Furthermore, tests of plutonium showed that it would work, but the gun method would be too slow. A plutonium bomb would have to use Neddermeyer's implosion method. Groves's factories could produce plenty of plutonium, but could Oppenheimer perfect implosion in time to use it? So far, Neddermeyer had made no progress. It simply seemed impossible to create a perfectly even explosion around the bomb's core.

Explosive lens. The answer came when British scientists joined the project. Among them was a young Englishman named James Tuck, who suggested using an explosive lens to direct the force just as a regular lens directs light rays. If such lenses were focused around the core, Tuck suggested, it should be possible to produce an even explosion. In the late summer and fall of 1944, Oppenheimer completely reorganized the implosion team, adding hundreds of scientists and speeding up tests and research.

Trinity. Gradually, the implosion bomb began to take shape. In early 1945, the army took over land for a test of it, uprooting the few ranchers in the area (some of whom had to be forced to leave). The deserted area, code-named Trinity, was south of Albuquerque—close enough to Los Alamos for easy transportation but isolated enough for safety and security. Early on July 16, 1945, Oppenheimer oversaw a successful test of the implosion weapon.

Shatterer of worlds. Under huge strain, Oppenheimer had lost weight, so that, while over six-feet tall, he weighed only 115 pounds. As he watched, a huge mushroom cloud and fireball ignited and spread across the sky, and the world entered the nuclear age. Later, Oppenheimer remembered the moment:

> A few people laughed, a few people cried, most people were silent. There floated through my mind a line from the *Bhagavad-Gita* [an Indian poem] in which Krishna is trying to persuade the Prince that he should do his duty: "I am become death, the shatterer of worlds." (Oppenheimer in Goodchild, p. 162)

Fateful decision. In May 1945, before the test, Oppenheimer had participated in a meeting to discuss the scientists' views on actually using the bomb. Germany had been defeated the previous year, which left only Japan as a possible target. The committee discussed other possibilities, such as demonstrating the bomb in front of Japanese officials.

Such a demonstration, Oppenheimer reasoned, might not work for a number of reasons. The Japanese might shoot down the plane that was going to drop the bomb. They might take American prisoners to the demonstration zone. The officials might downplay the weapon's strength on returning to Japan, or Japan might refuse to surrender anyway. American planes were already taking many Japanese lives in bombing raids on Tokyo and other cities. Furthermore, when American soldiers had to invade Japan, many could expect to be killed. The committee finally recommended that the bomb be used against Japan. The final decision, however, was President Truman's.

Hiroshima and Nagasaki. Truman decided to use the bomb. On August 6, 1945, the atomic bomb, code-named "Little Boy," was dropped on the city of Hiroshima, with devastating results. From 78,000 to 200,000 were killed, with over 60,000 buildings destroyed. The entire center of the city was wiped out in a fraction of a second. Later, thousands began dying of radiation sickness, the results of the bomb's radioactive fallout. Only three days later, on August 9, the second bomb was dropped on the city of Nagasaki. Over 100,000 were killed that day, again with more dying later of radiation sickness. On August 14, Japan surrendered.

Aftermath

"Father of the A-Bomb." As news of the secret work at Los Alamos became public, Oppenheimer was suddenly one of the most famous scientists in America: the "Father of the A-Bomb," as the press dubbed him. For most of the next decade, he acted as scientific advisor at the highest levels of government, helping politicians try to deal with the awesome new power that had been unleashed. He served on several committees that worked out U.S. policy on both atomic energy and atomic weapons. In 1947 he was appointed director of the Institute for Advanced Study at Princeton University.

As he had at Berkeley in the 1930s, Oppenheimer single-handedly built the institute into a top-notch physics research center.

Cold War hearings. By the early 1950s, Oppenheimer's blunt and often arrogant way of expressing his opinions had made him some powerful enemies. In particular, his opposition to the "H-Bomb" (a more powerful nuclear bomb that uses hydrogen rather than plutonium or uranium) angered both scientists and air force commanders. As anticommunist hysteria, spurred by Senator Joseph McCarthy, swept the nation, they saw their chance. In 1953 they used Oppenheimer's past ties to communism to get President Eisenhower to take away his security clearance.

In 1954 a month-long hearing, which in effect put Oppenheimer on trial as a Communist spy, ended in a refusal to return his security clearance. It was thought that he might have helped pass information to the Soviets while working on the Manhattan Project. He would never again be called on to advise the government, though his academic career at Princeton would continue. In response to the hearing, the scientific community rallied around Oppenheimer.

Fermi Award. In 1963 the Atomic Energy Commission and President Lyndon Johnson—as if making up for past injustice—presented Oppenheimer with the highly regarded Fermi Award for contributions to theoretical physics. Soon after, his health began to fail. Oppenheimer died of cancer on February 18, 1967, at the age of sixty-two.

For More Information

Goodchild, Peter. *J. Robert Oppenheimer: Shatterer of Worlds.* New York: Fromm, 1985.

Pagels, Heinz. *The Cosmic Code: Quantum Physics as the Language of Nature.* New York: Bantam Books, 1983.

Royal, Denise. *The Story of J. Robert Oppenheimer.* New York: St. Martin's Press, 1969.

Dorothy Thompson

1893-1961

Personal Background

Dorothy Thompson was born July 9, 1893, in Lancaster, a rural community in upstate New York. Her father, Peter Thompson, was an extremely kind minister, who welcomed anyone in need into his home. Margaret Thompson, her mother, was equally kind and, as Dorothy remembered, radiantly beautiful. At times the Thompsons, who had two other children, were so poor that the family ate only an apple or a cup of rice for supper. Yet they happily shared anything they had with friends or passing strangers. Dorothy was a sassy, bright child who loved knowledge as much as she enjoyed playing practical jokes on her brother and sister.

A childhood of hardship. Dorothy's first memory was of her father seated next to the fireplace, holding her younger brother in a blanket. The child was sick with whooping cough at the time. After he healed completely, the image of her father's loving and healing spirit never left Dorothy. The blanket in the minister's arms seemed to warm and protect the whole room, and the whole family. Later in her life, during hard times, Dorothy would recall this image to gain faith and hope for the future.

Unfortunately, she was forced to recall the memory quite often. When Dorothy was seven, her pregnant mother was killed accidentally by her grandmother. Dorothy's grandmother thought

▲ **Dorothy Thompson**

Event: World War II.

Role: One of the most accomplished journalists of the twentieth century, Dorothy Thompson used her talents to fight the spread of Nazism and the destruction caused by World War II.

that her daughter's fourth pregnancy would cause her too much pain and poverty and therefore gave her herbs to cause a miscarriage. The herbs proved too poisonous and killed Margaret Thompson and her unborn baby within two days. While on her deathbed, Margaret asked Dorothy to promise to take care of her father and the rest of the family. Dorothy agreed and fulfilled the promise as best she could until she was dealt another blow three years later. Her father got remarried to an unkind woman named Eliza Abbott.

Dorothy's stepmother treated her poorly, often calling her names and belittling her. One Christmas, Dorothy opened a present from Eliza containing a tiny baby bottle and a card that read: "Merry Christmas to a cry-baby" (Kurth, p. 27). Within two years, her stepmother sent her away to live with two aunts in Chicago, Illinois. Dorothy's respect for her father dwindled because he did little to try and stop Eliza from sending Dorothy away. She nevertheless remained grateful to him for encouraging her to read, a habit that helped her escape the pain of a difficult childhood.

A born journalist. Dorothy's life in Chicago was pleasant enough. In fact, her aunts gave her more attention than she received at home. She excelled in school and enrolled in junior college at the age of fifteen. In 1912 she entered Syracuse University in New York and graduated with honors in 1914.

Dorothy stayed in New York and almost immediately found a job. Women were seeking the right to vote at the time, and Dorothy went to work for the cause, stuffing envelopes at the New York State Women's Suffrage Party headquarters. An interest in writing, discovered during her college years, led to her producing dozens of papers—mostly on political and women's issues. She shared these writings with key people at the headquarters. Her friends here had connections in the state, and her work was excellent, which resulted in its being published frequently in local newspapers. Around this time, she decided to become a reporter, or journalist.

Thompson raised enough money to head for Russia via Europe in 1920. She reasoned that a woman was more likely to succeed as a journalist in Europe than in America. Also, the pull of a revolution in Russia was enough to attract Thompson. On the boat to London, England, she met a group of Zionists (people dedicated to reestablishing a Jewish state in Palestine). They were headed for a conference on the issue. Thompson began interviewing them and researching the Zionist cause, and when the boat landed in London twelve days later, she held in her hand the story that launched her career. The International News Service published her article on the struggle for Palestine. The story made Thompson an instant success. Afterwards she was engulfed in news assignments that spread across several countries. Thompson shelved thoughts of Russia, sensing that Europe needed her first.

Revolution. The following year, at the age of twenty-eight, Thompson went to Vienna, Austria, to report on the condition of Central Europe. Soon after she arrived, rioting broke out in the city over an emergency loan that was not delivered to the people of Vienna. Dressed in a fur coat that she had received as a gift, she headed for the center of the mob, where she was warned by a rioter that the symbol of luxury she wore on her back might excite some members of the crowd even more. So she took off the coat, learning one of her first lessons as a reporter: "Never wear a fur coat ... to a revolution" (Kurth, p. 74).

The twenty-eight-year-old reporter quickly discovered that there were very serious dangers in being a journalist at the time. In 1921, while she stood on a balcony during an uprising in Bulgaria, someone down below took a shot at Thompson. She was usually a tough reporter, but the experience caused her to faint on the spot. Thompson awoke to realize she had lived through one of the worst dangers a journalist of her kind had to face.

Sinclair Lewis and Twin Farms. After suffering through a brief, failed marriage to foreign correspondent Joseph Bard, Thompson fell deeply in love with novelist Sinclair Lewis. Lewis asked her to marry him the first night they met, and she accepted. They married in 1928, settling in Vermont with enough money from their successful careers to live in comfort. Lewis built Thompson two houses and named them Twin Farms. In one, she could write her regularly featured newspaper columns, and in the other, he could create his prize-winning novels. By this time, Thompson had become one of the most controversial journalists in America. Lewis, meanwhile, was a star in his own right. As a couple, they became the subject of media attention for many years.

The marriage, however, was less than happy. Lewis, an alcoholic, would fly into rages when he could no longer stand his wife's discussing politics with their friends. Thompson clearly put her career first, above marriage or anything else. In 1930 they had a son, Michael, and Lewis received a Nobel Prize. Perhaps, they hoped, these blessings would help the marriage survive. Unfortunately, Lewis withdrew even more than before and practically ignored their son. Meanwhile, Thompson thought nothing of leaving on assignments, by herself, for ten months out of the year. As her career soared, her family life crumbled. She received applause from a fellow reporter, who called her "the best journalist this generation has produced in any country" (Kurth, p. 159). But her personal life was failing. She had an unhappy, neglected child and a bitter husband who wanted a divorce.

Expelled from Germany. After her separation from Lewis, Thompson headed for Germany. Adolf Hitler agreed to do an interview with her in December 1931. Thompson, who found Hitler annoyingly difficult and small, predicted that this little man would never reach power. She published her dislike of him in several articles and a book called *I Saw Hitler!,* in which she attacked the Nazi cause and scoffed at Hitler's passionate desire for dictatorship. Of course, she was deeply embarrassed and disappointed when he later rose to power.

Hitler did not approve of Thompson either. After reading her repeated attacks on his character and political beliefs, he grew enraged. He vowed to take revenge on the journalist.

Thompson had decided to remain in Germany and report on Nazi events as they happened. In 1933 she began noticing a surge in support for the Nazi party. Standing on a German hotel balcony, she saw the first wave of storm troopers march by, shouting, "Perish the Jews!" (Kurth, p. 164). As she drove through the German streets, she noticed Nazi flags hanging from every house. She even stumbled upon a Hitler Youth camp, in which 6,000 young boys were being trained under a huge, swastika-marked flag that read: "YOU WERE BORN TO DIE FOR GERMANY!" (Kurth, p. 201). Horrified, she continued to report from Germany, pleading for America and the world to show open disapproval for the Nazis.

The following year, Hitler wanted to hear no more from Thompson. On August 25, 1934, as she finished breakfast in her hotel room, an agent from the Gestapo (Nazi secret police) handed her an expulsion order from Hitler. The order stated that her remarks against Germany had caused her to be expelled from the country and that she had twenty-four hours in which to leave.

The leading female voice. Thompson felt that Hitler was upset not about the attacks she was accused of making against his country but rather about her attacks against his character. She consequently fled Germany in a hurry. Her arrival in America was a celebrated event. Greeted with roses from other journalists, she also received praise from many Americans for her bravery. She came home as a leader in American journalism: she was the first of the foreign correspondents to be expelled personally by Hitler.

Building on her reputation, Thompson went on a lecture tour. She gained more fame with every stop, becoming known as a leading opponent of dictator governments and an expert on world affairs.

Her studies of Nazism inspired Lewis's *It Can't Happen Here,* a novel about the possibility of a dictatorship becoming the form of government in America. She became a radio commentator in 1936, a job she would hold until the end of the World War II. A year later, the pressures of approaching war, fame, and a final divorce with Lewis took their toll. At age forty-four, Thompson underwent a physical change; her hair turned completely white.

> ## Red, White, and Black
>
> While in Germany, shortly before she was expelled, Thompson described in her journal the Nazi flags of the country: "They hung from all the houses. They were bright red with a black swastika in a white circle in the middle, and sometimes they hung from the second storey [sic] to the ground. They gave the streets an odd Chinese look. There were often several on one house— one for every family who lived there." (Thompson in Kurth, p. 199)

Participation: World War II

Radio against Nazism. In 1938 Thompson declared that she would give her life to save Austria from a German invasion. She had the means to make such statements to America, in speeches heard regularly on the radio. By 1939 Thompson had three secretaries to help her prepare for her broadcast. Meanwhile, a new ritual was beginning in America. Every Monday night, 5 million people would gather around their radios to hear Thompson report on the war that had just broken out in Europe with the invasion of Poland by the Nazis. Following the news would be a commentary by Thompson, and these almost always became charged with emotion by the time the broadcast was finished. Thompson was waging her own war, through radio waves, against the Nazis.

Thompson Anticipates World War

"That we stand today possibly on the brink of another world war, is due to the fact that the last war [World War I] was never ended. And indeed this is not another war. This is the same old war. ... The Germans raise the cry that the goods of the world are badly distributed as among nations. They are indeed badly distributed. But it is no solution ... to take the preponderance [lion's share] of the goods of the world from one group of nations and give them to another group of nations." (Thompson, *America*, p. 13)

Thompson was making waves in person as well. She talked her way into a rally of the pro-Nazi German-American Bund, an association in New York. As she sat with journalists on all sides, typing away at the typewriters provided for them, Thompson began laughing out loud in the middle of an anti-Semitic speech. Police immediately rushed over to her and escorted her out of the building. Her laughter had disrupted the meeting, exciting the crowd. Clearly Thompson would not put up with Nazism anywhere, especially in her home country.

American affairs. Thompson contributed in other ways to the struggle in Europe. When she learned of people getting exiled from invaded areas, she opened the doors of Twin Farms to shelter and feed them. Sometimes her discussions with them would last all night. She proudly accepted the nickname "Cassandra," the character in Greek mythology who stood on the walls of Troy and predicted the coming of war. By 1940 the president himself, Franklin D. Roosevelt, acknowledged her intelligence and insight. He hired her as an adviser on foreign affairs. Hollywood too made a try at honoring Thompson when it based the 1942 movie *Woman of the Year* on her. However, Thompson was less enthusiastic about the movie. She felt that the Katharine Hepburn–Spencer Tracy film was unrealistic because the heroine gave up her journalism career, a move Thompson would never make.

Destruction, loss, and the end of the war. With the bombing of Pearl Harbor in Hawaii by the Japanese in 1941, America was thrust into the war. Thompson's involvement afterward reached levels she had never imagined. Her fight against the Nazis turned into a fight against the terribly destructive war. She remarked: "I am pro-human. Pro-reason. And pro-world cooperation after this war" (Thompson in Kurth, p. 358). Before it would end, she would lose a best friend and a stepson to the war, and countless friends to Nazi terrorism. The only way to fight back, she thought, was to broadcast directly into Germany, directly into the middle of the fighting there. Hired by Columbia Broadcasting System (CBS) to reach the Germans by shortwave radio, Thompson pleaded for an end to the slaughter. She hoped to reach Germans of all different backgrounds and political opinions. Perhaps she could inspire them to gather together and form a backlash against Nazi activity. But Germany continued to wage war until the Nazis surrendered on May 8, 1945. After Hitler's death the same year, Thompson rushed to tour and report on war-torn areas such as Dachau and Dresden. The experience was emotionally painful, as she saw the areas in which some of her closest friends were killed.

> ## Thompson's Commentary on October 31, 1938
>
> The *New York Times* announced that Germany was deporting Jews to Poland. Thompson broadcast her opinion on this and other events, ending with a comment on the rush for money in light of World War II.
>
> "Money. There is no money people say. Meanwhile the world will spend this year $18 billion for armaments. Armaments that will not feed a mouth, or shelter a child, or put a coat on a man's back or a dress on a girl's.... In 1932 the world spent less than $4 billion. The sum has more than quadrupled, and still it is not enough! We must spend more.
>
> "Yes, we must, if the world is to go on being made safe for lunacy." (Thompson, *Let the Record Speak*, p. 254)

The United States dropped atomic bombs on Hiroshima and Nagasaki to end World War II in 1945. By that time, Thompson was back home and exhausted by the overwhelming destruction that affected so many countries. The war had changed her. No longer was Thompson an idealist who believed good would triumph over evil. She was so disappointed in practically all political leaders and organizations that she wrote an obituary (death notice) for the earth: "It died because its inhabitants, being endowed with brains to penetrate the secret of all matter, preferred to perish rather than use them any further" (Thompson in Kurth, p. 381).

Aftermath

Politics. Thompson continued writing newspaper columns for two more years and published several books. She was pulled back into heavy reporting about politics and world affairs by the Korean War in 1950 and by the struggle for land ownership between the Arabs and the Israelis. Still deeply affected by world events, she admitted that the outbreak of the Korean War broke her heart. The Arab-Israeli struggle made her very angry at both parties, whom she spoke out against with little restraint.

Thompson once remarked, "I do believe that a woman in the White House could end the *Cold War*" (Thompson in Kurth, p. 405). Afterward, others kept urging her to run for president. She joked with Herbert Hoover about the possibility, then remarked that she wouldn't be fit to run for the local dogcatcher, much less president of the United States.

Disappointments. Thompson faced a few disappointments toward the end of her life. She felt that the invention of television was ruining the young minds of the world. In her opinion the programs were far too violent: "Every time I look at the television set somebody is shooting somebody. Boom Boom" (Thompson in Kurth, p. 386).

A Woman First

As a woman in a male-dominated field, Thompson was continuously compared to men. She reacted to this in a letter to another journalist: "I wish someone would say that I am a hell of a good housekeeper, that the food by me is swell, that I am almost a perfect wife.... In other words, I wish someone would present me as a female. I am tired of being told I have the brains of a man. What man?" (Thompson in Sanders, p. 248)

Thompson was also impatient with women. She wanted a better life for women in America and encouraged them to stand up for their rights. But often, when couples came over for conversation, only the men would enter into lengthy discussions with her. It upset Thompson that their wives did not join in the arguments; she wanted women to express their thoughts.

What disappointed Thompson most was the fate of the twentieth century. She had seen more war than she thought she would, and the possibility of further fighting was always lurking. She predicted more disaster in the coming years. "The twentieth century will be the earthquake and the fire to its very end" (Kurth, p. 433).

Thompson did not live to witness the accuracy of her words. While on vacation in Lisbon, Portugal, she suffered a heart attack alone in her hotel room at the age of sixty-seven. Before her death, she asked for a simple ceremony, flowers on her grave, and to be buried next to her third husband, artist Maxim Kopf. Softly, one of the "loudest" voices in journalism grew silent.

For More Information

Kurth, Peter. *American Cassandra: The Life of Dorothy Thompson.* Boston, Toronto and London: Little, Brown and Company, 1990.

Sanders, Marion K. *Dorothy Thompson: A Legend in Her Time.* Boston: Houghton Mifflin Company, 1973.

Thompson, Dorothy. *America: A Lecture by Dorothy Thompson.* Los Angeles: Ward Ritchie Press, 1939.

Thompson, Dorothy. *Let the Record Speak.* Boston: Houghton Mifflin, 1939.

Cold War

1945
▼
Allied leaders meet at Yalta to work out peace plans. Atomic bombs dropped on Japanese cities. World War II ends.

1945-1946
▼
France fights communist forces in Vietnam; begins to reconquer country.

1946
▼
George F. Kennan outlines U.S. "containment" policy against communism. Winston Churchill makes "Iron Curtain" speech.

1948
▼
Truman orders racial integration in the U.S. military; officially recognizes the state of Israel.

1948
▼
Soviets demand that Britain, France, and the United States withdraw from Berlin. They refuse.

1947
▼
Congress forms Department of Defense and Central Intelligence Agency (CIA).

1947
▼
President **Harry S Truman** establishes the Truman Doctrine of helping other countries resist communism.

1949
▼
John Foster Dulles helps form the North Atlantic Treaty Organization (NATO).

1949
▼
The Soviet Union develops its own atomic weapon. Communist revolution succeeds in China.

1950
▼
North Korean forces invade South Korea. War follows, involving U.S. and U.N. forces.

1951-1952
▼
United States develops a hydrogen superbomb.

1959-1960
▼
Fidel Castro leads successful revolution in Cuba; befriends the Soviet Union. Cold War nears U.S. borders.

1954
▼
France agrees to a divided Vietnam.

1953
▼
Korean War ends in a stalemate.

1951
▼
Truman fires **Douglas MacArthur** as commander of American forces in Korea; replaces him with Matthew Ridgway.

COLD WAR

The Cold War was a struggle between the United States and the Soviet Union for world leadership. The tension started during World War II with disagreements about the shape of the postwar world. For a time, the two powers shared a common interest—defeating Nazi Germany. This accomplished, their leaders met in the Soviet Union at Yalta, where their differences surfaced. The alliance had started to crumble even before the meeting, over issues such as what kind of government to set up in postwar Poland. The United States, a democracy, favored a system like its own. But the Soviets favored their system, communism, in which government controls all the industry and there is only one political party.

The Soviet government was anxious about the rebuilding of Germany. The Germans had invaded the Soviet Union twice in thirty years at the cost of millions of Russian lives. For protection, Soviet leader Joseph Stalin insisted on a shield of Eastern European governments that were friendly to the Soviet Union. The separate zones of Germany hardened, as did Russian influence over the nations of Eastern Europe. As Russian control stretched to the Balkan nations of Albania, Bulgaria, Greece, and Turkey, England's prime minister, Winston Churchill, spoke grimly of Russia's dropping an "iron curtain" across Europe. The phrase came to stand for Russia's tight-fisted control over the sweep of countries that it dominated—that is, for its policy of keeping noncommunist influences out of these countries.

Issues Leading to U.S.-Soviet Differences

- What type of government should be set up in Poland?
- Would America share the secret of the atomic bomb?
- How much and whom would the defeated nations pay for war damages?
- Would America make an unconditional loan to war-torn Russia?
- Who should occupy Germany?

The victors decided that Germany would be controlled jointly. Each Allied power would control one part, the Soviet Union taking a region in the east that included Germany's capital city, Berlin. Berlin, though located in the Soviet zone, would be parceled out among the victors, too. In 1948 the Soviet Union tried a blockade to oust the other powers from Berlin, but it failed. The others airlifted in supplies.

American leaders assumed that Stalin's goal was to upset regimes everywhere and replace them with communist governments. Like other politicians of his time, U.S. president **Harry S Truman** believed that the Soviets were masterminding revolutions around the world. He distrusted the Russians and, blunt leader that he was, told them so. In 1946 Stalin made a speech declaring that Russian communism and American capitalism were on a collision course. Soon after, an American diplomat in Russia, **George F. Kennan** wrote an 8,000-word telegram to the U.S. State Department, which would set America's Cold War policy for years to come. It spoke of containment—of preventing Soviet influence from spreading to any more areas beyond where it already existed.

This was a "Cold" War, in which there would be no direct combat between the United States and Russia. They would reach for indirect types of "weapons." European countries were shattered after the war. So one way to aid them, and fend off Soviet influence, was to provide money for defense and rebuilding. The United States had earlier stayed out of European affairs. But now Truman declared America's intent to help peoples maintain their independence against communist advances on their governments. Congress approved the new policy, known as the Truman Doctrine, granting the president's $400 million request for aid to Greece and Turkey to fend off communism. Such aid would also, it was felt, help prevent a return of the world-

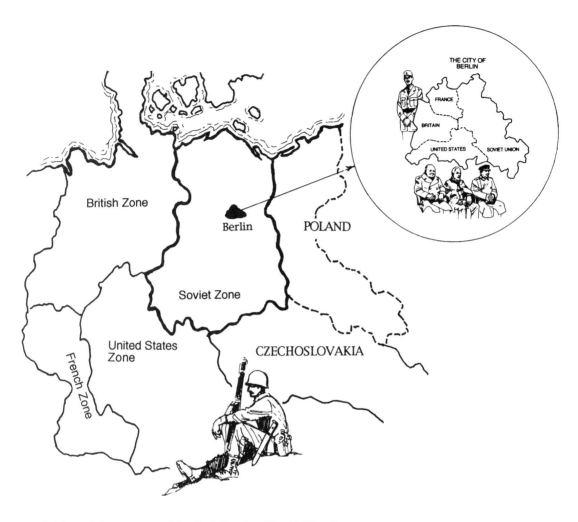

▲ **Division of Germany and Berlin following World War II**

wide depression. For the same reasons, Secretary of State George Marshall came up with a plan to aid much of western Europe. The Marshall Plan sent money to sixteen war-torn nations in Europe for recovery in agriculture and industry ($17 billion over four years). Such policies suggested a belief that the Americans could police the world—a dangerous notion, said newsman Walter Lippman. He predicted that it would thrust America into conflicts around the world, which indeed happened over the next few decades—from Korea to Vietnam, to the Middle East, and then to Cuba.

143

The bombing of Pearl Harbor, Hawaii, in World War II had caught America unprepared, after which it vowed never again to be surprised. In 1947 Congress formed a Department of Defense in the nation and a Central Intelligence Agency (CIA) to conduct spy activities. America's enemy became the Soviet Union instead of Germany, and a number of leaders (George Kennan, W. Averell Harriman, Dean Acheson) surfaced in the U.S. Department of State to help direct the conflict.

The Marshall Plan to aid western Europe went into effect in 1948. In 1949 western Europe and North America drew even closer by forming NATO, the North Atlantic Treaty Organization. It was a mutual defense group whose member nations vowed that an attack against one would be an attack against all, and they would fight back with joint force.

Containment, the Cold-War Policy

The Soviets, George F. Kennan argued, must "be contained by ... counter-force at a series of constantly shifting geographical and political points." (Gary Nash, *The American People,* vol. 2. [New York: Harper & Row, 1990], p. 897)

Adding to the conflicts of the time, a number of colonies in the world struggled to win their independence. Korea had been a colony of Japan before World War II. The Allies promised freedom to Korea at the end of the war, temporarily dividing the land at the thirty-eighthth degree of latitude. The area to the north fell under Soviet influence, and the Koreans set up a communist government there. The South fell under U.S. influence, and a free election, organized by the United Nations, led to a non-communist government there. Years passed, the temporary division becoming more and more permanent and each side hoping to reunite Korea one day under its government. Meanwhile, in 1949 there was a successful communist revolution in nearby China. The next year the North Koreans invaded South Korea. The Soviets, thought Truman, were testing how determined America was to contain communism.

Truman was convinced that America had to meet the challenge or the result would be World War III. So the president directed General **Douglas MacArthur** to South Korea. Along with U.S. troops came smaller forces from fifteen member countries of the United Nations, the new organization recently established to maintain world peace. Truman waged a limited war, without using atomic weapons. In 1949 the Soviet Union had developed its own Soviet atomic bomb and by 1953, when the fighting in Korea ground to a halt, both powers had invented even deadlier hydrogen bombs. These weapons could bring horrible destruction on the world.

MacArthur objected loudly to America's fighting a limited war until Truman finally took the celebrated general out of action, replacing him with General M.B. Ridgway. After three years and 54,000 American deaths (and 1 million to 2 million Korean deaths), the fighting ended in a draw. It was the first war in which U.S. troops were racially integrated and the first in which the deadly explosive napalm was used. After all the fighting, there was hardly any change in the boundaries, though, and at the awful cost of so many lives.

Before the Korean conflict ended, Dwight Eisenhower was elected the new U.S. president. He, like Truman, saw the Soviet Union as an enemy dedicated to the spread of communism. But unlike Truman, who built up U.S. atomic and common weapons, Eisenhower concentrated on atomic weapons. His secretary of state, **John Foster Dulles,** added a twist to U.S. foreign policy. He wanted to go further than George Kennan did in calling for communism to be contained. Dulles would have liked America to free countries already in the grip of the Soviet Union. Eisenhower instead continued the milder containment policy. But Dulles had an effect on the world and the nation. He toughened the U.S. stand by introducing nuclear weapons into discussions, making it clear that the United States would be ready to drop nuclear bombs on Russian cities to stop Soviet advances in the world. It was a tightrope policy, in which Dulles edged the nation to the brink of war without getting into it, a risk he saw as necessary. Truman had scared America with talk of a worldwide Soviet threat to democracy. Now Dulles increased fears with talk of nuclear warfare. They would be further aggravated during Dulles's last year in office by a revolution in Cuba that would soon bring the Cold War close to America's shores.

Harry S Truman

1884-1972

Personal Background

The four-term president. Franklin Delano Roosevelt had been president for three terms. During those twelve years, he had taken personal charge of attempts to rescue the United States from the Great Depression of the 1930s and had led the United States into World War II. For twelve years, Roosevelt had conducted the business of government with little communication between him and his vice presidents Jack Garner and Henry Wallace. As he campaigned for a fourth term, Roosevelt found himself faced with selecting a new vice-presidential candidate. He decided on a senator from Missouri, Harry S Truman, in part because few other politicians were available or desirable. Shortly after the two took office, Roosevelt died and a reluctant Truman took the oath as thirty-third president of the United States. His ignorance of the actions of the president were so great that he was not aware, until two weeks later, that the government had been involved in developing a superweapon, the atom bomb.

Early life. Harry S Truman was born in the farm community of Lamar, Missouri, May 8, 1884. His mother's father was *Solomon* Young and his father's father was Anderson *Shippe* Truman. As if to include both sides of the family, he was given a middle initial which stood for nothing in particular.

His father, John, worked at many occupations as the family moved around the area of Independence, Missouri. At various times

146

▲ **Harry S Truman**

Event: The Cold War.

Role: Vice President Harry S Truman was thrust unwillingly into the presidency of the United States upon the death of Franklin Delano Roosevelt. The move came in the midst of World War II. Truman was thus faced with ending a war and then helping to maintain world peace. He later supported the United Nations and its action against communist aggression in Korea.

he was a farmer, cattle and horse trader, night watchman, and dealer in grains. For a while, he was overseer of the roads of the county. By 1887 the family was living on the Solomon Young farm, and John Truman was managing it for the aging owners. Called "Peanuts" by his friends, John was a loyal and interested Democrat.

Harry's interest in politics began when, as a child, he accompanied his father to political meetings. The effect his father had on the boy was acknowledged by him in later years. "He was just as great as she [his mother Martha] was and had every bit as much influence on me" (Truman in Jenkins, p. 10). Perhaps his father was not given due credit for his influence on his son's life because of his size. John was two inches shorter than his wife, Martha. Also, her side of the family was far more prosperous than his. The Youngs owned more than 5,000 acres in Jackson County and had acquired a measure of wealth by running wagon trains west to Salt Lake City. Backed by her family, Martha brought security and strength to her children—Harry and later another son, John, and a daughter, Mary Jane.

Life on their grandparents' farm was pleasant. Grandmother Young remembered the sense of humor that Harry exhibited at the age of two as he chased a frog hopping about the farm. When he was six, the family moved to Independence, Missouri, so that Harry could attend a good school. At the time, Independence was a thriving town of 6,000, located only nine miles from bustling Kansas City, where the population was 55,000.

Six was also the age at which Truman began to wear glasses, as he would all his life. The glasses interfered with his playing sports, so Truman contented himself with reading. He was a frequent visitor to the small town library, paying most attention to books about history or the lives of great men. Mark Twain was his favorite author, but in the end he read nearly every book in the Independence library.

Meanwhile, the family attended church faithfully, and Truman was introduced to the Bible, a book he read through twice by the time he was twelve. From religion as well as his parents, he learned that people should take responsibility for their own acts. Years later, President Truman's desk would carry the sign, "The buck stops here."

▲ Downtown Independence, Missouri, 1951

When he graduated high school, there was little thought of Truman's going on to college. Their finances had sunk so low that the family had to move to Kansas City, where jobs were more available for Truman and his father. There Truman went to work.

Finding a job. Truman worked briefly at a Kansas City drugstore, spent a short time as a clerk for the city newspaper, and then became a timekeeper for the railroad. Lastly he took a job as a bank clerk. He was finally able to earn $100 a month.

While at the bank, he joined other workers in the national guard, unaware that the experience would benefit him in the future. After five years in Kansas City, Truman returned to his grandfather's farm, where he worked for the next ten years.

War service and marriage. Back when he was six, Truman met five-year-old Bess Wallace, who had since become one of the prettiest and smartest young ladies in the area. The two had kept contact and occasionally dated over the years. When he was thirty-three they agreed to marry. Theirs turned out to be a long engagement, however, for America was just entering World War I. Truman was called into the service, thanks to his national guard work, as a lieutenant in the 129th Infantry Regiment, in training in Oklahoma for service overseas. He was given command of a troop whose members had earned a reputation as both tough and poor soldiers. Short and bespectacled, Truman could nevertheless talk and play poker with these men. He soon established his authority and earned the respect of the unruly lot. His leadership won him a promotion to captain before war's end. The battalion saw little action.

Discharged when the war ended, Truman began job-hunting again. In June 1919, he and Bess had finally married and moved into the mansion where Bess's mother lived. (Bess's mother would stay with Bess and Harry the rest of her long life—even moving into the White House. Also, all her life she would remind her son-in-law that there were other men more fit to be senator and president than he was.) Truman needed to earn money. He and a friend named Eddie Jacobson decided to set up a men's clothing store. It was a success for a few months, then business dropped off, and after two years the partners closed shop.

Politics. Operating the store had allowed Truman to meet some influential people, among them James Pendergast, nephew of Tom Pendergast, the political boss of the area. With James's help, Truman secured a one-year appointment as overseer of the highways of Jackson County. He followed this up, in 1922, by becoming a judge of the Jackson County Court, his first elected position. From that time on his sights were set on a life in politics. The next election ended less happily.

In 1924 Truman lost his bid for reelection as judge and the income for his family at the same time that his only child, daughter Margaret, was born. Somehow, the family managed to survive until the 1926 elections, in which Truman won as presiding judge of the Jackson County Court. He would never again lose a political election. Reelected in 1930, he served the court until he was chosen by the Pendergast political machine to be their candidate for senate in 1934. One of his first major duties was to chair a senate committee to investigate wartime expenditures. The committee revealed unnecessary expenses that saved the American taxpayers $15 billion. Truman was reelected to the senate in 1940.

Franklin D. Roosevelt. The nation was at the time led by the immensely popular President Franklin D. Roosevelt. In 1943 Roosevelt was to run for a fourth presidential term. Henry Wallace had been his vice president and Roosevelt wanted him to run again. Other Democrats, including Eleanor, the president's wife, felt Wallace would not help win votes. William Douglas and James Byrnes were recommended, and so was Truman. Truman, however, did not want the job. He thought it would be a political dead end unless the president died and the vice president became president. And he certainly did not feel qualified to lead the nation. Finally, however, Roosevelt decided that his running mate should be Truman, who grudgingly accepted. It was the middle of World War II, and the nation could not afford a dispute over who should be the Democratic candidates.

In January 1944, Harry Truman became vice president. He had no previous knowledge of the workings of the executive section of government, and certainly Roosevelt, busy with the war, did little to make him aware of what was happening. Truman was not included in the meeting at Yalta, in Southern Russia, in which Roosevelt, Winston Churchill from Great Britain, and Joseph Stalin from the Soviet Union planned the end of the war in Europe. In fact, of the eighty-two days that Truman served as vice president, the president was in Washington, D.C., only thirty days. The vice president was left ignorant of wartime developments. Only later, two weeks after Roosevelt died, was Truman told about the nation's greatest secret, the making of an atom bomb.

President Truman. On April 12, 1945, President Roosevelt suddenly died, and Truman was thrust into the presidency. Truman had earned a reputation for plain speaking, honesty, and loyalty. Now he behaved humbly. He asked Americans to pray for him and beseeched the members of Roosevelt's cabinet and the late president's advisers to stay in their posts. Most agreed Truman was off to a good start as president, his personality contributing greatly to his success. He listened well to his advisers and proved much more direct and willing to act than his former boss. Soon Truman's popularity was greater than Roosevelt's had ever been.

He needed the support, for the country was developing controversial weapons, and World War II, although winding to an end in Europe, was still being fought by a capable foe, Japan. Almost at once, Truman found himself trying to deal with the leaders of England and the Soviet Union, who had made their agreements with Roosevelt. By July 6, 1945, he was participating in a conference with Stalin and Churchill at Potsdam in Germany.

Participation: Using the Atom Bomb

The allies and Japan. Japan continued to fight stubbornly and well in the war. Military leaders of the three allied countries estimated that it might take another eighteen months to subdue Japan and that invading her borders would be necessary. This was the situation at the time of the Potsdam conference. There was a new development to consider, too. The United States had successfully formed an atom bomb. Whether or not to use this new weapon was part of the Potsdam discussion. Truman, in Europe when he learned of the successful explosion of the first bomb, briefly pondered the question. Another eighteen months of war would cost numerous lives on both sides. Already, air raids had claimed countless lives—78,000 in Tokyo alone. Invading Japan, if the bomb wasn't used, would probably kill more than a million people on both sides. (The three allied leaders agreed to bring the war to an end quickly and warned Japan to surrender or be destroyed.) Finally Truman chose the path he felt would result in the fewest casualties; he ordered that the atom bomb be used to bring Japan to the peace table—but not dropped on the most heavily populated areas near Tokyo and Kyoto.

Dropping the bomb. On August 6, 1945, the atom bomb was dropped at Hiroshima. Some 75,000 people in this military city were killed and nearly 100,000 injured or declared missing. On August 8, Russia declared war on Japan—an action Stalin had resisted until events looked positive for the allies. The next day an American plane dropped a second atom bomb on the naval base at Nagasaki;

80,000 people were killed or injured. On August 14, Japan agreed to unconditional surrender with a single exception. The symbolic leader of Japan, Emperor Hirohito, would be able to remain on his throne. Japan, however, under military rule by General Douglas MacArthur, would be led toward a democratic government (see **Douglas MacArthur**). Afterward the United States offered the Soviet Union an agreement to destroy all nuclear weapons, but the Soviets refused.

Peace and Korea. There remained the question of how to take control of the land that Japan had seized on the Asian mainland. The question divided the allies even as they debated how to accept the Japanese surrender. The Soviet Union wanted the freedom to extend communism in Asia, while the United States was bent on establishing a foothold for democracy there. The two former allies bargained and finally agreed that Soviet military leaders would accept the surrender of Japanese forces north of the thirty-eighth parallel, while the United States, represented by General Douglas MacArthur, would accept the surrender of troops south of that line. Thus, the land of Korea was split into two nations. The Russians and Americans worked hard to establish their differing forms of government in the two Koreas despite a United Nations recommendation that Korea remain united. By 1949 both Russian troops and American troops had been withdrawn. North Korea was by then firmly communistic, with support coming in from China as well as Russia. South Korea had set up a democratic government that drew support from the United States.

> ## Truman's Impressions of Stalin and Churchill
>
> Stalin—"I can deal with Stalin. He is honest—but smart as hell."
>
> Churchill—"He is a most charming and a very clever person—meaning clever in the English and not the Kentucky sense. He gave me a lot of hooey about how great my country is and how he loved Roosevelt and how he intended to love me." (Truman in Jenkins, pp. 72-74)

Aftermath

Declining popularity. By this time, even though he had ended the war, Truman's popularity had declined. Fewer than 25 percent of the voters felt that he was doing a good job. For one thing,

▲ The U.S.S. *Santa Fe* offering assitance to the U.S.S. *Franklin* after the *Franklin* had been hit by a Japanese dive bomber, March 1945

they questioned his choice of government officials. As Roosevelt's former advisers left, Truman had to select their replacements. He was a man who made friends for life, and many of his friends joined him frequently in his great love for poker-playing. Now he began to reward these cronies with cabinet and other government positions. Few people recognized the names of cabinet members he chose, except for the stalwart General George Marshall who became Secretary of State. Soon Truman would have to explain his actions in a campaign for reelection. He, in fact, still felt poorly suited for the presidency. There was, however, no Democrat who seemed to stand a chance of replacing him.

Reelection. Truman waited until the last minute, actually just fourteen months before the election, to announce that he would be a candidate. His Republican opponent was Thomas Dewey, the poised and intelligent governor of New York. The American press exposed the feelings of the nation. Truman, the press predicted, would lose by a landslide. But Truman was a fighter. Once he had decided to run, he put his whole heart into the battle, making hundreds of speeches and traveling thousands of miles in a vigorous campaign. Still, on election eve, the American newspapers were predicting a landslide defeat. One magazine felt so sure of this that it prepared an issue to be released after the election with the headline "Dewey Wins." So embarrassed was this magazine after the election that it went out of business. There was no landslide. Truman, in fact, had won a second term as president.

Korea. In his second term, Truman faced a new problem. His assistant to the ambassador to the Soviet Union (see **George Kennan**) had outlined a foreign policy designed to prevent the spread of communism without risking World War III. It was this policy of containment that made the thirty-eighth parallel in Korea a dividing line. But suddenly the boundary became a battleground. Supported by Chinese reserves, North Korea's army marched across the border and invaded South Korea. In short order, the commu-

> ### Winston Churchill on Dropping the Atom Bomb
>
> "The historic fact remains ... that the decision whether or not to use the atomic bomb to compel the surrender of Japan was never even an issue. There was unanimous, automatic, unquestioned agreement around our table; nor did I ever hear the slightest suggestion that we should do otherwise."
> (Churchill in Jenkins, p. 73)

nist north had swept across the south, leaving the South Korean army penned up in a small section around Pusan in southeast Korea.

Truman's general in command of the Pacific, MacArthur, had supervised the reorganization of government in Japan and returned to his post in the Philippines. Truman ordered MacArthur immediately to Korea, where he took personal command of the troops.

Instead, however, of directly counterattacking the North Koreans in the southeast, MacArthur planned a ground and water landing near the capital city of Seoul just below the thirty-eighth parallel. Personally leading troops in a landing at Inchon, MacArthur cut across Korea south of the parallel and soon threatened to cut the northern army's supply lines to the south. North Korean troops were forced to retreat. MacArthur's army chased them across North Korea nearly to the Yalu River border with China. But then hundreds of thousands of Chinese "volunteers" rushed to the sup-

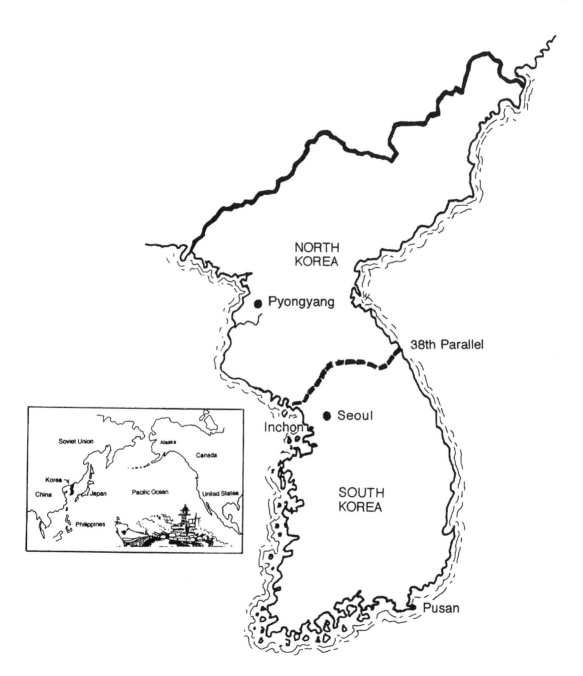

port of North Korea and forced the United Nations army, led by MacArthur, back below the thirty-eighth parallel.

MacArthur had demonstrated his bravery and courage in fighting in the Philippines in World War II, and now he wanted to destroy the North Korean capability for war. He asked Truman for permission to again enter North Korea. This time he wanted to be supported by bombing raids on the military bases of China and by the army of Taiwan, which he proposed should distract China by attacking the Chinese mainland. Truman disagreed; he was committed to containing communism without the risk of starting a third world war. When it appeared that MacArthur might charge ahead with his plan anyway, Truman fired him.

It was a bold move by the president, for MacArthur was a tremendously popular American. Truman, however, held to his position. He had done what he thought necessary—without consulting Congress and without asking for the financial support his advisers thought he needed for the military stalemate in Korea. (Even before the Korean conflict, they had recommended that the military budget needed to be raised from $14 billion a year to $40 billion.) Nor had he asked Congress for permission to station naval ships in the Pacific to prevent Taiwan from invading mainland China.

In the end, both sides agreed to establish a buffer zone along the thirty-eighth parallel and to hold their positions north and south. Truman had worked within the policy of containment to stop a communist takeover of South Korea and had done so without risking a third world war.

Retirement. Congress had grown cautious about a president serving so many terms as Roosevelt had, passing a law that limited the president to two terms in office. Truman, who had never wanted the job in the first place, signed the bill into law. When his second term was up, he with some misgivings supported Adlai Stevenson as the candidate. When nominated, Stevenson began immediately to change the leaders of the Democratic party. Truman, always loyal to his cronies, was offended, more so because Stevenson seemed to ignore his strong support. Finally Truman wrote to the

◄
The divided Korea

A Page in History

"TRUMAN EXPLAINS MacARTHUR OUSTER.

". . . Mr. Short said that the President *was asleep at Blair House* when the news was made public at *a hastily summoned press conference at 1 a. m.*"—New York Times, April 12, 1951.

(Editor's Note—Mr. Short is the White House Press Secretary. The news referred to was General MacArthur's dismissal.)

SO—*President Truman* was asleep when *Secretary of State Acheson* "fired" General MacArthur.

Thus a page in history—a dark, disgraceful page—was written in the midnight hours of April 11.

General MacArthur was fired—no doubt about that.

But did *the President* fire him? THAT IS DOUBTFUL.

———

NEWSPAPER MEN in Washington were suddenly summoned to an unscheduled *"press conference."*

This was quite unusual.

Naturally, it was expected that the President himself would be *"on the job."*

BUT HE WAS NOT.

He was *"asleep in Blair House."*

Now, how could that happen?

What put President Truman asleep at the very crisis of his own career?

Maybe the State Department gave him some kind of mental or neural anodyne.

For certainly the State Department was not inactive while Mr. Truman slumbered and General MacArthur was being immolated on the un-American altars of British Socialism and Russian Communism.

"Just before the announcement was made," reports the New York Times, *"Secretary of State Dean Acheson and Mr. Rusk began calling the ambassadors of the 13 other United Nations countries who had sent troops to fight in Korea to notify them of the command change."*

ALL THIS WHILE THE PRESIDENT SLEPT!

The State Department has long been General MacArthur's leading enemy.

Its midnight strategy in Washington resembled its devious "strategy" in Korea, which reduced General MacArthur to mere "tactics."

And the State Department strategy is a disloyal hybrid.

It derives directly from the State Department's own pro-Communist policies which betrayed Chiang Kaishek and delivered China to the Reds.

AT PRESENT IT IS DICTATED BY THE BRITISH SOCIALISTS.

———

SOCIALIST Britain has *"recognized"* the Chinese Communists, and hopes to seat them in the United Nations, in order to trade with them through Hong Kong.

Consequently—

Socialist Britain opposes the winning back of North Korea;

Socialist Britain opposes a blockade of the Chinese coast;

Socialist Britain opposes bombardment of the Communist *"privileged sanctuary"* in Manchuria and

Socialist Britain opposes the utilization of the large and strong Formosan army against the Reds.

In sum, the Socialist politicians want to end the Korean war on TACTICAL terms, and surrender the STRATEGIC benefits to Russia.

Therefore Socialist Britain and our Communist-infected State Department conspired to get rid of General MacArthur and of the MacARTHUR STRATEGY OF VICTORY.

▲ Truman explains ouster of Douglas MacArthur

new candidate, saying he believed he had become an embarrass-ment to the new Democrats. As soon as the election was over, he quietly packed his bags and went home to Independence. He left in the same condition as when he entered the presidency—not much richer and as humble as before. When reporters asked what he did as soon as he and Bess arrived home, his answer was that he carried their bags up to the attic.

Unusual for a president, Truman retired with no major job offers, only proposals to buy his name for commercial purposes. All of these he refused. Nor did he immediately collect a government pension. He and Bess sold part of their farm property for a shopping center and he earned a small fee for the publication of two volumes of memoirs.

A 1962 poll asked historians to rate the presidencies of the United States. Labeled as "great presidents" were Abraham Lincoln, George Washington, Franklin D. Roosevelt, Woodrow Wilson, and Thomas Jefferson. "The near greats" included Andrew Jackson, Theodore Roosevelt, James Polk, Harry Truman, John Adams, and Grover Cleveland. Truman was pleased. "I don't know how they came to put me so high up on the list," he wrote, "but I appreciate it nevertheless" (Truman in Jenkins, p. 214).

Truman lived quietly with Bess in their old Independence home until his death December 26, 1972. His headstone merely lists, in order, the government positions in which he served.

For More Information

Jenkins, Roy. *Truman.* New York: Harper and Row, 1986.

Miller, Merle. *Plain Speaking, an Oral Biography of Harry S. Truman.* New York: G. P. Putnam, 1950.

Truman, Margaret. *Harry S. Truman.* New York: William Morrow, 1973.

George F. Kennan

1904-

Personal Background

The Kennan family. George Frost Kennan was born February 16, 1904, in Milwaukee, Wisconsin. In his own memoirs, he describes his family as coming from a long line of farmers, people who had always worked as independently as possible. According to his memory, no one in the family had ever worked for someone else for wages and, in any emergency, the Kennan family had always looked to God rather than the government for help. The family survived and grew but without distinction, except for a cousin of his grandfather, also named George Kennan. This distant relative explored Siberia in the 1880s—along with artist George Frost—to investigate the Russian practice of exiling unpopular citizens to Siberian work camps and prisons. Distant cousin George Kennan had written a popular book about this expedition.

Early life. Not much in Kennan's early life indicated that he would have a profound effect on America. Although he did well in school, he felt caught between dreams and reality as a child. He was always independent, enjoying a day spent observing nature or dreaming of strange beings as much or more than one spent playing with the other children. Kennan was more likely to have one or two good friends than to be part of the general crowd of children his age.

▲ George F. Kennan

Event: The Truman Doctrine and the Marshall Plan.

Role: Making his career in international relations, George F. Kennan served in Germany and Eastern Europe and was assistant to Ambassador W. Averell Harriman in Russia. His observations led him to suggest an American policy for containing communist influence. Kennan's ideas were the basis of the postwar aid to Europe known as the Marshall Plan.

Education. Kennan ended his early education at St. John's Military Academy, where he prepared for entrance to college. Entering Princeton in 1921, he soon isolated himself from the other students. The last to be enrolled in the freshman class, he was assigned living quarters some distance from the school. He became even more distant from student activities on campus when, after the Christmas break, he developed scarlet fever. It was then a very serious illness and kept him from returning to school until long after the second semester had begun.

One college incident illustrates his independence of spirit. He had enrolled in an English class and become bored with it. The instructor, as was common, would have his students read passages of literature and then analyze the passages from a grammatical and literary point of view. Kennan was more interested in what the particular literature said about the time in which it was written and thought the class should discuss the social meaning of the writing. He began to cut classes and was in danger of failing until the professor cornered him outside class and demanded to know what was wrong. Given this personal interest in him, Kennan agreed to attend class and study.

Soon after the incident, the students were assigned to write an essay. Kennan chose to write about his disagreement with the way the English classes were taught and to give his own ideas about what was important to look for in literature. For the essay, he earned the highest grade in the class. Kennan continued at Princeton, studying history and international relations with the idea of entering the diplomatic service.

Entering the foreign service. Graduating from Princeton in 1925, Kennan immediately went to Washington to prepare for the exam taken before entering the foreign service. It was a difficult examination, one that demanded taking a special course just to prepare for it. Kennan enrolled in the course and passed the examination only to find more schooling ahead. He spent much of 1926 in Foreign Service School, then was assigned to the diplomatic corps in Geneva, Switzerland.

At the end of the summer of 1927, Kennan was given a permanent post as vice counsel at Hamburg, Germany. Although he remained there only six months, he credits this experience with expanding his interest to events outside his own life. It was during this period that Kennan began to feel that his education had not really prepared him for foreign service. He felt a need to return to America for more formal education. In the winter of 1928, he returned to Washington, D.C., to resign from the diplomatic service.

Fortunately, an old teacher in the Foreign Service School helped him change his mind. William Dawson reminded Kennan that he could continue his education while remaining in the foreign service. He had only to volunteer for training as a specialist in one of the lesser known foreign languages—Japanese, Chinese, Arabic, or Russian. European universities were more advanced in this sort of study. He would attend a European university for three years of graduate study.

That same year, Kennan applied for special training in Russian and was accepted. Before starting his university education, he was assigned a brief field experience in a Russian-speaking environment. Russia was closed to foreign students, but three small nations had recently been separated from Russia—Latvia, Lithuania, and Estonia. These countries still had Russian-speaking populations. After a brief assignment to Berlin, Kennan began tours of the capitals of the three nations. For more than five years, he would study the language and customs of Russia in Berlin, Tallinn (Estonia), Riga (Latvia), and Kovno (Lithuania).

Marriage. While studying at the university in Berlin, Kennan met a Norwegian girl who was visiting the city. In 1931 Kennan and Annelise Soerensen were engaged to be married. The wedding took place in September at Kristiansand, Norway, and the newly-weds left immediately for Kennan's assignment in Latvia. They lived there in a second-story apartment built over an old factory until 1933. The couple's first daughter, Grace, was born that June. Three years later, the couple's second daughter would be born at Kennan's sister's home in Highland Park, Illinois.

Tracking events in Russia. From 1931 to 1933, Kennan worked in the small research group in the American embassy at Riga. His job consisted of studying Russian newspapers and magazines and reporting about conditions in the Soviet Union. It was a time of international distrust mixed with the feeling by leaders in the West that the Soviet Union could be a cooperative ally.

During this period, for Kennan a period of more study, he realized the great difference with which the Soviet Union and the United States viewed treaty arrangements. The Soviets regarded agreements, such as one made with Germany concerning the treatment of prisoners, as a convenience—to be observed only if doing so would advance Soviet goals. In addition, the Soviets acted as if they were under attack, limiting every kind of information to foreigners. For example, information about crops and industrial production were supposedly open to foreigners but were, in fact, part of Soviet long-term plans, which were secret. Communication with Soviet leaders was difficult. Wording of messages to the Soviets needed to be very clear, otherwise their country would interpret it in the most convenient way. Kennan came to recognize the wide differences between the governments and goals of the Soviet Union and the United States. Finally, in 1933, he was assigned to the diplomatic force in Moscow. He arrived there in 1934 and began a long crusade to convince western powers to think differently about the Soviet Union.

World War II. During the early part of World War II, Kennan was assigned to Berlin, then to Portugal. His activities took him throughout Europe before his return to Moscow from 1944 to 1946. The war in Europe was winding down during these two years, and using the atom bomb ended the fighting with Japan. To deal with a new peace in Europe and Asia, the Allied forces agreed to form a Council of Foreign Ministers. Kennan had long realized that the objectives of the Soviet Union and of England and the United States were so different that cooperation among them would not really occur. He had written notes to superiors in the State Department suggesting that cooperation in a war effort did not necessarily mean that the Soviet Union and the United States shared common post-war goals. He began to write down his ideas for dealing with the Soviet Union, basing them mostly on distrust of the political leaders there. He even developed a set of rules for dealing with Soviet leader Joseph Stalin and the Soviet government. The ideas were never completed and never used.

Kennan believed that the Soviet Union was set on influencing the entire world with a communist philosophy of government, which was at odds with the government of the United States. In the past, he had fumed over events he did not approve of until near the boiling point and had then fought for his own ideas. Once, in Portugal, he had objected to a presidential order about military bases in that country. Kennan finally challenged the president's order, then was recalled to Washington, D.C., to explain his actions to the president. President Franklin Roosevelt agreed with his explanation and his action. Now he was prepared to bypass his immediate bosses to win attention to his own ideas about dealing with the Soviet Union.

Participation:
The Truman Doctrine
and the Marshall Plan

The Kennan view of Soviet goals. For eighteen months before February 1946, Kennan had been talking with anyone who would listen about Americans misunderstanding the Soviets. Few listened. The American government was committed to the idea that the Soviet Union and the western nations could work together in harmony. However, in February, the Soviets refused to participate in the new World Bank and International Monetary Fund. State Department plans based on a cooperating Soviet Union seemed to collapse at this point.

The refusal came while Kennan was in charge of affairs in Moscow in the absence of the ambassador there. He thus was the one to receive requests from upset leaders in the U.S. State Department for an explanation of the Soviet action. He had been writing notes about this for years without anyone paying attention. Suddenly it was Kennan's opportunity to be heard:

Kennan's Rules for Dealing with the Soviets

A. Don't act chummy with them.

B. Don't assume a community of aims with them which does not really exist.

C. Don't make fatuous [foolish] gestures of good will.

D. Make no requests of the Russians unless we are prepared to make them feel our displeasure in a practical way in case the request is not granted.

E. Take up matters on a normal level and insist that Russians take full responsibility for their actions on that level.

F. Do not encourage high-level exchanges of views with the Russians unless the initiative comes at least 50 percent from their side.

G. Do not be afraid to use heavy weapons for what seems to us to be minor matters.

H. Do not be afraid of unpleasantness and public airing of differences.

I. Coordinate, in accordance with our established policies, all activities of our government relating to Russia and all private American activities of this sort which the government can influence.

J. Strengthen and support our representation in Russia. (Kennan, *Memoirs, 1925–1950*, pp. 291-293)

Now, suddenly, my opinion was being asked. The occasion, to be sure, was a trivial one, but the implications of the query [inquiry] were not. It was no good trying to brush the question off with a couple of routine sentences describing Soviet views on such things as world banks and international funds. It would not do to give them just a fragment of the truth. Here was a case where nothing but the whole truth would do. They had asked for it. Now, by God, they would have it. (Kennan, *Memoirs, 1925–1950,* p. 293)

The Long Telegram. Kennan began a telegram answering the question about the Soviets and the World Bank by stating that the response was so involved, delicate, and strange to American thought that a direct answer would risk oversimplification. The telegram then went on to explain the Soviet World Bank action in terms of the goals of the Soviet Union as he saw them. The "Long Telegram," as it became known, required 8,000 words and was divided into sections so that it could easily be read. The first section outlined the Soviet world outlook and goals after the war. Other sections gave historical background for the Soviet plans and discussed what might happen there on a political level. The telegram also explained Soviet "unofficial" behavior, that is, Soviet actions around the world through communist organizations and pro-communist individuals in other countries.

The telegram was sent in 1946. When he read it again in the 1960s, Kennan was surprised at his own writing: "Much of it reads exactly like one of those primers put out by alarmed congressional committees or by the Daughters of the American Revolution, designed to arouse the citizenry to the dangers of the Communist conspiracy" (Kennan, *Memoirs, 1925–1950,* p. 294).

The timing was right. With their dreams of Soviet and American cooperation after the war crumbling, leaders in the State Department read the telegram. So did the secretary of the navy, James Forrestal and President Truman. Here was a different view of the Soviet Union. According to Kennan, Soviet politics had long been governed by uneasiness and defensiveness about conditions both within and outside of that country. Soviet politics were thus to a large degree secretly handled. The actions of the Soviet Union indicated a plan for world domination. Still, having been very seriously battered in World War II, the superpower, Kennan felt, would pursue its plan for world domination through steps short of another great war. What was needed was a United States plan to contain communism. This could be done, advised Kennan, by strongly upholding American positions and by supporting noncommunist countries wherever help was needed. Kennan felt that eventually the Soviet insecurity would lead to problems of managing the countries within their sphere of influence and that the Soviet Union would collapse.

The Long Telegram persuaded Americans almost immediately. As Kennan said, "Six months earlier this message would probably have been received in the Department of State with raised eyebrows and lips pursed in disapproval. Six months later, it would probably have sounded [like] ... a sort of preaching to the convinced" (Kennan, *Memoirs, 1925–1950,* p. 295). Now it prompted immediate action. America's plans for a "Cold War" began to take shape.

Conditions after the World War. After World War II, U.S. representative General Douglas MacArthur joined representatives of the Soviet Union in making peace with the Japanese. Temporarily, the Soviets would handle arrangements with the Japanese north of the thirty-eighth parallel (latitude) and the western nations would do the same south of it. This parallel now became the boundary for containing communism in Asia.

In the Middle East, the Allies had agreed to remove their troops. The Soviet Union, however, was slow in leaving Iran. It became a testing ground for Kennan's idea that the Russians would stop short of another war if the West took firm stands. Iran, Britain, and the United States strongly demanded Russian withdrawal from Iran, and the Soviet Union withdrew.

Greece was another trouble spot. Unless British troops stayed in that country, some felt that it would fall to communism. Undersecretary of State Dean Acheson felt that if this happened "A highly possible Soviet break-through [in Greece] might open three continents to Soviet penetration" (Boorstin, p. 584). Kennan's Long Telegram had resulted in a firm stand against the Soviet Union's dreams of world domination, but now Kennan began to feel that the United States had overreacted. Many influential Americans were regarding communism everywhere as the same—a threat by the

Soviet Union to take charge. Such a view resulted, Kennan thought, in some overly strong responses by the United States.

His educational telegram had started a plan to contain the Soviet Union, but Kennan now disagreed with U.S. policymakers. He did not view international issues as fixed in time and place; he saw them as constantly changing. Plans, he felt, should be altered as conditions changed, always measured in the real interest of the United States in whatever part of the world was in question.

Aftermath

The Truman Doctrine. President Truman responded to the imagined threat in Greece by calling on Congress to provide money and weapons to support the Greek government. That might have been in keeping with the Kennan plan of containment, but the president went one step further. He told a frightened Congress that it must be the policy of the United States to support free peoples who are resisting domination by armed minorities or by outside pressure. These free peoples should be allowed to work out their own destinies. This plan became known as the Truman Doctrine. Secretary of State George Marshall began to support the doctrine by spreading aid to the many nations struggling to rebuild a capitalist economy. This "Marshall Plan" and the Truman Doctrine, Kennan felt, went too far. It had failed to consider the cost to the United States of becoming a supporter of the world.

> ### Some Books by George F. Kennan
>
> *Realities of American Foreign Policy* (1954)
>
> *Russia, The Atom and the West* (1958)
>
> *Soviet Foreign Policy, 1917–1941* (1960)
>
> *On Dealing with the Communist World* (1964)
>
> *Democracy and the Student Left* (1969)
>
> *The Cloud of Danger: Current Realities of American Foreign Policy* (1977)
>
> *The German Problem: A Personal View* (1989)

In preparing for the Marshall Plan, George Marshall had created a Policy Planning Commission in the State Department. Kennan became leader of that commission, which produced numerous documents recommending actions to the secretary of state. In the next few years, however, anticommunism in America would reach such heights that Kennan felt himself more and more out of tune with the actions taken by the United States.

By 1953 Kennan had fallen out of step with the State Department, this time because he felt many of the actions to contain the Soviet Union were unnecessary or too costly. He left the State Department and began a university career, teaching and researching. He also set down his ideas about American diplomacy in writing.

Kennan continued to study and to monitor international politics. Frequently, he found U.S. actions unacceptable and spoke out against them. For instance, he felt that the organization of NATO for the protection of Europe was threatening to Russia and that NATO should not be armed with nuclear weapons. He disliked the quarreling over how to deal with postwar Germany, feeling that this would weaken western influence and strengthen Soviet influence. In the 1950s he felt that the United States had no reason to have military personnel in Korea and later, as conditions changed, he felt that the United States and the Soviet Union would be able to peacefully coexist. In 1957 he proposed that the two German countries be united and remain an unarmed neutral state, and in the 1960s, he spoke out strongly against American involvement in the Vietnam War, it was too high a cost for protecting the few American interests there.

Realistic diplomacy. Although some leaders (see **John Foster Dulles**) strongly disagreed with Kennan's idea of containment, others felt that Kennan deeply influenced diplomatic relations between the Soviet Union and the United States. In 1957 he was invited by the British Broadcasting Company (BBC) to deliver a series of lectures, the Reith Lectures, which allowed him to express his views to a great number of listeners. He himself has regarded his constant effort to create a realistic and long-range American foreign policy as a failure. "I have gone my own way and attracted no great body of followers.... I have always been regarded by the United States Establishment as an oddball" (Kennan in Polley, p. 157).

For More Information

Boorstin, Daniel J., and Brooks Mather Kelley. *A History of the United States.* Lexington, Massachusetts: Ginn and Company, 1983.

Kennan, George F. *George F. Kennan: Memoirs.* Boston: Little, Brown and Company, *1925–1950,* 1967; *1950–1963,* 1972.

Polley, Michael. *A Biography of George F. Kennan: The Education of a Realist.* New York: The Edwin Mellen Press, 1990.

Douglas MacArthur

1880-1964

Personal Background

Perhaps no one in American history has been as confusing a character as General Douglas MacArthur. Few have risen to command as much power as he held in the Pacific Ocean after World War II, and even fewer were as prepared throughout their young lives for such distinction.

Arthur MacArthur. Douglas MacArthur was born January 26, 1880, in Little Rock, Arkansas. His mother, Mary Harding MacArthur, came from Virginia. His father, Arthur MacArthur, had been a first lieutenant in the Twenty-fourth Wisconsin Infantry during the Civil War. At the battle of Missionary Ridge, Arthur earned the Congressional Medal of Honor. He temporarily left the service at the end of the war, having risen by then to the rank of lieutenant colonel.

Arthur reentered the regular army in 1866, again as a first lieutenant. By the time the Spanish-American War erupted in 1898, he was a brigadier general in charge of volunteers. One of his assignments during this war took him to the Pacific Ocean area. He led the opposition to Filipinos resisting the American takeover of their country, then became military governor of the Philippines. In the position of governor, he earned the respect of the Filipinos for his efforts to restore justice to the nation. By the time he retired in 1909, Lieutenant General MacArthur had become commander of

▲ Douglas MacArthur

Event: The Korean War.

Role: As commander of the U.S. Army in the Pacific and commander of the combined United Nations forces, General Douglas MacArthur directed the campaign to push North Koreans and Chinese "volunteers" out of South Korea in the 1950s.

the U.S. forces in the Pacific. So committed was he to the military service that even after his retirement he expressed a desire to die in the front of his troops. His wish was, in fact, granted. Arthur MacArthur died while speaking at the fiftieth reunion of his original regiment in 1909. By then he had launched his son on an equally distinguished military career.

Early life. Douglas MacArthur was the third son in the family. While his older brother Arthur received his father's name, Douglas was the one who took an early liking to the military. He was born at a military station, and for much of his early life his family moved from post to post. Douglas spent three early years, from age four to six, at Fort Selden near the Mexican border, watching the drills and parades of the fifty soldiers stationed there. He remembered learning to ride and shoot at Fort Selden even before he could read or write. While his father concentrated on the military, his mother took over the task of training the boys. She taught them to have a sense of obligation for service to others and held them to two unyielding rules—never lie and never tattle. That last rule would almost endanger young Douglas's military career. Mary spent much of her time persuading her son that he was special and destined for greatness. As a result, Douglas was, from an early age, a leader and an achiever. He earned high grades and found time to be active in sports but never participated much in the social activities at school. An acquaintance later said he was arrogant, or overly proud, from the age of eight.

Military career begins. From Fort Selden, the family moved to Fort Leavenworth and then to St. Paul, Minnesota. Douglas spent important years in St. Paul and grew to claim it as his home. It was there that his father decided his son should prepare to enter West Point.

In 1899, at the age of nineteen, Douglas MacArthur entered the military academy at West Point. In those days, it was the practice of upper classmen to "haze," or play pranks on freshmen, sometimes viciously. Because he was Arthur MacArthur's son, he joined Ulysses S. Grant III in receiving more cruel hazing than the other cadets. That year Congress decided to investigate the hazing practices of the academy, and MacArthur was called to testify. When asked to name the upper classmen who had mistreated him, he remembered his mother's teachings and refused to supply the names. MacArthur spent some uncomfortable days worrying about his future before other freshmen supplied the names, and he was relieved of the pressure.

At West Point, he continued to earn top grades while playing baseball and managing the football team. He even, in his senior year, served as president of the student body of West Point. MacArthur graduated in 1903 with a grade average of 98.14 percent, first in his class. It was the beginning of a series of firsts in his military career.

MacArthur rose rapidly in the service. His first assignment was in Leyte in the Philippines as an aide to his father, who was an American military observer of the Russian-Japanese War. By 1911 he had risen to the rank of captain. In 1913, after serving as an aide to President Theodore Roosevelt and with war brewing in Europe, MacArthur found himself in Vera Cruz, Mexico, with the Corps of Engineers. The next year, he was promoted to the rank of major, at first supervising the State Department Building in Washington and then joining the general staff of the army. He was on the general staff in 1917 when the United States entered World War I.

Major Advances of Douglas MacArthur

Youngest division commander in World War I

Youngest superintendent of West Point

Youngest active major general in the army

Youngest full general

First American field marshall of a foreign army

First American commander of a United Nations force

World War I. Still only a major, MacArthur was a decidedly junior officer among the generals on the army staff. Yet he now began to show the arrogance and determination that would mark his military career.

The wartime army needed more men. One way to get them was to enlist the National Guard into the regular army. MacArthur was strongly in favor of this move, but most generals on the staff felt that the guard was not properly prepared and so were opposed to it. In meetings about the issue, MacArthur argued so violently that one superior officer threatened to block any more promotions for him. Still, the argument was carried to Newton Baker, Secretary of War. MacArthur was so convincing that Baker decided to ask President Wilson to hear the young officer's side.

MacArthur planned to bring the National Guard into the army in such a way that it would unite the entire nation behind the war effort. He proposed to form a single battalion from National Guard volunteers of every state—a "Rainbow Battalion." President Wilson liked the idea and soon MacArthur found himself a colonel helping to form the Rainbow Battalion and then a brigadier general leading the battalion into battle. Winning medals for his bravery and leadership, MacArthur was wounded twice and disabled by a gas attack once during World War I. One of his officers in the battalion was future president Harry Truman.

Postwar duty. Returning after the war, MacArthur was appointed superintendent of West Point. He stayed in that position for three years until, in 1923, he followed his father's footsteps on assignment to the Philippines. Back in the United States a year later, he took command posts of several army corps before returning to the island nation in 1928. In 1930 he became chief of staff of the army.

MacArthur served the army well as its directing officer. He tried to persuade Congress to provide more money for the military, worked to unify the commands of the army and navy, spoke out for tanks and other machinery for a new kind of warfare, and pressed for more air support for the troops. His work was so impressive that President Franklin Roosevelt asked him to stay in the position until 1935—one year beyond the normal tour for a chief of staff.

Field Marshall. MacArthur was now fifty-five years old and able to retire but still ambitious and in good health. He had survived an unsuccessful marriage to Louise Brooks in the 1920s and now suffered the loss of his close companion, his mother. "My loss has partially stunned me.... For the first time in my life, I need all the help I can get" (MacArthur in Petillo, p. 176). Two years later, in 1937, MacArthur would wed Jean Marie Faircloth, and this second marriage would be lasting, happy, and blessed with the birth of a son, Arthur MacArthur III.

Also in 1937, General MacArthur retired from the U.S. Army. His old friend Manuel Quezon, then president of the Philippines, had asked him to serve as a military adviser. He became a field marshall in the Philippine army, with an assistant appointed by the U.S. Army, a young major named Dwight D. Eisenhower. (The United States at this point in Philippine history was in charge of the island nation's defense and so could make such appointments.) As usual, the field marshall had great plans. Given enough time before a major battle in the Pacific, he would be able to arm and train 40,000 troops to defend the islands. But another world war was already brewing.

Pacific commander. Since the Spanish-American War at the end of the 1800s, the Philippines had been a U.S. territory working toward independence. It was about to become a free country in 1940 when it appeared that the United States would soon be involved in World War II. MacArthur was at this point needed in the U.S. Army. In 1941 President Roosevelt recalled the field officer, appointed him a major general, and one day later promoted him to lieutenant general in charge of the U.S. forces in the Pacific. MacArthur would include the Philippine army as part of these U.S. forces.

General MacArthur had proven to be a fearless and able commander in battle, but he now showed a weakness. Perhaps his own personality got in the way of good communication, or perhaps his intelligence staff was not as capable as necessary. For whatever reason, MacArthur felt that the Philippines were not threatened by the war. If Japan did join Germany and Italy in war, he thought, it would not attack the Philippines. He held to this idea even after, on December 7, 1941, Japanese airplanes struck Pearl Harbor in Hawaii. Ten hours later, the Japanese struck Clark Field in the Philippines, destroying most of MacArthur's planes.

A Japanese invasion and takeover of the Philippines followed, with forces far beyond the numbers the U.S. leaders thought possible. MacArthur and his troops were penned up in the jungles with little possibility of escape or reinforcement. Still, MacArthur took personal command of his army's defenses and refused to leave the desperate situation until he was commanded to go by President Roosevelt. The general took with him a few of his men who could not become Japanese prisoners because they knew key military secrets and in 1942 left the Philippines for Australia. Typically and perhaps arrogantly he sent a last message to the Japanese and Filipinos. In the message, he used the words "I shall return" instead of the army's recommendation, "We shall return."

While some took such gestures as proof that he was vain, others disagreed. MacArthur had a complicated personality. There were critics who called him haughty, overly serious, and emotionally distant; his close staff meanwhile described him as modest and warm-hearted with a sharp sense of humor. It was, in any case, universally agreed that the man had a brilliant mind, especially when considering military matters, which was almost all the time.

Two years after he left, in command of the army in the Pacific, MacArthur did return to the Philippines. He had won out over other officers who preferred to bypass the Philippines on the way to an invasion of Japan. He returned to Leyte Island and immediately broadcast to his Filipino friends, "People of the Philippines, I have returned" (MacArthur in Long, p. 152). MacArthur had made himself a hero in the Philippines. Now from his base in the island nation, he directed the army in the final days of the war to victory over the Japanese.

Adviser to Japan. The dropping of the atom bomb on Hiroshima and Nagasaki ended the war, calling for major decisions by the Allies. Who should receive the surrender of the Japanese and what should be done about the government of Japan? Although MacArthur had begun to suspect that Asia might be a testing ground for communism and should be taken over by the United States, it was finally agreed that the Soviet Union would accept the surrender of Japanese troops north of the thirty-eighth parallel and the United States would accept the surrender south of that parallel (the present boundary between North and South Korea). As commander of the U.S. forces and of the Allied forces in the Pacific, General MacArthur accepted the Japanese surrender. He was then charged with building a new government in Japan.

The old government had been based on a belief in an emperor chosen by heaven and a government dominated by the military. General MacArthur, as usual, was prepared. He had planned to turn Japan into a democracy. His arrogant ways in this instance proving useful, he marched into Tokyo with a handful of aides, all without weapons, and established his office there. The emperor was allowed to continue as the symbol of unity for the Japanese but without any power to govern. MacArthur directed the emperor and his officials in a change toward elected government.

For five years, General MacArthur held several positions—commander of the U.S. forces in the Pacific, commander of the Allied and then the United Nations forces, and military commander of Japan. He worked seven days a week long into the night to form a Japanese constitution and a form of government much like that of the United States. All the while, he ruled Japan with a firm but gentle hand so effectively that at least one Japanese historian praised MacArthur's "imperious aloofness and lordly graciousness" (Kawai, p. 6).

Perhaps because he was too busy with his many tasks in Japan, or perhaps because his intelligence officers were not alert, General MacArthur was not prepared for the 1950 uprising in Korea.

Participation: The Korean War

By 1950 the new communist nation of North Korea had built an army of 135,000 soldiers, trained by Russian advisers. The force was well armed, with 120 tanks supplied by Russia along with 40 fighter aircraft and 70 bombers. Meanwhile, the American generals in Asia guessed that Russia would soon take its forces out of southern Asia and that there was little danger of war there. Consequently, the United States had begun to disarm and the American military in South Korea had become so careless that most of the officers took weekend leaves from their troops. No one seemed concerned when the North Koreans announced in June that in August they would have a meeting in Seoul, the capital of South Korea, for the purpose of forming a government of a unified Korea. Nor were the South Korean and American troops aware that the North Koreans were gathering their forces along the border. By June 25, North Korea had 90,000 soldiers prepared to attack across the border. They faced 10,000 unprepared South Korean and American troops.

North Korea invades. On June 25, 1950, North Korean troops moved to capture the South Korean capital. Artillery fire began the war and was followed by thousands of North Korean soldiers attacking along the border. The attack was so sudden and so unsuspected that within a few days the capital city of Seoul was threatened and U.S. forces were fleeing south. The American army, now joined by United Nations troops, established a defense line around Pusan, in the far south of the peninsula, but by September even this line was being threatened.

MacArthur defends South Korea. General MacArthur was determined to control the communist drive and limit its influence in Asia. Even though he had been caught unprepared, he now planned a counterattack. Inchon was a port city near Seoul in the area over-ridden by the communists. Rather than fight back from the base at Pusan, MacArthur would lead a landing at Inchon and attempt to cut off the North Korean army from its supplies in the North. Although he was more than seventy years old and had been a military leader in both world wars, MacArthur took personal command of the invasion.

So effective was MacArthur's plan that the North Korean forces were soon in retreat. By September 30, 1950, the communist army had been driven back to a few miles south of the Han River, which flows through Seoul. MacArthur's forces moved quickly and by the end of October had advanced far into North Korea. It appeared that the war would end quickly with a United Nations victory. The North Koreans, however, regrouped and were joined by thousands of "volunteers" from China. These heavy forces again pushed South Korea's defenders well south of the thirty-eighth parallel and appeared on their way to taking the country.

Again General MacArthur carried out an excellent battle plan and pushed the invaders north of the border. Now the general wanted to destroy communism in Asia completely. He proposed to bombard China and to give help to the Chinese who had escaped to the island of Formosa (Taiwan), help that would allow those non-communist Chinese to invade the mainland. MacArthur was in effect proposing to take on China directly. To do anything else, he felt, would lead to a draw or stalemate in the war, and the communist threat would remain in Asia.

American policy. For many years, the United States had followed a policy of "containment," a plan to stop the progress of communism without threatening World War III. George Kennan had

MacArthur (center) comes ashore at Inchon, South Korea, 1950 ▶

introduced the idea, and the American presidents oversaw the carrying out of the plan (see **George F. Kennan**). Such action as MacArthur proposed, many thought, would lead to all-out war with China and the Soviet Union—in other words, World War III. Cautious of over anxious generals, President Harry Truman had directed all military leaders to refrain from making any plans contrary to the president's directions and declarations of foreign policy.

Fired. Very capable in battle and very self-assured, MacArthur had more than once taken action without the approval of his superiors or of the president. Now he began to speak out against the president's actions. President Truman, himself a strong leader, felt that this airing of differences would not help the country. Military and political leaders in Washington agreed, and on April 11, the president fired his most famous and popular general, replacing him with General Matthew Ridgway. The message of dismissal read:

> I deeply regret that it becomes my duty as President and Commander-in-Chief of the United States military forces to replace you as Supreme Commander, Allied Powers; Commander-in-Chief, United Nations Command; Commander-in-Chief, Far East; and Commanding General, U. S. Army, Far East. You will turn over your commands, effective at once, to Lieutenant General Matthew B. Ridgway.... My reasons for your replacement will be made public concurrently with the delivery to you of the foregoing order. (Long, p. 221.)

Douglas MacArthur had served in the military for fifty-two years. He had won nearly every medal for valor and courage awarded by the United States. He had been the highest-ranking officer in the military forces of another nation and had earned great respect for the defense of the Philippines and the peace in Japan. He served his nation so continuously that he had been out of the United States for sixteen years. At seventy-one, he was still a strong man. Being fired by the president of the country he had so stoutly defended must have been an emotional blow. But MacArthur was always a military man. His reaction to the firing was to accept it from his superior. When the news was brought to him, his only response was to his wife, "Jeanie, we're going home at last" (MacArthur in Long, p. 222).

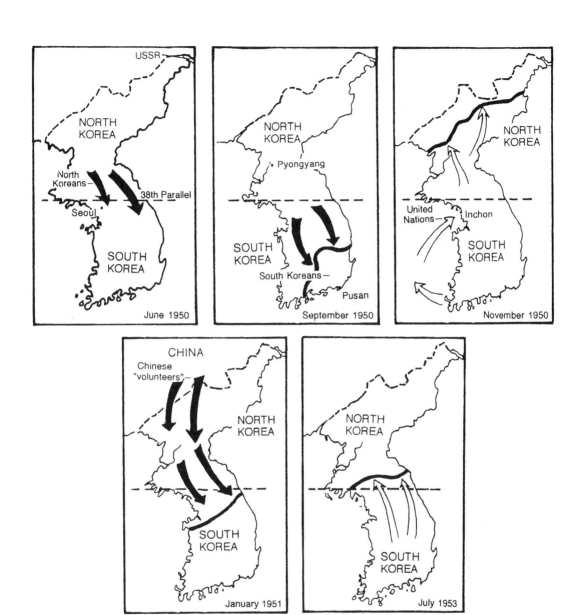

▲ The seesaw battle for Korea

Aftermath

A career change. General MacArthur returned to Washington, D.C. Though he arrived after midnight, 20,000 admirers were

on hand to welcome him. He was invited to speak to Congress, where he denied that he had acted in opposition to the president's directives. Most of the military men in Washington agreed with him. He became a popular speaker throughout the country. But his working career was not over.

MacArthur soon became the chairman of the Remington Rand Corporation and led that company for several years. Meanwhile, he remained active as a speaker against communism. MacArthur felt that communism and democracy were at war and that in war there was no substitute for victory. Not finishing the dispute in Korea, he felt, would lead other nations to feel that the United States was weak and would result in other conflicts. He would soon prove to be correct, when U.S. forces battled communist forces in Vietnam.

Outcomes. General Ridgway was a brilliant military leader. Yet the war in Korea dragged on for another year. In 1953 the two enemies decided to stop fighting without declaring a victory for either side, again as MacArthur had predicted.

In May 1962, General MacArthur returned to West Point to speak to the cadets and to be awarded the Sylvanus Thayer Medal, the highest award given by the Association of Graduates of West Point. Although he would live another two years, this was to be his last speech. MacArthur died April 5, 1964, at the age of eighty-four. One of his final visitors was President Lyndon Johnson. MacArthur advised Johnson, as he had John F. Kennedy, not to send ground forces to Vietnam or anywhere else in mainland Asia. General Leonard Heaton, the surgeon general of the army, observed that MacArthur showed great grace during his dying days. Before the funeral, in keeping with his own request, his body was dressed in one of his old tropical uniforms decorated with only the U.S. and five-star general insignias. He once said that if history a hundred years in the future remembered him only briefly for contributing to the advance of peace, he would gladly "yield every honor which has been accorded by war" (James, p. 690).

For More Information

James, D. Clayton. *The Years of MacArthur*. Vol. 3. Boston: Houghton Mifflin, 1985.

Kawai, K. *Japan's American Interlude*. Chicago: University of Chicago Press, 1960.

Long, Gavin. *MacArthur as Military Commander.* Princeton: D. Van Nostrand Company, Inc., 1969.

MacArthur, Douglas. *A Soldier Speaks.* New York: Praeger Publishers, 1965.

Petillo, Carol Morris. *Douglas MacArthur: The Philippine Years.* Bloomington: Indiana University, 1981.

John Foster Dulles

1888-1959

Personal Background

Birth. John Foster Dulles was born February 25, 1888, into a distinguished family. His mother was Mary Foster Dulles, whose father, John W. Foster, claimed to be a descendant of the Frankish emperor Charlemagne. Furthermore, members of the family played key roles in American politics. Grandfather Foster was secretary of state under President Benjamin Harrison, and "Uncle Bert" Robert Lansing was chief counsel to the Department of State under President Woodrow Wilson.

John Foster Dulles's father, Allen, was a successful Presbyterian minister. As the birth date of his first child approached, he was moving from a church in Detroit, Michigan, to one in Watertown, New York. Expecting to give birth at any moment, Mary Foster Dulles chose to stay with her parents in Washington, D.C., while the move was completed. So John Foster Dulles was born in the nation's capital city.

Early experiences. The family had always had a deep religious interest. The other grandfather, John Welsh Dulles, was an early missionary to Madras, an area in southern India. And the newly born John Foster Dulles would be brought up in a strict religious atmosphere. He accepted this responsibility fully, attending several religious services a week and learning the hymns and Bible verses

▲ **John Foster Dulles**

Event: The Cold War.

Role: As secretary of state under President Dwight Eisenhower, John Foster Dulles directed the American foreign policy that aimed to contain communism. He was involved in finding an end to the Korean War, uniting Europe under the North Atlantic Treaty Organization, and reaching a settlement of the conflict in Vietnam.

taught in the Presbyterian Sunday School. So well did John Foster learn his religious lessons that at age twenty-four he was asked to participate in a grand debate between "modern" ministers and the "fundamentalists," who believed in an exact, literal interpretation of the Bible. Leading the fundamentalists was the great orator William Jennings Bryan. John Foster's father was a "modern" preacher. He believed firmly that new knowledge in science, for example, could expand information beyond the scope of the Bible. Given this background, John Foster was an able participant in the debate.

Family life. Grandfather Foster was fond of taking the family to a summer retreat at Henderson Harbor on Lake Ontario. There John Foster and Allen, his younger brother, and his sisters (Margaret, Eleanor, and Natalie) learned to fish and sail. John Foster was always the leader in their childhood activities and often the teacher. At home in Watertown in the winter, John Foster spent time on winter sports, wood carving, and nature expeditions. His brother, five years younger, and his sister Eleanor were his most constant followers. John Foster's role as leader of the other children would continue into their adult lives.

Family vacations to Europe were common. John Foster spent weeks there several times in his youth, and as a teenager, lived with a family in Switzerland for a year, learning to speak French fluently. In later years, he would also learn Spanish.

Education. John Foster, or Foster as he was often called, was an able student. Sizing up his mind, his mother described its strength. "He reasons with a clearness beyond his age" (Hoopes, p. 11). He developed a reputation, even in childhood, for being cold and decisive, believing that his reasoning was always right. Certainly, his brother and sisters envied his ability to earn good grades with very little effort. Even out of school, young Foster showed a knack for planning and reasoning. One story tells of his interest in a bird's egg laid in the top of a very large tree. He spent much time circling the tree and identifying the branches he thought would support his weight. His plan made, he climbed up by the path he had laid out, collected the egg, and carried it safely down by holding it in his mouth.

Foster enrolled in Princeton University at age sixteen. From the beginning, he seemed destined for a career as a diplomat. While he was still at Princeton and only nineteen years old he was given his first international assignment. In 1907 representatives of forty-four nations were to attend a convention in Holland to discuss arms limitations and world peace. Attending this convention would give him an opportunity to meet diplomats from around the world. His Grandfather Foster, still a powerful man in Washington, D.C., helped him get a job as secretary to the delegation from China.

Law and marriage. Grandfather Foster was to help his grandson in other ways. John Foster Dulles returned from the convention and enrolled in law school. Then, with his grandfather's influence, he found a job as a clerk for the law firm of Sullivan and Cromwell. His pay, in 1912, was $50 a month, but that would soon change. Dulles had learned to speak, read, and write Spanish, and the law firm did a great deal of business in Latin America. Soon Dulles was assigned to Latin America and his monthly salary grew to $100. From that beginning, Dulles rose steadily to become a senior partner in the firm.

Just after he started work at Sullivan and Cromwell, Dulles married Janet Avery. The two had met as teenagers. In fact, for a short period Dulles and his younger brother, Allen, had vied for Janet's attention. But Allen soon found her uninteresting. Some friends and acquaintances thought Janet too empty-headed to be a good wife to Dulles, but he was devoted to her and she to him until his death in 1959. At the time, Janet told friends that her life had stopped along with his.

International diplomacy. In 1917, on the eve of America's entrance into World War I, Dulles was working for the law firm in Panama when he received a new opportunity for government service. American interests in Panama were threatened by disagreements between the American minister there, the commander of the U.S. military forces guarding the Panama Canal, and the officer in charge of the canal. The disputes grew into a full-fledged feud. President Woodrow Wilson called on Dulles to settle the issue, and he succeeded in getting the three men to cooperate with one another. It was the beginning of a long service in international affairs.

Peace advocate. After World War I, Dulles returned to his law practice and became a very successful Washington, D.C., attorney. Meanwhile, he pursued his interest in international relations. He joined U.S. presidents and cabinet members in the discussions of the Council on Foreign Relations. And in the 1930s he began to actively promote world peace and international cooperation. Meanwhile, his law firm was doing business in Germany. Coworkers pressured him to stop because of Hitler's mistreatment of the Jews. But he did not think the situation serious enough to warrant the loss of his law firm's German business or U.S. involvement in a European war. German mistreatment of Jews, he reasoned with cool detachment, was but a momentary glitch in history. His staff prevailed, however, forcing him to stop doing business there.

In 1939 Dulles wrote a book (*War, Peace, and Change*) describing methods by which peaceful change could be used as a substitute for war. The next year, he was named chairman of the National Council of Churches' Commission on a Just and Durable Peace. In the early 1940s, he began to speak for a united commonwealth of Europe and for placing European colonies under international rule. Unity and anticolonialism would remain the causes he championed throughout his life.

Politics. All this time, Dulles was becoming increasingly interested in the politics of the Republican party. In the late 1930s, he met Thomas E. Dewey, a lawyer who had risen to political fame as a crime investigator. Dewey would become a candidate for president three times, in 1940, 1944, and 1948, but would never be elected to the office. He nevertheless encouraged Dulles in his political ambitions. It was on Dewey's behalf in the 1944 campaign that Dulles met the then Secretary of State Cordell Hull. Thereafter, Dulles was appointed to the team of American delegates who met with other nations in San Francisco to establish the United Nations.

John Foster Dulles During World War I and After

During the war

- Helped to round up potentially dangerous German citizens in Panama
- Was a member of the War Trade Board

Immediately following the war

- Served as legal counsel for the United States at the Versailles peace conference
- Proposed that the Germans be required to pay only for acts that clearly violated international law and for damages to civilian property
- Helped found the Council on Foreign Relations, a "think tank" that promoted American involvement in international affairs

---

Adviser to the state department. Dulles had now handled three difficult assignments for the United States and had been successful at all of them. Both political parties respected his ability, and he rose steadily up the political ladder. In 1949, Dewey, then governor of New York, appointed him to fill a vacant United States senate seat from that state. Losing the job in the next election, he was appointed by President Harry Truman to be a consultant to the State Department, then led by Dean Acheson. In this position, he drew on his experience at the peace table to form an agreement that set the terms for peace with Japan after World War II. It was 1951 when the treaty was signed and the Cold War (a United States term for acts to curb the spread of communism) was just heating up. Fighting was again breaking out in Korea, and there still had been no formal agreement with the Japanese on how to end World War II. Dulles succeeded in blocking those who wanted to impose heavy payments on Japan and won Japan's approval for keeping American soldiers there. He wrote and signed the final agreement on the terms of Japanese surrender in San Francisco.

Secretary of State. The next year, Dulles supported Dwight D. Eisenhower in his presidential campaign. The campaign gave Dulles a chance to once again air his view on putting down communism, and for that matter, any form of international force throughout the world. Truman's policy, he claimed, only aimed at containing communism and would result in a longtime stalemate between communism and democracy. Instead the United States should use its superior technology to maintain a weapons advantage and should use this weaponry in a bold policy aimed at freeing nations threatened with communism. Dulles thought of such nations as captive peoples. The key to their liberation, in his view, would be diplomacy, propaganda broadcasts, and aid programs, backed up by United States power. He repeated this idea as he presented more than twenty speeches in support of Eisenhower for president. When Eisenhower took office in 1953, he appointed John Foster Dulles secretary of state.

Participation: The Cold War in Asia

The Soviet Union. Dulles worked closely with President Eisenhower to shape America's foreign policy in a difficult period of history. Communism had taken charge in the Soviet Union in 1917 and had later spread through many other countries. Dulles became convinced that the Soviet Union intended to spread communism throughout the world. A few days after his appointment as secretary of state, he appeared on television to explain how the Soviet Union was planning to encircle the United States. However, his immediate concern was Korea, which had been divided in 1945 with the Soviet Union dominating the north and the United States, the south. Two new governments had been formed in 1949, and war broke out between them in 1950. The other countries of the world tried to promote peace in the area, with talks about the Korean issue beginning in 1951.

Korea. The first order of business for the new secretary of state was to bring an end to the war between North and South Korea. Peace talks were deadlocked and neither side was gaining in battle. By now George Kennan, who inspired the U.S. policy of containment of communism, had spoken out strongly against American involvement in Korea, as he would later against the war in Vietnam (see **George Kennan**). Dulles, however, paid little attention to Kennan.

President-elect Eisenhower had visited Korea immediately after his victory. Now he met with Dulles and other members of his staff aboard the cruiser *Helena* to discuss the situation. Their decision was that the United States should try for a permanent cease-fire from both sides. Since the United States fought on the side of South Korea, American leaders could persuade it to make peace. The North Koreans were, however, supported by the Soviet Union and China. Should these nations block a cease-fire, the United States proposed to employ Dulles's strategy of force. Perhaps there would even be an attack on China to gain a military victory. Dulles wanted China to know of this decision before deciding about the cease-fire.

Two Faces of John Foster Dulles

John Foster Dulles led the Department of State through many crises of the Cold War. He became greatly respected for his skill in challenging the Soviet Union without committing the United States to a third world war. But the brilliant, respected, and not very well-liked Dulles was sometimes proven wrong. For example, he:

- Felt that Nazi mistreatment of the Jews was a short-term event.

- Believed that the Chinese would not become involved in the Korean War.

- Approved his brother's plan to invade Cuba and defeat Fidel Castro.

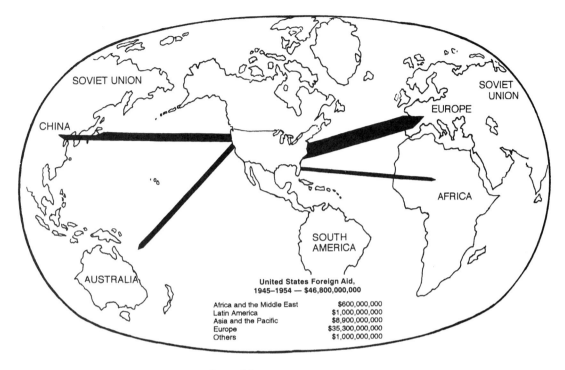

United States Foreign Aid, 1945–1954 — $46,800,000,000	
Africa and the Middle East	$600,000,000
Latin America	$1,000,000,000
Asia and the Pacific	$8,900,000,000
Europe	$35,300,000,000
Others	$1,000,000,000

▲ **United States foreign aid during the Cold War**

On a visit to India, Dulles told Prime Minister Jawaharlal Nehru of the plan. Within two weeks, news had reached China and the communist side agreed to meet to discuss a permanent cease-fire. Meanwhile, Dulles and Eisenhower put pressure on the Chinese by withdrawing naval vessels that were preventing the Chinese on the island of Taiwan from raiding the coast of the Chinese mainland. Under this pressure, the meeting between North and South Korea was successful. A cease-fire took effect on July 27, 1953.

Vietnam. Eisenhower and Dulles faced a difficult problem in Southeast Asia, where the French had been fighting communist guerrillas since 1946. Dulles thought that losing Indochina (Vietnam, Laos, Cambodia, and their neighbors) to the communists would cause the Japanese to begin rethinking their agreements with the west. He thought that the French should either have increased their military strength in the area or freed Vietnam, Laos, and Cambodia from French rule.

Despite being upset with France, the United States continued to pay 80 percent of the military costs of fighting communism in Indochina. But France's efforts were ill planned. Hoping to achieve an easy victory over the communists, France had sent 12,000 men to battle at Dien Bien Phu, a remote post in the mountains of northwest Vietnam. The French were soon surrounded and helpless. They appealed to the United States to bomb communist positions. Although the chairman of the Joint Chiefs of Staff, Admiral Arthur Radford, approved the idea, Dulles and Eisenhower had by this time changed their minds. They wanted no more situations like Korea in which the Americans did most of the fighting in a local war. Dulles still wanted to stop communism but now proposed that British soldiers and some Asian allies join the United States in supporting the French. But it was an idea the British rejected. Without them, Dulles and Eisenhower did not commit United States aid.

Vietnam had grown to be an international issue, and a conference of foreign ministers was called to meet in Geneva and discuss solutions for all of Indochina. The day before the conference, May 7, 1954, Dien Bien Phu fell to the communists. Knowing that now the conference would make an agreement that would turn millions of people over to the communists, Secretary of State Dulles left the meeting and returned home.

Dulles had lost. President Eisenhower now directed him to fly to Paris to meet with the French prime minister. The two agreed to a compromise in which the communists would receive all the land north of the seventeenth parallel. Vietnam would, like Korea, be divided. Dulles then threw his support to the leader of South Vietnam, Ngo Dihn Diem, and bolstered America's sagging influence by joining other anticommunist nations in a Southeast Asia Treaty Organization. The situation would stagger along for many years with the United States becoming more and more involved in South Vietnam. Eventually the whole country fell to communism.

Aftermath

Europe. Back in the 1950s, as he was busy resolving the Korean issue, Secretary of State Dulles pushed for a united defense of Europe through the formation of a European Defense Commu-

▲ Dulles

nity (EDC). Major stumbling blocks to this defense community were France and West Germany. West Germany, seen as a threat by France, had not been allowed to rearm after the war and thus was not able to help with the defense, even though the country was in a strategic position to block the communists. Dulles again used threats to obtain results. He notified the French that unless that

193

country joined EDC, the United States would have to create a separate armed defense effort against communism by allowing West Germany to arm. A compromise quickly resulted. West Germany was recognized as a new nation and Allied occupation there, which had gone on since the end of World War II, was stopped. West Germany gained the right to some rearmament (without battleships, heavy bombers, or nuclear weapons), and Great Britain received permission to keep British troops in Germany for fifty years.

Egypt. The Middle East was another trouble spot. There Dulles formed a Middle East defense block that included Turkey, Iran, Pakistan, and Iraq and was known as the Baghdad Pact (1955). Left out, Egypt's President Gamal Abdel Nasser saw the pact as a dangerous expansion of American influence. He began to seek arms from the Soviet Union. At the same time, Egypt needed to build a large dam for flood control and energy, and President Nasser was short of money for the building. The United States offered to loan the money and Nasser was about to agree to the terms when Dulles canceled the offer. Thereafter, Nasser decided to seize the Suez Canal and charge large fees for its use to pay for the dam. The decision created an international incident. Great Britain became involved to keep the canal open, and the Soviet Union agreed to loan the money for the dam.

Continued strategy. Dulles continued to push for aggressive action to stem the tide of communism even though he believed that the communists would fall from their own weight as they tried to support more and more people around the world. His actions even took the form of a CIA military action to overthrow a budding communist government in Guatemala. While temporarily victorious there, he failed to prevent another communist leader, Fidel Castro, from taking over Cuba at the end of the 1950s. Still, he called for economic action that would "activate the strains and stresses within the Communist empire so as to disintegrate it" (Beal, p. 312). As he grew older, Dulles had come to believe that diplomacy and aid programs would defeat communism more quickly than military uprisings. He had, in other words, moved closer to the "containment" idea on which at first he so seriously disagreed with Truman.

Sputnik I. Diplomatic challenges continued to confront the secretary of state. His notion that the United States would be victorious through superior technology received a sharp blow when the Soviets launched Sputnik I, the first spaceship. Dulles refused to join the Soviets in a conference about space after that defeat.

Iraq and Lebanon. On July 14, 1958, the pro-Western government of Iraq was overthrown at the same time that civil war grew more intense in Lebanon. This time, Dulles responded with arms. U.S. troops landed in Lebanon, and Dulles was satisfied that he had prevented the fall of another friendly government.

Berlin. Finally, in 1958, Soviet leader Nikita Khruschev announced his intention to force western troops from Berlin (the United States, Britain, and Russia had divided the city after World War II). Dulles refused Soviet demands that they be given rule of Berlin and began to make preparations to protect the American and British troops there. But his health was failing.

Illness and death. In 1956 Dulles had been hospitalized with cancer. In February 1959, doctors found that the cancer had spread and prescribed radical treatment. President Eisenhower granted the secretary a leave of absence, but soon other spots of cancer were found. Dulles resigned as secretary of state on April 15, remaining as a foreign policy adviser to the president even in his illness. He had called a conference of foreign ministers to deal with the Soviet threat in Berlin. Though the conference was held in the spring of 1959, Dulles did not attend. He died May 24, 1959.

For More Information

Beal, John Robinson. *John Foster Dulles: 1888–1959.* New York: Harper and Barnes Publishers, 1959.

Hoopes, Townsend. *The Devil and John Foster Dulles.* Boston: Little Brown, 1973.

Immerman, Richard, editor. *John Foster Dulles and the Diplomacy of the Cold War.* Princeton, New Jersey: Princeton University Press, 1990.

Krieg, Joann P., editor. *Dwight D. Eisenhower—Soldier, President, Statesman.* New York: Greenwood Press, 1987.

McCarthy Era

1940
▼
Congress passes the Smith Act, making it a crime to call for the overthrow of the U.S. government or belong to an organization that does.

1947
▼
President Harry S Truman begins Federal Employee Loyalty Program. Truman Doctrine defines communism as the enemy.

1950
▼
Accused of having belonged to a communist spy ring, former U.S. official Alger Hiss is found guilty of perjury.

1950
▼
McCarran Internal Security Act makes it illegal to contribute to forming a dictatorship in America.

1947
▼
The Congressional House Committee on Un-American Activities (HUAC) investigates people in the motion picture industry.

1950
▼
Senator **Joseph R. McCarthy** begins a four-year "witch hunt," naming so-called communists in the U.S. government.

1950
▼
Julius Rosenberg and **Ethel Rosenberg** are arrested for passing secrets on the atom bomb to the Russians.

1951–1953
▼
HUAC investigates additional motion picture workers about communist ties.

1953
▼
The Rosenbergs are executed.

1955–1956
▼
Supreme Court reverses loyalty-security laws, moves to protect citizens' constitutional rights.

1954
▼
Atomic bomb scientist J. Robert Oppenheimer is put on trial as a communist spy.

1954
▼
McCarthy calls U.S. Army men communists; McCarthy Hearings are televised. Congress condemns McCarthy.

MCCARTHY ERA

After World War II, President Harry S Truman announced the Truman Doctrine, which promised aid to other nations to help them resist communism. With it came a new view of the Soviets, from wartime ally and friend to deadly enemy. A Cold War developed, pitting the United States against the Soviet Union in what was seen as a contest for supreme world power.

Especially from 1945 to 1954, a Cold War was also being waged within the United States. A few leaders began to suspect that some U.S. government employees and entertainers and writers were communist spies. Both the president and Congress took action based on these suspicions. In 1947 President Harry Truman set up a Federal Employee Loyalty Program. Brought before a loyalty review board, suspects were put on trial for their politics. Such questioning was a clear invasion of their freedoms as U.S. citizens, but the public supported it, as fear of communism spiraled out of control.

Both houses of Congress engaged in the near-hysteria that gripped much of the nation. In 1947 the House Committee on Un-American activities (HUAC) began an intense investigation of the motion picture industry. Witness after witness was called before the HUAC to answer questions about personal beliefs and activities and to inform on others.

Adding to the anticommunist furor were the activities of the Federal Bureau of Investigation, which opened files on numerous suspects.

A Victim Scolds Congress

"There are law enforcement agencies to arrest and try citizens who commit crimes. But this Committee [has] operated not in the field of crime but in the field of ideas ... in the very field forbidden to it by the Constitution and the Bill of Rights." (Robert Vaughn, *Only Victims* [New York: G.P. Putnam's Sons, 1972], pp. 244–45)

With their fears fueled by policies such as the Truman Doctrine, many Americans saw communism as a deadly threat and were truly frightened for their country's survival. They read books and magazines of the time in which anticommmunists were cast as the heroes and communists as the villains. Such images resulted in public support for the government's anticommunist activities. Becoming "friendly" witnesses, some of the suspects called before Congress cooperated with its questioning. They even supplied names of other individuals with communist ties. In contrast, "unfriendly" witnesses refused to answer questions or identify other suspects.

Some Suspects in the McCarthy Era

Pearl Buck
Charlie Chaplin
Dashiell Hammett
Lillian Hellman
Ernest Hemingway
Paul Robeson
Carl Sandburg
John Steinbeck

Some American citizens did, in fact, have communist ties. Earlier in the 1900s, particularly during the New Deal years, a number of citizens had joined groups that were linked to communist thought. Their intent in joining them was generally to better U.S. society, not to overthrow the government. But Congress feared otherwise.

Both the House and the Senate acted on their fears. The Smith Act (1940) had made it a crime to call for the overthrow of the U.S. government, and close to 100 citizens were charged with breaking this law in the early 1950s. Then the McCarran Internal Security Act (1950) outlawed behavior that would contribute to establishing a dictatorship in the United States. Along with the acts, the House continued its investigating through the HUAC, and the Senate formed its own committee. Led by Senator **Joseph R. McCarthy,** the body had a lengthy name—the Permanent Investigations Subcommittee of the Senate Committee on Government Operations. In the next four years, it became known simply as the McCarthy Committee. McCarthy's accusations were questionable from the start. He first claimed that 205 U.S. officials belonged to the Communist Party. By the next day the list dropped to 57. Along with shifting numbers, he changed facts or operated without them in making accusations. McCarthy, whose tactics have been described as both brutal and vulgar, nevertheless wielded great power in the nation for more than four years. With his help, citizens were persecuted for their politics and judged guilty if they associated with a communist group.

An earlier case seemed to indicate that there was good reason for all the suspicion. In 1950 Alger Hiss, a former U.S. official, was convicted for lying under oath about knowing a member of a communist spy ring named Whittaker Chambers. Chambers accused Hiss of belonging to the same spy ring and of passing on secret government documents. Also there was the case of **Julius Rosenberg** and **Ethel Rosenberg.** In 1949 the Soviet Union exploded an atom bomb, an impossible achievement, thought many Americans, unless secrets about the U.S. atom bomb had been smuggled to the Russians. Arrested in 1950, the Rosenbergs were tried and convicted for passing atomic secrets to the Russians. Both the Hiss and Rosenberg trials, far from being open-and-shut cases, have remained subjects of controversy.

Blacklisting

Witnesses in the motion picture industry who refused to cooperate with Congress were blacklisted. Branded as disloyal, they could not find jobs in Hollywood for years.

Becoming an Informer

Playwright Lillian Hellman, a witness investigated by Congress, refused to inform on others: "I am most willing to answer all questions about myself.... But I am advised by counsel that ... I must also answer questions about other people and that if I refuse to do so, I can be cited for contempt.... I am not willing, now or in the future.... To hurt innocent people whom I knew many years ago in order to save myself is to me inhuman and indecent and dishonorable." (Hellman in Robert Vaughn, *Only Victims* [New York: G.P. Putnam's Sons, 1972], p. 162)

▲ The McCarthy hearings in the U.S. Senate

Roy Cohn, a lawyer against the Rosenbergs, became a key aide to Senator McCarthy. Together they carried McCarthy's crusade against communism farther than the rest of the nation would accept. Congress, especially conservative Republicans, had backed McCarthy for many months. At the height of his power, about half the public was behind McCarthy and he had attracted public support for other Republicans too. Even they, however, felt that McCarthy was going too far when he began to investigate the U.S. Army. Televised, the Army-McCarthy Hearings of 1954 revealed the senator's brutal ways to the public and destroyed his career. That same year, atomic-bomb scientist J. Robert Oppenheimer, charged with helping to pass secret information to the Soviets, was put on trial as a communist spy. Some citizens objected to this trial too.

The next year, the Supreme Court made decisions that reversed or changed loyalty laws to protect civil rights. McCarthy reacted by calling Chief Justice Earl Warren a friend of the communists. Few people took McCarthy seriously or were even listening to him at this point. Yet many still believed that hunting down communists was necessary. They would continue to believe this in the 1960s, growing suspicious if new leaders did not criticize the Soviet Union. Martin Luther King, Jr., a main leader in the struggle against segregation, would be one example of Americans who fell victim to such suspicions.

Joseph R. McCarthy

1908-1957

Personal Background

Early life. Joseph Raymond McCarthy was born November 14, 1908, in a log cabin near the small rural town of Grand Chute in northeastern Wisconsin. One of seven children, Joe attended the Underhill Country School and worked on his father's small farm. Outgoing and willing to take risks, he left school and the family farm at age fourteen and set up his own chicken farm. Joe ran his farm for five years, then, when it failed, found a job managing a grocery store in Manawa, Wisconsin.

A friend soon encouraged him to return to school. Nearly twenty years old, Joe left his management job and enrolled in Little Wolf High School. While attending school, he supported himself by working in the grocery store and as an usher in the local theater. He managed, in spite of all this work, to complete his high school requirements in one year. He then enrolled as an engineering major at Marquette University in Milwaukee, Wisconsin. Once more he worked his way through school, this time taking jobs in restaurants and at a gas station.

Politics. Interested in politics by this time, McCarthy changed his major to law after one year and earned his degree in 1935. His independent spirit prompted him to open his own law practice in another small Wisconsin town, Waupaca. Within a year,

▲ Joseph R. McCarthy

Event: The McCarthy hearings.

Role: Joseph R. McCarthy, a United States senator, gained national attention in 1950 when he began a personal crusade against communists and government workers who might be security risks. As chairman of a senate committee, he conducted a series of sensationalized hearings for which he was himself investigated and officially scolded.

he had been invited to join the firm of the successful attorney M. G. Elerlein. Elerlein became his advisor, although McCarthy seldom took anyone's advice about his career.

A Democrat and a strong supporter of Franklin Roosevelt, McCarthy became an outspoken champion of the New Deal. In the 1936 presidential election, he campaigned vigorously for the president's reelection. Having caught the fever of politics, he decided that year to seek the district attorney office, even though Ederlein thought it unwise. McCarthy lost the election but, three years later ran again, this time in an election for circuit judge. Again Elerlein and friends in the Democratic Party advised him not to run. After all, his opponent had been in the office for twenty-four years and current office holders were easily reelected, as a rule. But McCarthy campaigned hard and won the election. He was still serving as judge when the United States became involved in World War II.

World War II service. McCarthy was thirty-three years old in 1941, too old to be drafted into the military. Nevertheless, he left his judgeship and enlisted in the Marine Corps. He was commissioned a lieutenant and assigned to intelligence. His job was to gather data about enemy forces in the Pacific area from fighter and bomber pilots returning from raids over enemy territory. Going on seventeen flights within eighteen months, he made a few of them himself, serving also as a tail gunner. He returned to the United States with awards for his devotion to duty, a Distinguished Flying Medal and an Air Medal. He would later use his war effort in politics, campaigning as "tail gunner Joe" and referring to a leg injury from a shipboard fall as a "war wound."

While he was still a Marine but now a Republican in politics, friends back in Wisconsin nominated him to run for the Senate. He lost the 1944 election but regained his old job as a judge when the war ended. He immediately prepared for a race against Senator Robert M. LaFollette, Jr. LaFollette had held the seat of his father, the famous Progressive [liberal] leader "Fighting Bob" LaFollette, since the elder LaFollette's death in 1925. Again McCarthy was advised not to run against such a strong opponent, and again, after a strong campaign, he upset the overconfident LaFollette with an unexpected victory. He took his place in the Senate in 1947.

The senate. McCarthy's first few years in the Senate were unspectacular. Still independent, his quarreling with other senators cost him an assignment on the powerful Senate Banking Committee. Instead, he finally was made a member of the rather inactive and weak Government Operations Committee. This committee sometimes reviewed the spending patterns of some of the government offices.

Communists. A wave of communist activity swept the United States after World War I and reached its peak in the 1930s. By the time McCarthy joined the senate, this activity had long been declining. Franklin Roosevelt, however, concerned about what appeared to be Soviet plans to expand throughout the world, had asked the Federal Bureau of Investigation (FBI) to uncover communists in the government at the end of the 1930s. A communist victory in China and the Soviet Union's first nuclear explosion had encouraged FBI Director J. Edgar Hoover to continue the investigations.

McCarthy later told his aide Roy Cohn that he suddenly developed an interest in communism in late 1949, when three men showed him a document from the FBI describing Soviet spying in the United States. The State Department had ignored the report, and the men hoped that McCarthy, whom they saw as young and courageous, would take the report to the public. McCarthy proved a willing crusader against communism.

Beginning charges. In a speech to a group of Republican women in Wheeling, West Virginia, on February 9, 1950, McCarthy charged that a number of communists were working in the State Department. These sensational charges immediately captured headlines. He repeated his charges in speeches that followed, declaring that he would tell the story of communist penetration of the State Department "over and over again until the public gets so tired of it the administration will clean up the mess" (McCarthy in Cohn, p. 3). In a speech to the Senate on February 20, he said that eighty-one loyalty and security risks were employed at the State Department.

Tydings Committee hearings. The Democrats expected the Republicans to follow the McCarthy lead. They were likely to use communists-in-government as an election issue. However, the

Democrats, who controlled Congress, saw in McCarthy's charges an opportunity to discredit, or bring down, both McCarthy and the communists-in-government issue. Senator Scott Lucas and other Democratic senators decided to set up a subcommittee to investigate the charges.

Accordingly they set up a committee consisting of three Democrats and two Republicans. The chairman, Millard Tydings, a powerful senator from Maryland, said, "Let me have him [McCarthy] for three days and he'll never show his face in the Senate again" (Oshinsky, p. 119). McCarthy had only a few days to prepare for the hearings. A network of conservative and anticommunist journalists, commentators, pamphlet writers, and activists began supplying him with information.

McCarthy's Style of Exaggeration

In accusing the State Department of employing communists, McCarthy first claimed to have a list of 205 communists in the department. When questioned by the Senate, he reduced this number to 57. Even then, McCarthy refused to name the 57, distinguishing one from another in reports to Congress by case number. Some of the case numbers were conveniently omitted from his reports. Others listed suspected communists, homosexuals, and foreign-born workers without regard to actual communist ties.

The hearings began poorly for McCarthy. Tydings heckled McCarthy during his opening speech. Also, Tydings insisted on public meetings, denying McCarthy's request to hold the hearings in executive [closed] sessions. McCarthy made charges against nine people, most of whom were security risks but none of whom were communists. Some appeared at the hearings and defended themselves, often very well.

On March 30, 1950, McCarthy named Owen Lattimore, a professor and sometime State Department consultant, as the top Russian agent in the country. He soon withdrew the Russian agent charge but insisted that Lattimore was the chief planner of the Truman administration's foreign policy failures in the Far East. His case against Lattimore was at first unconvincing. Senator Kenneth Wherry, one of his strongest supporters, remarked that he had "gone out on a limb and made a fool of himself" (Oshinsky, p. 147). Furthermore, Lattimore spoke strongly before the committee in his own defense. At this point, McCarthy appeared to have been discredited.

▲ McCarthy at the senate hearings, June 1954

Suddenly McCarthy produced a surprise witness. Louis Budenz, former editor of the Communist Party newspaper *The Daily Worker,* testified that Lattimore belonged to a communist unit in the Institute for Pacific Relations, an influential research institution. However, he denied that Lattimore was a Russian agent. Many at the hearings were convinced by Budenz's testimony, although much of his information was based on hearsay. Another ex-communist witness, Freda Utley, said that she found a pro-Russian bias in Lattimore's writings but did not believe him to be a spy.

Later, the Senate Internal Security Subcommittee would conclude that Lattimore was indeed a tool of a Soviet conspiracy. Lattimore became an outspoken opponent of McCarthy and coined the term "McCarthyism" to refer to sensational and unsupported accusations. The term survived McCarthy's death.

The Tydings Committee hearings dragged on for six more weeks. Afterward the committee issued a report denying the charges against each of McCarthy's targets and charged him with starting a fraud and a hoax. The Republicans on the committee refused to sign the report, but the Senate voted to adopt it.

The Independent Joe McCarthy

Throughout his life, Joe McCarthy resisted taking advice from others, always working independently. For example, as he began his investigation of communists in government, he became acquainted with another famous "red" hunter, Richard Nixon, from the earlier days in which communists were more active. Nixon advised McCarthy to tone down his investigation and only report on his suspicions of those he could actually prove had been members of a known communist organization. Yet McCarthy continued to investigate and report any rumor of possible leanings toward communism.

McCarthy, a celebrity. Far from being discredited, McCarthy was now a celebrity. The clear and sharp manner in which the Democrats dominated the hearings probably worked against them. The outbreak of the Korean War, which saw communist North Koreans sweeping through South Korea just as the hearings ended, only heightened public concern over communism. In the fall of 1950, McCarthy campaigned for Republicans, and his efforts were at least partly responsible for Tydings and Lucas being defeated for reelection.

McCarthy continued to capture headlines with his sensational attacks. In 1951 he suggested that Secretary of State Dean Acheson, whom he felt was soft on communism, move to the Soviet Union. He charged that General George Marshall, who was a powerful influence in both the Roosevelt and Truman administrations, had knowingly promoted the communist takeover of Eastern Europe and China. Although widely criticized for these remarks, he remained popular with many voters and won reelection to the Senate in 1952.

Participation: The McCarthy Hearings

The Government Operations Committee. Republican McCarthy was now in line for a committee chairmanship in the Senate. The leaders there assigned him to the unimportant Government Operations Committee, and Senator Robert Taft commented that "We've got Joe where he can't do any harm" (Oshinsky, p. 252). Taft was wrong. The committee had the authority to review government activities at all levels and McCarthy would soon launch a series of investigations aimed at finding traitorous government employees and security risks everywhere.

One of his first investigations, a probe into the International Information Agency, the government's information and propaganda service, yielded mixed results. An investigation into the *Voice of America,* a radio program whose broadcast reached into communist areas, found almost nothing.

Another investigation, which brought McCarthy heavy criticism, was a probe into libraries in Europe that the International Information Agency managed. As part of this investigation, two of McCarthy's aides, Roy Cohn and G. David Schine, made a tour of these libraries. Hordes of newspeople followed them as they conducted their searches for, among other things, books by communist authors.

The tour for the most part went badly. Freda Utley, who was herself investigating the libraries for a magazine article, described Cohn and Schine as poorly behaved. However, the two did find some instances of loose security. Followings hearings into the matter, McCarthy's committee found that the libraries contained an inexcusably large number of books by communists and procommunists.

In August 1953, an investigation of the U.S. Government Printing Office by the committee resulted in the removal of a bookbinder who assembled classified documents. The bookbinder was found to have a record of past communist activity. The Government Printing Office's loyalty board, which had cleared the bookbinder for hiring, was also fired.

In another case, McCarthy had been investigating shippers' trading practices with communist countries. He apparently threatened the shippers with Senate hearings. On March 28, 1953, he announced that he had reached agreement with Greek owners of 242 merchant ships to stop using their ships for trade with China, North Korea, and other communist countries. His interference angered the State Department, which accused him of meddling in international affairs. He also angered the British, who used the ships for trade with communist nations. Still, in the United States he won praise for protecting American soldiers in Korea. Even liberal reporter Drew Pearson, a McCarthy enemy, praised him for this accomplishment.

Investigating the U.S. Army. McCarthy took a break from the hearings to marry Jean Kerr in September 1953. A member of his staff, Kerr played a key part in all of his anticommunist activities. In October 1953, McCarthy launched an investigation of the U.S. Army that would eventually bring him trouble. It began with a look at the Army Signal Corps station at Fort Monmouth, New Jersey. Radar systems and guided missile controls were being developed there. The Senate committee found that communists had wormed their way into the base in the past but was unable to find any currently active spies, only a few security risks. Nevertheless, the base's secret operations were later moved to Arizona because officials believed that Fort Monmouth had, indeed, housed communist informers.

Next McCarthy took up the case of Irving Peress, a captain who had been promoted to the rank of major. Peress had refused to answer a questionnaire about possible associations with undesirable political groups. Threatened by McCarthy's probing, the army soon recommended Peress's dismissal and gave him a hasty honorable discharge.

McCarthy, thinking that the army might be using the discharge to cover up a scandal, ordered hearings on the matter. In February 1954, he summoned Peress's former commander, General Ralph Zwicker, to testify. Zwicker had been a World War II hero. On the stand before the committee, he was evasive and uncooperative. Earlier that day, McCarthy had been in an automobile accident in which his wife was injured. He was in a sullen mood and became angry with Zwicker, saying that he was not fit to wear his country's uniform.

Shortly afterwards, at a supposedly secret meeting in Senator Everett Dirksen's office, Secretary of the Army Robert Stevens signed a memorandum of understanding in which he agreed that the committee was within its rights to question Zwicker, and that he would furnish the committee with the names of those involved in Peress's promotion and discharge. The press quickly learned of the meeting and labeled it an army surrender. McCarthy saw it as an instance of splendid cooperation with the Senate committee.

In any case, Stevens's agreement with the Senate committee angered President Dwight Eisenhower, who increasingly came into conflict with McCarthy. The president now decided to fight McCarthy from behind the scenes.

The Army-McCarthy Hearings. Two aides to McCarthy became involved in his downfall. In 1953 one of these aides, G. David Schine, had been drafted into the army. The other aide, Roy Cohn, believed that Schine, a Harvard graduate who had served in the Merchant Marine, should be given a commission. Instead Schine was brought into the army as a private. Cohn continued to pressure the army, but it refused to give Schine special treatment.

The president and his advisers now saw a chance to bear down on McCarthy. White House aides and army officials drafted an anti-McCarthy document that described Cohn's attempt to influence the army and accused McCarthy of improper behavior. The army tried to use this information to blackmail Senator McCarthy into calling off the investigation of the army and firing Cohn. The senator refused to budge, and the army released the anti-McCarthy document. McCarthy responded by disclosing the army's attempt at blackmail.

These charges and countercharges led to demands for public hearings into the matter. It was arranged that McCarthy's committee would conduct an investigation of its own chairman with Senator Karl Mundt assuming temporary chairmanship. The televised hearings opened on April 22, 1954.

McCarthy and Cohn performed poorly before the television cameras. Noting this, President Eisenhower tried to prolong the

JOSEPH R. MCCARTHY

The Red Scare

McCarthy played upon the "red scare" that had bothered Americans since World War I, his investigations bringing pain to innocent victims. The lives of many U.S. citizens were destroyed or damaged by McCarthy's hinting that they were communists. As a result of McCarthy's suggestion that he was a communist, Aaron Coleman was thrown out of the army. Twenty years later, in 1973, the army found him innocent of the charges and gave him back his old job.

211

hearings. Soon, however, it appeared that the president's office might be exposed for setting up the dispute over Cohn and Schine. Eisenhower barred testimony of conversations, communications, and documents relating to administration officials. McCarthy criticized this presidential decree, and shortly afterwards the hearings ground to a halt.

McCarthy's downfall. The Republican committee members found McCarthy innocent of wrongdoing. The Democrats maintained that he had not objected to Cohn's actions, which were improper. Both parties criticized the army, yet Cohn, now a drawback for McCarthy, soon resigned. Meanwhile, McCarthy's enemies prepared to move against him.

On July 30, Senator Ralph Flanders, a Vermont Republican, introduced a resolution to condemn, or censure, McCarthy for conduct unbecoming a senator and contrary to Senate traditions. A select committee headed by Senator Arthur Watkins was set up to study the charges against McCarthy. On September 15, 1954, the committee recommended that he be censured for:

1) showing contempt for the Senate for refusing to testify before a committee examining his finances and by insulting one of its members, and

2) his reprehensible, or shameful, behavior toward General Zwicker.

McCarthy defended himself vigorously. He blasted the Watkins committee for being an unconscious handmaiden of the Communist Party. His supporters called the move to censure him unconstitutional and political. Senator Barry Goldwater and others tried to get McCarthy to apologize to the senators he had insulted, but he angrily refused to do so.

Three and one-half months later, the Senate finally approved a resolution of censure by a vote of 67–22. By that time, the Zwicker charge had been dropped to be replaced by a charge that McCarthy had abused the Watkins committee. Even before the censure, McCarthy's investigations were losing their thunder.

McCarthy now lacked the support of the Senate but the stubborn senator refused to stop his investigations. McCarthy's committee resumed its hearings on communists in the defense industry and, on December 7, McCarthy defiantly apologized for having supported Eisenhower in the 1952 election.

Aftermath

McCarthy's actions, although often based on fantasy, had stirred the Congress. In 1954, with only a few "nay" votes, Congress passed the Communist Control Act. The act was designed to outlaw the Communist Party and went far beyond anything McCarthy had ever proposed.

Anticommunist to the end. By January 1955, McCarthy lost his committee chairmanship. A few months later, the committee closed its probe into the army. The administration had already begun to steal the McCarthy thunder. Security was tightened at the State Department and in other agencies. Still McCarthy remained an outspoken critic of the administration and a champion of hard-line measures against communists at home and abroad.

Meanwhile, his health was declining. McCarthy suffered from medical problems for years and was also a heavy drinker. Beginning in 1954, he began feeling weaker and weaker. Yet he ignored his doctor's orders to stop drinking and to rest. On May 2, 1957, McCarthy died of a liver infection at Bethseda Naval Hospital, near Washington, D.C.

For More Information

Cohn, Roy. *McCarthy: The Answer to "Tail Gunner Joe."* New York: Manor Books, 1977.

Goldwater, Barry M. *With No Apologies.* New York: William Morrow and Co., 1979.

Greenstein, Fred I. *The Hidden Hand Presidency—Eisenhower as Leader.* New York: Basic Books, Inc., 1982.

Lewy, Guenter. *The Cause that Failed—Communism in American Life.* New York: Oxford University Press, 1990.

Matusow, Allen J., editor. *Joseph R. McCarthy.* Englewood Cliffs, New Jersey: Prentice-Hall, Inc., 1970.

Oshinsky, David M. *A Conspiracy So Immense: The World of Joe McCarthy.* New York: The Free Press, 1983.

Ethel Rosenberg

1915-1953

Julius Rosenberg

1918-1953

Personal Background

Ethel Greenglass. Ethel Greenglass was born on the Lower East Side of New York City on September 28, 1915. It was a mostly Jewish neighborhood, and she grew up in one of its many overcrowded "coldwater flats," along with her parents and three brothers—David, Sam, and Bernard.

A working-class family, the Greenglasses were typical of the area. Ethel's father operated a sewing machine repair shop in front of their apartment on Sheriff Street, while her mother tended the home and children. Ethel and her brothers were raised in a strictly Jewish household and were sent to Hebrew and public schools.

Boys preferred. Though close and affectionate with her father, Ethel received little attention from her mother. Described as cold toward her only daughter, Mrs. Greenglass showered affection on her youngest son, David, and the other two boys but remained noticeably distant from Ethel. Whatever money there was for secondary education went to David and his brothers. Ethel was a very bright student and had planned to attend college, but instead, at sixteen, she was instructed by her mother to learn something "useful"—secretarial skills, for example—and get a job, which she did.

The actress and singer. Although Ethel did not get much positive attention at home, she did receive it at school and in the

▲ **Ethel and Julius Rosenberg**

Event: The Rosenberg case.

Role: Convicted as the first American "atomic spies" of the Cold War era, Ethel and Julius Rosenberg were executed in 1953. The Rosenbergs maintained their innocence until their death. Today they are generally believed to have been framed by government officials (most notably Senator Joseph R. McCarthy and J. Edgar Hoover, head of the FBI) who were bent on waging the Cold War and promoting fear of Russian communism in America.

theater. She was a small but outgoing girl and possessed a strong, high soprano voice. She liked to sing and act and dreamed of performing on Broadway someday. As a teenager, she joined several East Side theater groups and performed in musicals as well as dramas. According to a friend and fellow actor, "She was in love with art ... and hardly noticed the world around [her]" (Gardner, p. 20).

Work and singing on the side. After graduating from high school in 1931, Ethel did as her parents wished. She enrolled in a typing course and got a job as a stenographer (taking dictation). She worked at an office up to twelve hours a day but kept her theater dreams alive by singing in local talent competitions at night—frequently winning top prizes of a few dollars. While her office paycheck went to her family, Ethel's prize money enabled her to buy a secondhand piano and take voice lessons from an instructor at Carnegie Hall. Ethel's talent soon earned her an offer to become a professional singer for forty dollars a week, but her parents disapproved of the idea and insisted that she keep her "more respectable" seven-dollar-a-week secretarial job. Though this was the opportunity Ethel had been dreaming of, she again did as her parents wished and turned down the offer. Crushed, Ethel officially abandoned her Broadway ambitions just as she'd given up her college dreams. She quit her voice lessons and plunged herself into work and the budding labor movement, of which, up to that point, she had been largely ignorant.

Julius Rosenberg. Julius Rosenberg was born in Harlem on May 12, 1918, to Harry and Sophie Rosenberg. With his parents, brother and two sisters, Julius soon moved to the Lower East Side, where Harry Rosenberg worked as a patternmaker.

Though they did not know each other as children, Julius grew up just two blocks from Ethel and both shared many of the same childhood experiences. Both came from poor, working-class families. They attended the same high school and Hebrew school (though not at the same time), lived in the same set of overcrowded, dilapidated tenements, and routinely walked past the thousands of overworked and underpaid garment workers who labored in sweatshops throughout the neighborhood. They lacked opportunity and lived in dingy surroundings. Yet each of them was an extremely hopeful, caring individual who made friends easily.

Religious and idealistic. Julius was an especially religious young man and continued Hebrew classes long after he was required to take them. Like his father, he was a great storyteller and often took on the role of teacher both at school and in his home. He would study Old Testament passages for up to five hours a day and read everything else he could lay his hands on, too.

Like Ethel, Julius was a good student and a dreamer. His goals were to become a mechanical engineer and to be the first of his family to graduate from college. But unlike Ethel, Julius was fortunate enough to have parents who encouraged him in all he did and made sacrifices to send him to college. Julius was very close to his parents and forged a particularly strong bond with his father, whom he greatly admired and tried to imitate. Mr. Rosenberg was a hardworking, religious man who put others first and taught Julius to do the same.

Teacher's influence. Julius—called "Julie" by his family and friends—was also profoundly influenced by one of his Hebrew teachers. The teacher (who remained anonymous out of fear of being persecuted after the couple's execution) had a unique way of comparing Bible stories to current political events. For example, Julie's teacher related the story of Isaiah to a strike by garment workers occurring at the time. He told his students that Isaiah, like the factory owners, did not pay his workers a living wage or treat them humanely. Therefore, God did not want money or other contributions from Isaiah or the factory owners until they agreed to treat their employees fairly.

Julie's teacher continually stressed the importance of helping one's fellow man and community service, and, according to him, "Julius believed it" wholeheartedly (Gardner, p. 48). He was a sensitive young man and developed a deep sympathy for workers and a strong interest in the ongoing labor movement. But his teacher feared he may have become too idealistic. He noticed how self-sacrificing and trusting Julius seemed as a teenager and feared that in the future he would be gravely disappointed by people and events that did not live up to his high expectations.

College. In 1934, sixteen-year-old Julius entered City College of New York (CCNY) to become a mechanical engineer. The campus was alive with political activity at that time. Students were protesting international events, such as the takeover of Spain by a fascist dictator and the rise of the Nazis. Also supported by students of the time were the labor movements and strikes throughout New York City. In this politically charged atmosphere, Julius became strongly pro-union and antiwar. He believed in workers' rights and social equality.

Julius joined the CCNY students' chapter of the Federation of Architects, Engineers, Chemists, and Technicians (FAECT) and distributed leaflets for the union on campus. It was quite "natural" for Julius to become involved in the labor movement and to believe in social welfare. The majority of students at CCNY and throughout the nation acted and believed as he did. President Franklin Delano Roosevelt himself was promoting social welfare programs in the United States to ease the Great Depression, and the Russian government, which had just undergone a workers' revolution, was not yet treated as a fearsome enemy the way it was by many following World War II.

Ethel's union activity. While Julius was attending college, Ethel, who worked as a shipping clerk, also became active in the labor movement. In 1932 she got a job with the National New York Packing and Shipping Company as a clerk. Working twelve-hour shifts for only a few dollars a week, the shipping clerks scribbled receipts as fast as they could until their hands turned raw, while their employer made huge profits. Finally, after three and one-half years of this, Ethel encouraged her fellow clerks to go on strike for shorter working hours and better pay. On August 30, 1935, approximately 150 women, including Ethel, laid down in the middle of West 36th Street, blockading the entrance to the shipping company's warehouse and preventing company trucks from making deliveries. The women succeeded in shutting down the business for a day. Ethel was fired for her efforts, but the National Labor Relations Board got her rehired with back pay, and the strike led to the establishment of the Ladies Apparel Shipping Clerks Union.

A romance kindled. By 1937, both Ethel and Julius were regularly attending union meetings and political rallies throughout the city, but they still had not met each other. Finally, at a New Year's Eve dance held for the International Seamen's Union, the two came into contact.

Ethel had agreed to sing at the event but was very nervous because it had been so long since she had performed in public. Julius spotted her across the room—seated apart from everyone else and staring nervously at the stage. He had a friend make formal introductions. Julius could see that something was troubling Ethel, and she confessed to him how nervous she was about singing later that evening. Immediately taken with her, he suggested she practice in front of him in another room to calm her nerves and clear her voice. As Ethel sang, Julius's heart melted. He confessed, "I knew she was for me, if she'd have me, and I have loved her ever since that night" (Julius Rosenberg in Gardner, p. 62).

After their initial meeting, Julius and Ethel went everywhere together. They discovered they had a great deal in common and began attending union meetings and other East Side functions with each other. They wanted to get married right away, but their parents insisted that Julius graduate from college first. In February 1939, he received his degree in electrical engineering, and on June 18 he and Ethel were married.

Participation: Rosenberg Case

Poor but happy. Once married, the Rosenbergs moved into their own East Side flat, not far from where they both grew up. Julius got a job with the Army Signal Corps as a junior engineer for $2,000 a year, and Ethel started working for the East Side Defense Council, which was raising money and gathering supplies for the Allies' war effort to defeat Hitler. Their apartment was ice cold in the winter and unbearably hot in the summer, and it had little light or air year round. Yet Ethel and Julius were very happy there. They did not care much for material things and were too involved in outside activities and in each other to dwell on their economic state.

Family concentration. In 1943 the Rosenbergs' first son, Michael, was born, and Ethel quit working for the Defense League. Thrilled to have a child on whom she could shower the attention she never received as a girl, motherhood became Ethel's full-time occupation. For the next five years, both she and Julius cut back on their involvement in the labor movement and other political activities and focused the bulk of their time and attention on their family, which by 1947 included a second son, Robby.

David Greenglass. In 1945, accused of belonging to the Communist Party—which he denied—Julius was dismissed from his union (FAECT), and he lost his job in the Signal Corps. Shortly thereafter, he started his own machine shop and took in Ethel's younger brother, David Greenglass, as a partner. The business was not successful, largely due to poor workmanship on the part of Greenglass. But Julius, as his childhood Hebrew teacher feared, was self-sacrificing to the extreme and kept David on for years despite the financial drain on the shop. Finally, by 1950, Greenglass moved west with his wife, Ruth, and the future seemed to brighten for the Rosenbergs. But the sunny times were not to last for long.

Cold War begins. From 1940 to 1950, while the Rosenbergs were raising their young family and struggling to make their machine shop profitable, some major events occurred in the United States. Harry Truman became President, the "Manhattan Project" produced the world's first atomic bomb, and Truman used it to end World War II.

The creation of the world's first nuclear weapons sparked the "Atomic Age," which brought with it new power struggles and a great shift in the political thought of the U.S. government. The United States and Russia had emerged from World War II as the world's two superpowers, and the United States no longer considered Russia her ally. Instead, a rivalry that became known as the "Cold War" developed between the two nations, and a far-reaching and rapid campaign against communism was begun in the United States.

Senator Joseph R. McCarthy, a Republican from Wisconsin, led the attack. On February 9, 1950, he declared that communism not only threatened capitalism economically but that Russia was a moral enemy of the United States. The difference between the western Christian nations and the nonreligious communist world, McCarthy argued, was not political but moral. He became the first U.S. official to make such a public claim. McCarthy, along with FBI director J. Edgar Hoover, insisted that the Cold War was a direct attack on a government unconcerned with what was right and proper, or on Russian communism.

McCarthyism. Though they had no evidence to back up their claims, McCarthy and Hoover were convinced that communist

▲ Julius Rosenberg in custody

spies were working in the U.S. government and were selling nuclear weapons secrets to the Russians. They called for the investigation and arrest of all suspected communists, and, after a British member of the Manhattan Project, Klaus Fuchs, was arrested for supposedly selling information about the atomic bomb to Moscow, McCarthy and Hoover began a massive "witch-hunt" for his American counterparts.

The case against the Rosenbergs. Incredibly, the witch-hunt led to Julius and Ethel Rosenberg. Their names were supplied to the government by Ethel's brother, David Greenglass, who was arrested in New Mexico and charged with being a long-time member of "Fuchs' atomic spy ring." In a press release, Hoover stated that in 1945 Greenglass had "turned over classified information he had secured from the Atom Bomb Project at Los Alamos, New Mexico, where he was stationed at the time as a soldier" and that his brother-in-law, Rosenberg, had helped him do it (Schneir, p. 80).

On July 17, 1950, Julius was arrested after Greenglass, who it is said, agreed to tell what he knew and turn in other members of the "spy ring" in exchange for a reduced sentence (Schneir, p. 79). Greenglass named Julius and claimed that he was not only a member of the ring but had recruited Greenglass and arranged for him to sell the diagram of an atom bomb to a Russian agent for $500 (the act for which Greenglass was arrested).

Completely taken off guard when the FBI showed up at his apartment while he was shaving, Rosenberg vigorously denied the charges leveled against him by Greenglass, but the FBI arrested him anyway and illegally searched his apartment. Attorney General Irving H. Saypol used Rosenberg's past union activity and dismissal from the Signal Corps to level against him the additional charge of Communist Party membership. He concluded also that Ethel must be a spy and arrested her twenty-five days later on August 11.

Tried in the press. Running newspaper stories that claimed the Rosenbergs were involved in a world communist conspiracy and that Julius had betrayed his own country, the press doomed the Rosenbergs before their trial even began. Public sentiment shifted strongly against the so-called atomic spies, and the few friends they did have were afraid to show support publicly or even admit they knew the couple. Within the United States, only the *National Guardian* ran stories favorable to the Rosenbergs and suggested that they were framed, though in Europe many publications were making those claims and public support for the Rosenbergs was strong.

The trial. The trial commenced in 1951, but Julius and Ethel by this time realized they would not receive a fair hearing and that a guilty verdict was likely. Julius told his lawyer, Emmanuel Bloch, that he believed a guilty verdict was a way for the government to intensify hatred for the Soviets while at the same time keeping social activists at home quiet.

The government's attorneys built their case on two key factors, that the drawing Greenglass supposedly sold to the Russians at Rosenberg's request threatened national security, and that the Rosenbergs made money from the sale of national defense secrets to the Russians. Neither of these points were proven—most scientists admitted that the drawings were "worthless." And an "expensive table" that the Russians supposedly gave the Rosenbergs as payment for supplying information was proved to have been bought at Macy's by the Rosenbergs for $14.95 (it was the only nice piece of furniture they owned). Furthermore, the government's lawyers never established a link between the Rosenbergs and other members of the so-called spy ring other than Greenglass.

Despite its failure in these areas, the prosecuting attorneys, as Julius predicted, secured convictions for both Rosenbergs. Judge Irving R. Kaufman sentenced them to death in the electric chair. The sentence was designed to force the Rosenbergs into confessing their crime in order to receive a lighter sentence but, since they insisted they had done nothing wrong, the Rosenbergs refused to assume guilt—even to save their own lives. Ethel explained:

> We are innocent. We stand convicted of the conspiracy with which we are charged. We are conscious that were we to accept this verdict, express guilt, penitence and remorse, we might more readily obtain a mitigation [lightening] of our sentences. But this course is not open to us. We are innocent ... and to forsake this truth is to pay too high a price for even the priceless gift of life—for life thus purchased we could not live out in dignity and self-respect. (Ethel Rosenberg in Schneir, p. 187)

223

▲ A group of Rosenberg supporters

Aftermath

Execution. Though the case was appealed to the Supreme Court and pleas were made by Bloch and the Rosenbergs' children to President Dwight D. Eisenhower, the Rosenbergs were put to death at Sing Sing prison on June 19, 1953. Michael and Robby, ages ten and six, were sent to several foster homes and were finally adopted by Anne and Abel Meeropol in 1957.

Reopening the files. In 1975 Robby and Michael filed suit under the Freedom of Information Act to obtain the FBI files on their parents. In July of that year approximately 200,000 pages were released to them that helped to shed light on what actually occurred in the case. However, many of the files have yet to be released by the FBI and much of the information in the files has been deleted for "national security reasons."

Review of the material in the FBI files has led many to assert that they "contain no tangible proof that the alleged crime actually occurred" (Fund, p. 6). It certainly was not proved in court that any spy ring actually existed, that the supposed transfer of information to the Russians in any way threatened U.S. national security, or that the Rosenbergs had any part in it. But it is a fact that Julius and Ethel Rosenberg were executed in 1953. Their deaths serve as a painful reminder of the potential danger of overly enthusiastic government officials and illustrate a national defense policy that had gone terribly wrong. As their son Michael Rosenberg Meeropol cautions, it is the responsibility of all Americans to keep a close eye on government activities and "not to permit this to happen again" (Fund, p. 2).

For More Information

Fund for Open Information and Accountability. *Our Right to Know.* New York: FOIA, Inc., 1983.

Gardner, Virginia. *The Rosenberg Story.* Masses & Mainstream, 1954.

Meeropol, Robert, and Michael Meeropol. *We Are Your Sons.* Boston: Houghton Mifflin Co., 1975.

Schneir, Walter, and Miriam Schneir. *Invitation to an Inquest.* New York: Doubleday & Co., Inc., 1965.

Sequence of the Events in the Rosenberg Case

1950

February 3, Klaus Fuchs, British member of Manhattan Project, confesses to giving atomic information to the Soviet Union.

May 23, Harry Gold, an American chemist, confesses to being Fuchs's messenger.

June 15, David Greenglass signs confession he helped Gold in 1945.

June 25, Korean War begins—a war against communism in which Russia becomes a U.S. enemy.

July 17, Julius Rosenberg arrested and charged with recruiting Greenglass into spy ring; he denies all charges.

August 11, Ethel Rosenberg is arrested on the charge of aiding husband's spy activities.

1951

March 6, Rosenberg trial begins.

March 29, guilty verdict is returned.

April 5, Rosenbergs are sentenced to death (Greenglass gets 15 years in prison; Gold, 30).

1953

February 11, President Eisenhower refuses to lighten the sentence.

June 15, Supreme Court refuses to retry case.

June 19, Rosenbergs are executed.

Desegregation

1942
Black leaders form Congress of Racial Equality (CORE) to combat racism in the United States.

1946
Thurgood Marshall argues his first desegregation case before the Supreme Court—*Morgan* v. *Virginia*.

1953-1954
U.S. government conducts Operation Wetback, deporting 1.1 million Mexicans who are in the nation illegally.

1951
Oliver Brown sues the school board of Topeka, Kansas, to allow his daughter to attend a school for whites.

1948
President Harry S Truman ends segregation in the military; presents civil rights program to Congress.

1947
CORE workers help conduct freedom ride on bus to test *Morgan* v. *Virginia* court decision.

1953-1958
U.S. government adopts termination policy to end Indian reservations as legal units in the United States.

1954
Marshall wins *Brown* v. *Board of Education* case, which upsets the "separate but equal" doctrine.

1955
Rosa Parks breaks the law by refusing to give up her seat on the bus to a white man in Montgomery, Alabama. Bus boycott begins.

1960
Congress passes second civil rights act.

1957
Congress passes civil rights act. Martin Luther King, Jr., forms Southern Christian Leadership Conference (SCLC) to coordinate protest activities in Southern cities.

1957
President Dwight D. Eisenhower calls in federal troops to desegregate Central High School in Little Rock, Arkansas.

DESEGREGATION

Segregation, the separation of races, still existed in the United States after World War II. It was legally enforced in public and private facilities in various parts of the country. Laws demanding segregation were most common in the South. There, blacks and whites were restricted to their own sections of buses and lunch counters and to separate restrooms and swimming pools. Signs on benches and water fountains read "Whites Only" or "Colored Only."

Legally the divisions were based on an 1896 Supreme Court case, *Plessy* v. *Ferguson*. The decision declared that separate railroad cars for Louisiana's blacks and whites were legal if the cars were equal, setting a policy that would prevail in the South for decades.

"Separate but equal" became the accepted rule, but it was not observed completely. Facilities for whites were usually higher in quality because of racism, the notion that they were superior. Whites were granted privileges and rights denied to others on the grounds of race alone. Local laws, for example, set up special poll taxes and reading and writing

▲ A segregated theater

tests to keep blacks from voting. Those unable to pay the taxes or pass the tests—which local authorities made harder for blacks—could not register to vote.

During World War II, black leader A. Philip Randolph had threatened a march on Washington to gain rights for African Americans. U.S. troops were segregated at the time, and black workers were passed over or given lowly jobs in defense factories. Just the threat of the march won rights for blacks in the factories. Had the march taken place, it would have used a tactic in the struggle for civil rights—direct action.

Another tactic, legal action, was already being used by civil rights workers. Chipping away at segregation, the National Association for the Advancement of Colored People (NAACP) began in the early 1900s to bring cases to court on inequalities in housing, education, and interstate travel. The 1946 case *Morgan* v. *Virginia,* argued before the Supreme Court by a black lawyer named **Thurgood Marshall,** became a legal victory for the NAACP. The court declared that segregation on interstate buses was against federal law.

In 1947 blacks used direct action to test the Morgan decision. Members of an organization called Congress of Racial Equality (CORE) helped conduct a "freedom ride," across a few southern states. Sitting in any section of the bus, they met southerners who tried to punish them for this behavior. One rider, Bayard Rustin, later a major civil rights leader, was sentenced to a month-long jail term on a North Carolina road gang. The incident did not, however, attract national attention. It would take seven more years and another black bus rider named **Rosa Parks** to do so.

Meanwhile, the U.S. government entered the struggle against segregation. In 1947 a committee formed by President Harry S Truman issued a report on civil rights. The report documented the unequal treatment received by blacks in every area of life, from education to housing to medical care. Acting on the report, Truman presented a civil rights program to Congress. Not since the post–Civil War era sixty-five years earlier had such a program been considered, and little was done with it now. The president used his powers, however, to issued an executive order that ended segregation in the U.S. military. And, working under him, the Justice Department began bringing cases to court, adding to NAACP efforts there.

The United States was waging a Cold War against the Soviet Union for world supremacy at this time. Americans hoped to attract the newly independent nations of Asia and Africa to their side but were handicapped by segregation within U.S. borders. In words that stung Americans, the Soviet Union made fun of a "democracy" that allowed segregation. A number of southerners, sensitive to these comments, became more willing to ease segregation laws to gain allies in the Cold War.

While the Cold War exerted outside pressure, the NAACP kept up the pressure against segregation within the nation. Focusing on education in the 1940s, it brought cases to court to eliminate segregation in the public schools. In 1951 Oliver Brown, the father of eight-year-old Linda Brown, sued the school board of Topeka, Kansas, to allow his daughter to attend a local school for whites. The case grew and on May 17, 1954, was argued by Marshall, the NAACP lawyer, before the Supreme Court. Public schools in twenty-one states and in Washington, D.C., were segregated at the time. Suddenly, because of one ruling, segregation in these schools became illegal. *Brown v. Board of Education* overturned the Plessy decision, which had made "separate but equal" the policy in the South for fifty-eight years.

Impact of
Brown v. Board of Education

Though about schools, the Brown ruling suggested that segregation was not legal in any public facility. Supreme Court decisions made in later cases would support this view.

Civil rights cases continued to be brought before the Supreme Court, which under Chief Justice Earl Warren issued more groundbreaking decisions. But people were slow to put the decisions into effect. Exasperated, civil rights workers embraced the tactic of direct action. Rosa Parks, a black seamstress and NAACP worker, sat on a bus one day and refused to budge when ordered to give up her seat for a white man. Her arrest led to a community-wide bus boycott in Montgomery, Alabama, and the rise of a local minister, Martin Luther King, Jr., to leader of the American civil rights movement. It also popularized nonviolent civil disobedience (used by Henry David Thoreau 100 years earlier to protest slavery).

There was resistance, however: 100 congressmen from the South joined in condemning the Supreme Court for its rulings, and white citizens' councils were formed to stop blacks from entering white schools. In 1957 Governor Orval Faubus placed National Guardsmen by Central High School in Little Rock, Arkansas, to keep out the first few black students. President Dwight D. Eisenhower, refusing to let Faubus defy the law, sent in federal troops to protect the black students. "Two, four, six, eight, we ain't gonna integrate," chanted hostile mobs outside Central High (Gary Nash, *The American People*, vol. 2

▲ Civil rights leaders Martin Luther King, Jr., and A. Philip Randolph meet with President Dwight D. Eisenhower (center)

[Harper and Row, 1990], p. 948). But the courts and civil rights workers pressed on. Tallahassee, Florida, and Birmingham, Alabama, began movements like the Montgomery bus boycott. And in 1957 King established the Southern Christian Leadership Conference (SCLC) to coordinate direct-action activities in cities around the South. Congress followed the president's lead, finally passing two civil rights acts in 1957 and 1960. But they were weak and progress was slow. By 1960 only about 10 percent of school districts in the South had heeded the direction to integrate with all deliberate speed. The major work in desegregation was yet to be done.

Rosa Parks

1913-

Personal Background

Rosa's family history. Rosa Parks was born Rosa McCauley to Leona Edwards and James McCauley on February 4, 1913, in Tuskegee, Alabama. Rosa was a frail child who inherited her parents' striking beauty. Their parents separated when she was very young, just after her younger brother, Sylvester, was born. Rosa's father left to find work, and her mother took her and Sylvester to live with their grandparents in Pine Level, Alabama, near Montgomery.

Named after her maternal grandmother, Rose, Rosa had a mixed heritage. Her mother was a bright, young teacher; her father, a skilled carpenter. At least three of her ancestors were slaves who came from Africa. Another was a Scottish-Irish indentured servant, one was a soldier who fought in the Civil War, and one was a white plantation owner. Rosa's grandfather, Sylvester Edwards, was the son of that plantation owner and a slave housekeeper. When his parents died, Edwards was treated very badly by a white overseer who used to beat and starve him. This caused Edwards to form a very passionate hatred for all white people, although he himself was half white and very light-skinned and he often passed for white. The hatred lasted into the post–Civil War years.

While Rosa was growing up, her grandfather wouldn't even let her play near white children, although she didn't mind it. Though

▲ Rosa Parks

Event: Desegregation of the South.

Role: By refusing to give up her seat on a Montgomery, Alabama, bus to a white man, Rosa Parks triggered a year-long bus boycott by African Americans in the city. The boycott helped civil rights supporters to pass laws to end segregation in the South and to build the civil rights movement in America.

Rosa never learned to hate whites like her grandfather did, she did learn from stories of his experiences "that you don't put up with bad treatment from anybody" (Parks, p. 15).

Growing up in the South. Being raised in the South, Rosa needed her grandfather's toughness and her mother's intelligence to fight the feeling of white superiority, or racism, that surrounded her. She learned quickly that things weren't the same for black children as for whites. Since educational opportunities were so limited for blacks, Rosa was for many years taught by her mother at home. Some of the local white children would taunt the black children, including Rosa and Sylvester. Name-calling and threats against them were a common part of their childhood.

Despite the cruelty, Rosa was not afraid of the white children. One day, a white boy began taunting Rosa and threatening to hit her. She picked up a brick and dared him to do it, at which point he ran away. Later, Rosa's grandmother scolded her for wanting to fight back. She said that it was too dangerous for a black girl to put up a fight because there was a good chance such defiance would lead to her being lynched by a mob. A black child could in those years get killed for acting as Rosa had. According to her grandmother, "you just didn't talk to white folks or act that way around white people. You didn't retaliate [fight back] if they did something to you" (Parks, p. 22). Rosa did not completely agree with this. She did come to understand that her grandmother, out of fear for Rosa's safety, was trying to protect her. But Rosa never forgot the brick incident. She had fought back, and that boy had backed down.

The children of Alabama did not seem to be much of a problem compared to the adults. When Rosa was still a little girl, in the beginning of the 1920s, the white racist organization known as the Ku Klux Klan would ride in their white robes and pointed hoods down the road in front of her house. The men's screams, their horses' hooves, and the light from the fire on their torches kept Rosa awake for hours, night after night. Rosa's grandfather slept with his hand on his gun in the next room, expecting to be targeted. Rosa knew that the Ku Klux Klan could ride up to her door and lynch her whole family and nothing would happen to the Klan members. She also knew that underneath those hoods could be anyone who hated African Americans, including her Alabama neighbors, politicians, or policemen.

School days and segregation. When she was eleven, Rosa was sent to school in Montgomery, Alabama. She rode in the back of segregated streetcars, on which the races were separated, to get there. If she wanted to stop for a drink of water, she would have to find the drinking fountain marked "colored." When Rosa first saw a drinking fountain with a "colored" sign, she thought that the water that came out was all different colors. She soon learned differently—the fountains were segregated, just like the schools, churches, and neighborhoods.

Rosa's school was held in a very small, brick building, which white racists had burned down and looted several times. Rosa appreciated her teachers, a few of whom were white. Aware that they were receiving death threats for wanting to teach blacks, Rosa thought these women were very brave. She went to a few different schools until she had to drop out at age sixteen in order to take care of her ailing mother and grandmother.

Marriage and activism. A few years after she dropped out of school, Rosa met and married a black worker for the National Association for the Advancement of Colored People (NAACP) named Raymond Parks.

Shortly after their marriage, the couple moved to Montgomery, where Parks recruited Rosa into becoming a member of the NAACP. At first, the president of the NAACP, E. D. Nixon, was not pleased with the idea of a woman becoming a member, but he let Rosa join. She attended meetings, and even held some at her house, a dangerous undertaking, given the threat that the Ku Klux Klan might discover where the NAACP met. Describing the first meeting held at her house, she remembered how it made her feel: "The table was covered with guns.... I was very, very depressed about the fact that black men could not hold a meeting without fear of bodily injury or death" (Parks, p. 67).

Rosa went back to school and received her high school diploma in 1933, which was an extremely rare occurrence then. She worked hard for the NAACP and took jobs as a seamstress for many years until she was able to get a job in 1941 at an army air force base. Rosa could ride an integrated trolley, on which the races were not separated, while she was on the army base. But she had to ride in the back of segregated buses to and from work, which upset her deeply.

The grip tightens. In 1943 Nixon invited Parks to become the secretary for the NAACP, a job she readily accepted. Part of her work was to document and keep files on any trouble the whites were causing the blacks. There were more than enough incidents to keep Parks busy. She recorded hundreds of instances of blacks being persecuted, murdered, and lynched in Montgomery.

Parks experienced one instance herself when she tried to register to vote. It took the city two years, and Parks three tries, before she was finally registered at the age of thirty-two. Twice the city said she didn't pass the test without giving her the results. Even if the law said African Americans had certain rights, it seemed next to impossible to claim them.

Parks also experienced trouble on the segregated buses. The law was that blacks had to pay their fare at the front of the bus first, then get off and reboard at the back of the bus, which was often very crowded. Sometimes after a person had paid their fare and tried to board through the back door, the driver would leave without letting them on. One day, after Parks paid her fare, the driver told her to get off and go around the back. She refused, and he took her by the coat sleeve and told her to get off his bus. Not wanting any more trouble, she left. She "never wanted to be on that man's bus again" (Parks, p. 79).

The Highlander Folk School. Years later, at the age of forty-one, Parks met a white woman named Virginia Durr, who was very active in helping African Americans. Although it was the same year that the *Brown* v. *Board of Education* case declared segregated schools unconstitutional, blacks were still suffering from racism in other areas. Durr helped Parks try to battle inequality by paying for her to attend an anti-segregation workshop at a place called the Highlander Folk School in Tennessee. There Parks had experiences she had never dreamed of before: sitting together with whites in meetings where they all brainstormed on how to end segregation. The workshop gave Parks a sense of hope.

"You're under arrest." When Parks arrived home from Highlander, she had to continue riding the segregated buses. It was 1955, and Parks had heard about a woman named Claudette Colvin who refused to give up her seat in the middle section of the bus (in a row technically reserved for blacks but used for whites when the white section was filled) to a white person. Colvin was arrested, and the NAACP immediately prepared to take her case to the federal courts to try and prove her arrest unconstitutional. Colvin was pregnant at the time, and unmarried, and the NAACP knew if this fact were discovered, she would be ridiculed and their case would be ruined, so Nixon decided not to pursue it. The NAACP had to sit back and wait for a better case.

On the evening of December 1, 1955, a distracted Parks boarded a bus in Montgomery, expecting to be driven home down Cleveland Avenue as on any other day. She was concentrating on her work for the NAACP and when she paid her fare hadn't even looked up to notice that the driver was the same one who took her sleeve and put her off the bus twelve years earlier. By the time she noticed him, the bus was moving. She took a seat in the front row of the black section, next to two women and one man. At the next stop, several whites boarded the bus, and the seats filled up so that one white man was left standing. When the driver noticed this, he stopped the bus and told Parks and the rest of the people in her row to stand up and let the white man take a seat. If one white person wanted to sit down, the whole row had to stand up because whites and blacks were not allowed to even sit in the same row. At first, the whole row refused. The driver said, "Y'all better make it light on yourselves and let me have those seats" (Parks, p. 115).

As the rest of the people in the row gave in and stood up, Parks moved to the window seat, looked outside, and thought back to when the Ku Klux Klan would frighten her community, or when that little white boy threatened to hit her, and she decided that enough was enough. She looked up at the driver, who was standing above her, and firmly said, "No." He warned her that he was going to have her arrested. She answered, "You may do that" (Parks, p. 116). The driver called the police and stood outside of the bus to wait for

▲ **Parks being fingerprinted**

them. Parks waited calmly in her seat, trying not to think about what the police might do to her when they arrived.

Two policemen came to arrest her. As they did so, they asked her why she didn't give up her seat. She answered with another question, "Why do you all push us around?" (Parks, p. 117). One officer said, "I don't know, but the law is the law and you're under arrest" (Parks, p. 117).

A test case is born. The two policemen drove her to City Hall, where at first she was refused her two requests: a drink of water and a telephone call. She was fingerprinted, mug shots were taken, and then she was led to a cell.

Parks was eventually allowed one phone call. She called home, where her husband and mother both were. The news of her arrest had spread so quickly, a man was already on his way to pick up her husband so that he could bail her out. Soon after, he and a few others posted her bail, and the prison guard let Parks out.

Nixon was already making arrangements to use Parks's arrest and trial as a test case for the NAACP. This meant that she would have to plead "not guilty" to force a "guilty" verdict to be handed down. Only cases with a guilty verdict could be appealed to a higher court, where the hope for a change in the laws could become a reality.

Parks's trial was scheduled for the following Monday, December 5, 1955. She was a perfect candidate for a test case, because, as Nixon pointed out, "She was honest, she was clean, she had integrity" (Parks, p. 125). Parks likewise thought hers would be a good higher court case. In her words, "The white people couldn't point to me and say that there was anything I had done to deserve such treatment except to be born black" (Parks, p. 125).

Within moments of Parks's arrest, practically everyone in the black community of Montgomery began working on the case. A woman named Jo Ann Robinson of the Women's Political Council and an attorney named Fred Gray called a midnight meeting that same day. There, knowing that blacks made up about 70 percent of the bus riders in their town, a group of people drafted a flyer calling for a black boycott of all the buses in Montgomery on Monday, the day of Rosa's trial. Part of the flyer read: "We are ... asking every Negro to stay off the buses Monday in protest of the arrest and trial. Don't ride the buses to work, to town, to school, or anywhere on Monday" (Parks, pp. 126-27). The group ran off 35,000 flyers that night and prepared to hand every one of them out to all the black students in Montgomery, so they could bring the flyer home to their parents.

The next morning the flyers were being distributed to every school in Montgomery. The local newspaper, the *Montgomery Advertiser,* ran a story about Parks's arrest and the plans for the boycott. Taking a cab to work, Parks met with Gray during her lunch hour to discuss her case. Nixon called for a meeting of Montgomery's black ministers, including Dr. Martin Luther King, Jr., so that they could help spread the word of the boycott at their churches. The Women's Political Council was already at work on a shortened version of the original flyer, which was printed on the front page of the Sunday paper the day before the boycott.

The Montgomery bus boycott. Parks was both excited and nervous when Monday morning came. As she and her husband looked out the window of their home, they caught a glimpse of the first bus of the day. They didn't see one black person on it. The same was true for the second bus, and all the buses that followed. Without black passengers, the buses were practically empty. Instead of riding them, people took cabs owned by blacks who, during the boycott, charged the same rate for a cab ride—ten cents—as the bus rate. The cabs came around to all the regular bus stops in order to pick up all the boycotters and take them to work. The first united protest against segregation in Montgomery was under way.

When Parks arrived at the courthouse for her trial, she was surprised to see a large crowd of people gathered in front to show their support. One of the women in the crowd yelled in a high-pitched voice, "They've messed with the wrong one now" (Parks, p. 133).

Parks was found guilty of violating segregation laws, a verdict she and her lawyers expected. She was fined and released. During her trial, a group of ministers was forming the Montgomery Improvement Association (MIA) and electing as its president Dr. King. That evening, the MIA held a meeting in a Baptist Church to decide if the boycott should continue. So many people attended that a loudspeaker had to be set up so everyone outside could hear. King made a speech urging the crowd to stand for nothing short of justice and freedom. A reverend read the list of demands the MIA was going to present to the city, conditions that had to be met before blacks stopped boycotting the buses. One was

---

Front-Page News

On the day before the scheduled boycott, a notice was reprinted on the front page of the *Montgomery Advertiser*. The notice urged blacks to stay off the buses to protest Rosa Parks's arrest:

Don't ride the bus to work, to town, to school, or any place on Monday, December 5.

Another Negro woman has been arrested and put in jail because she refused to give up her bus seat.

Don't ride the buses to work, to town, to school, or anywhere on Monday. If you work, take a cab, or share a ride, or walk.

Come to a mass meeting, Monday at 7:00 p.m., at the Holt Street Baptist Church for further instruction. (Parks, p. 130)

▲ **Painting by Marshall D. Rumbaugh of Parks in custody, 1983**

to be treated courteously on the buses. The second was to have first-come, first-served seating. The third was to hire black bus drivers for the black routes. The reverend asked for the crowd to vote, by standing up if they wanted to enforce these demands and continue the boycott. People began rising and didn't stop until every person, inside and out, was on their feet and cheering in unity. The boycott was to continue until their demands were met.

A hard road to desegregation. The boycott went on, although the city leaders and the police made it very difficult for the blacks.

241

Cab drivers who were not charging the normal fare for boycotters riding to work began getting arrested. Insurance was suddenly canceled on cars that brought blacks to and from work. Police arrested dozens of blacks as they waited at the bus stops for cabs and other cars, saying they were a public nuisance. Carpool drivers were arrested for minor traffic violations. Still the boycotters successfully managed to find ways to drive 30,000 people to and from work for 381 days. There were so few riders on the buses, and such little income, the bus company had to completely shut down several of its routes.

Parks, her husband, and many others lost their jobs because they supported the boycott. The Parkses both went to work full time as volunteers for the MIA, whose demands had been flatly refused by the city. Life became difficult and dangerous for the boycotters and for the members of the MIA and NAACP. Both King's and Nixon's homes were bombed. And the Parkses received many threatening phone calls.

By February 1956, some white attorneys had found an old law prohibiting boycotts. Rosa Parks was rearrested, along with King, some ministers of the black churches and members of the MIA, and many citizens. The MIA paid all the bail, and everyone was released until the trials, which were held the following month. King was the only one who was tried, convicted, and fined, because before more trials could begin, a federal district court, in an answer to the suit against bus segregation, ruled two to one in favor of the boycotters. The city immediately appealed the decision, the boycott continued, and the case went to the Supreme Court. Finally, on November 13, 1956, the Supreme Court ruled that bus segregation was unconstitutional. Overjoyed yet cautious, the black community waited for the written order. As Parks remembered, "We stayed off the buses until it was official" (Parks, p. 155).

Aftermath

The family moves. Shortly after the bus boycott ended, Parks, her mother, and her husband moved to Detroit, Michigan, to join her brother, Sylvester. In Detroit, Parks spent a good deal of time traveling, making appearances and speaking about the boycott and desegregation.

Activism and loss. Parks remained active for many years. She attended meetings, marches and demonstrations of the Southern Christian Leadership Conference (SCLC). She kept in close contact with King and his wife. She was elected to the board of directors for the NAACP. At the age of fifty, she attended the March on Washington for civil rights. At fifty-two, she again marched for civil rights, this time from Selma to Montgomery, Alabama. The same year, 1965, just after her acquaintance Malcolm X was assassinated, she went to work for African American congressional candidate John Conyers.

Three years later, Parks was stunned and crushed by the assassination of King. Within the next decade, she lost her husband, brother, and mother, yet continued her work.

In 1987 Parks established the Rosa and Raymond Parks Center for Self-Development, an organization to help young people discover how to help their communities and themselves. The following year, she supported Jesse Jackson as a candidate for President at the 1988 Democratic National Convention. He introduced her with these words: "Rosa Parks. We all stand on her shoulders" (Celsi, p. 28).

The road that was known as Cleveland Avenue, on which Rosa used to ride the bus home, has since been named Rosa Parks Boulevard, after the woman who said of the act that helped end segregation, "I just couldn't accept being pushed even at the cost of my life. I was raised to be proud" (Parks, p. 174).

For More Information

Parks, Rosa, and Jim Haskins. *Rosa Parks: My Story.* New York: Dial Books, 1992.

Celsi, Teresa. *Rosa Parks and the Montgomery Bus Boycott.* Brookfield: The Millbrook Press, 1991.

Siegel, Beatrice. *The Year They Walked.* New York: Four Winds Press, 1992.

Young, Andrew. *Rosa Parks: The Movement Organizes.* Englewood Cliffs: Silver Burdett Press, 1990.

Thurgood Marshall

1908-1993

Personal Background

Family life. Thurgood Marshall was born on July 2, 1908, in Baltimore, Maryland, to William Marshall and Norma A. Williams. The youngest of two boys, Thurgood grew up in a lower middle class neighborhood, bordered on one side by homes of the white upper class and on the other by the city's slums. It was a racially divided city: "The only thing different between the South and Baltimore was trolley cars. They weren't segregated. Everything else was" (Goldman, p. 143). But, as a boy, Marshall was not overly concerned with segregation, or the separation of races. Though his parents were antisegregationists, they taught him to "go along with it, not to fight it unless you could win it" (Goldman, p. 144). However, if anyone ever called him names or made slurs against blacks in his presence, Thurgood was instructed by his father to fight, which he did.

Parents' influence. Thurgood—originally named Thoroughgood after his paternal grandfather, a freedman and a Union Army soldier during the Civil War—was strongly influenced by both his parents. His mother, a kindergarten teacher, encouraged his educational pursuits, and his father, a Pullman Car waiter and amateur writer, taught Thurgood the art of debate. Though moderately comfortable, the Marshalls wanted the best for their children and sacrificed in order to send their sons to college. Mrs. Marshall sold her engagement ring to pay Thurgood's college expenses. Mr. Marshall,

▲ **Thurgood Marshall**

Event: Desegregation, 1930–1954.

Role: As chief counsel for the NAACP and as a Supreme Court justice, Thurgood Marshall dedicated his life and career to achieving desegregation and increasing civil rights for minorities in the United States. Marshall, before serving as a justice himself, argued and won the landmark *Brown* v. *Board of Education* decision, which overturned the "separate but equal" doctrine that had allowed segregation to persist in the nation.

without necessarily intending to, prepared Thurgood for a career as a lawyer by constantly forcing his son to prove every point he made. As Thurgood recalled:

> He never told me to become a lawyer, but he turned me into one. He did it by teaching me to argue, by challenging my logic on every point, by making me prove every statement I made. (Marshall in Bland, p. 4)

Occasionally Mr. Marshall even took his son to the local courthouse to watch trials.

School. Thurgood's interest in the law was also encouraged at school, but not because he was a superb student. By chance, his elementary school was located next to a police station, and Thurgood often heard officers beat black prisoners, which made him realize the lack of rights suffered by accused black men. But, more importantly, because he liked "horsin' around" and telling jokes in class he was often sent to detention and made to read the United States Constitution as punishment (Bland, p. 5). As a result, he memorized the document, and by the time he graduated from high school, already had a good grasp of constitutional law.

College. Though interested in the law, Thurgood did not immediately consider attending law school. Instead, his mother encouraged him to become a dentist and he enrolled as a pre-med student at Lincoln University in 1925. His failing biology made it apparent that he was not cut out for medical school, and he turned his attention to getting into law school. He joined the Forensic Society debate team and at once his grades and dedication to study vastly improved.

Marriage and law school. A young woman who attended the University of Pennsylvania also helped Marshall settle down. Vivian "Buster" Burney, whom Marshall met on a weekend trip with his debate team, was an energetic young student and very supportive of Thurgood's goals. She and Marshall began dating, fell in love, and were married on September 4, 1929. The following year, Marshall graduated from Lincoln with a degree in humanities and tried to enter the University of Maryland Law School. Though academically qualified, he was rejected solely because he was black (desegregating this law school would later be his first victory for the National Association for the Advancement of Colored People [NAACP]). But Marshall was accepted by Howard Law School, a respected, all-black college in Washington, D.C., and it was there that he began to develop into the outstanding constitutional lawyer he became.

Howard and Houston. At Howard, Marshall was challenged intellectually and influenced deeply by both his professors and course of study. The vice dean of Howard Law School, Dr. Charles Hamilton Houston, had an especially strong impact on Marshall and became a mentor, or special guide, to him. Both encouraging him and pushing him to research and study harder than everyone else, Houston taught Marshall how to use the law to defeat discrimination. Houston showed Marshall that through the legal system, and in particular by using the Constitution to back their claims, civil rights could be increased for minorities in the United States without riots, bloodshed, or any form of civic protest. For Marshall, this was a startling revelation that changed his life.

Marshall knew that he had to be better than the average white lawyer in order to win cases as a black attorney. Guided by Houston, he poured himself into his studies and became the most hardworking student in his class. Marshall dug deep into law books, uncovering obscure cases and precedents (previous rulings). He worked hard to develop unique arguments to challenge legal precedents and studied the courtroom techniques of Houston, who was considered a master at his craft.

Marshall, loud and energetic as well as hard-working, learned other lessons from Houston during his years at Howard, too. He was taught to never enter a courtroom without being fully prepared, which meant never asking questions which hadn't been thoroughly thought out and debated in advance. Marshall learned this lesson well and was known throughout his legal career for the depth of his research. But perhaps the most important lesson Houston taught Marshall was that "lawyers were to bear the brunt of getting rid of segregation" (Goldman, p. 145). It was an obligation that Marshall took seriously. Once out of law school, he began a career as a civil rights attorney to do just as his instructor had suggested.

Marshall graduated at the top of his class in 1933. He and Vivian moved back to Baltimore to be close to their families, and Marshall opened his own practice there. However, the Great Depression made it difficult for his practice to succeed; he found himself taking most of his cases "gratis," or free. Though not very profitable, his first years as a young lawyer gave him courtroom experience on a wide variety of cases, from criminal to civil, that later proved invaluable.

NAACP. In 1934 Marshall volunteered his services to a local NAACP chapter and began taking his first civil rights cases—one of which happened to be desegregating the University of Maryland, which had barred him from entering on racial grounds five years earlier. In 1935, when Marshall won that case, the national NAACP headquarters noticed this promising young attorney. Houston, who had become the Counsel-General of the NAACP Legal Defense and Educational Fund, Inc. in 1934, encouraged the NAACP to hire Marshall at its offices in New York, and in 1936 Marshall was named Houston's assistant counsel.

Thurgood Marshall's Outlook on Life and Work

"You either work to improve society, or you become a parasite on it."

"I intend to wear life like a very loose garment and never worry about nothin'."

"The Court fails in its constitutional duties when it refuses ... to make even the effort to see [what it is like to be poor]. For the poor, education is often the only route by which to become full participants in our society."

"I enjoy the fight. I agree with the old saying 'I love peace, but I adore a riot.' You've got to be angry to write a dissent" [opinion disagreeing with the majority opinion of the judges]. (Marshall in Goldman, pp. 177, 179, 181)

Participation: Desegregation

Legal strategy for desegregation. Once Marshall was in New York and back together with his good friend and teacher, his career began to thrive. Now able to put into practice what they had talked about at Howard University, Houston and Marshall plotted the course they would take to end segregation. Along with attorney William Hastie, the three began researching the background of *Plessy* v. *Ferguson,* 163 U.S. 537 (1896), the case that established the "separate but equal" doctrine and made segregation legal. The doctrine stated that public places and transportation—for example, schools, restaurants, and buses—could be segregated and have

▲ A colored-only store in Belle Glade, Florida, April 1945

"separate but equal" facilities. *Plessy* was considered a legal precedent. Therefore, the only way to outlaw its content was to get the decision overturned by the Supreme Court. And that is what Marshall and his coworkers set out to do.

Marshall began researching the history of civil rights legislation and NAACP lawsuits, successful and unsuccessful, to find a solid and original argument against *Plessy*. The attorneys also began looking over cases brought to the Fund, to determine which could get them to the Supreme Court to begin chipping away at the *Plessy* decision. Their plan was to bring numerous cases before the court that would slowly break down the precedent and demonstrate that the "separate but equal" doctrine was completely unconstitutional.

Research skills pay off. The first case they brought to the Supreme Court was *Missouri ex. rel. Gaines* v. *Canada,* 305 U.S. 337

(1938), in 1936. It was the first time the NAACP challenged the constitutionality of segregation in public schools, and it proved to be a huge victory for the association. Marshall played a key role in the success of the suit. He prepared the brief that argued the case, declaring that school segregation was unconstitutional because Missouri had no separate and equal law school for blacks, and the Fourteenth Amendment states:

> No State shall make or enforce any law which shall abridge the privileges or immunities of citizens of the United States ... nor deny to any person within its jurisdiction the equal protection of the laws. (Prentice Hall, p. 810)

Marshall's argument, using the Constitution he knew so well to back his claims, proved highly persuasive. His thoroughness of preparation and research skills paid off when the Supreme Court ruled for the NAACP's client, Gaines, on December 12, 1938. It was the first key decision that opened the door for the elimination of the "separate but equal" rule, but Marshall realized it was just a single victory and now the war had begun.

Counsel-General. In 1940 Marshall became the chief attorney or Counsel-General of the Fund, and for the next decade he directed an attack on *Plessy* from all angles. He assembled experts from a variety of professions, including sociologists, historians, and psychologists, to determine the negative effects of segregation on society. He wanted to mount more than just a legal assault on segregation; he wanted to show the human toll it was taking on *all* members of society, white and black. He encouraged white and black Americans to work together to end segregation and called all those who believed in desegregation into action:

> We must not be delayed by people who say "the time is not ripe," nor should we proceed with caution or fear of destroying the "status quo." Persons who deny to us our civil rights should be brought to justice now.... The responsibility for the enforcement of these statutes [constitutional guarantees] rests with every American citizen regardless of race or color. (Marshall in Bland, p. 34)

First case. As always, Marshall practiced what he preached. In 1946 he brought to the Supreme Court the first in a series of desegregation cases that he personally argued. This initial case, *Morgan* v. *Virginia,* 328 U.S. 373, involved a black woman, Miss Irene Morgan, who refused to move to the back of a bus when it passed through a segregated county. The bus was traveling from Virginia to Maryland—in and out of segregated or "Jim Crow" counties—and when Morgan repeatedly refused to move, she was arrested and fined ten dollars. Marshall argued that not only was this extending racism to a national level, but it also placed an "undue burden" on transportation businesses, which had to continually move their passengers. Marshall remarked: "The national business of interstate commerce is not to be disfigured by local practices bred of racial notions alien to our national ideals" (Marshall in Bland, p. 43). He further argued that the U.S. had just joined the United Nations and agreed to promote "universal respect for, and observance of, human rights and fundamental freedoms for all without distinction as to race, sex, language, or religion," and it needed to start practicing these ideals at home (Marshall in Bland, p. 43). The case was decided in favor of Morgan and dealt a deadly blow to segregation. But Marshall and his team persisted, not content until all public facilities in America were desegregated and *Plessy* was no longer legal on any grounds.

School desegregation. Marshall's next line of attack was on public schools at the primary level. Major victories had already been achieved for graduate schools and universities, but elementary and high schools had yet to achieve integration. Marshall developed his argument that education could not be "separate but equal" because there was no way to equally duplicate factors such as a school's prestige (standing), quality of teachers, and an institution's reputation. Marshall brought numerous school desegregation cases to the Supreme Court through 1954, arguing that "segregation has been used historically and is being used at the present to deny equality of educational opportunity to Negroes" (Marshall in Bland, p. 62). He attacked the practice of segregation in schools, calling it un-American and unconstitutional and used the arguments he had gathered from the experts to show how damaging separation of the races is to society. Segregation, he argued, promotes a caste system of higher and lower levels of society and alienates or separates Americans from each other in spirit as well as body.

Brown decision. By 1950, Marshall had won a series of key victories but needed one big case to overturn *Plessy* once and for all. Stating that children could not afford to wait "twenty, thirty, or forty years before the Jim Crow school might wither away," Marshall and his coworkers brought cases to court in Kansas, Virginia, Delaware, and South Carolina (Bland, p. 70). These four cases, filed on behalf of local black schoolchildren to gain admission to segregated white elementary and secondary schools, were eventually combined into one lawsuit brought before the Supreme Court. Known as *Brown* v. *Board of Education,* 344 U.S. 1 (1954), the lawsuit won for Marshall the landmark decision he had been working for his entire legal career.

In preparation for the case, Marshall again assembled a panel of experts and held mock trials at Howard University Law School to test and refine his arguments. In 1952 the case went before the Supreme Court with Marshall as lead counsel. Marshall, now as skillful in the courtroom as his one-time teacher, Houston, forcefully argued that:

> The significance of the legislative history of the Fourteenth Amendment is that there can be no doubt that the framers were seeking to secure and to protect the Negro as a full and equal citizen.... The Court decisions in aid of this fundamental purpose, we submit, compel the conclusion that school segregation ... is at war with the [Fourteenth] Amendment's intent. (Bland, p. 79)

Marshall's argument carried the day and on May 17, 1954, Chief Justice Earl Warren announced the *Brown* victory. Writing for the Court, Warren found segregation to be unconstitutional and therefore, *Plessy*'s "separate but equal" doctrine no longer lawful or valid as it applied to education. His writing maintained that to separate black children solely because of race produces a feeling of being inferior and added that separate schools are because of their separateness unequal.

Black Americans were ecstatic. While sixty-nine southern congressmen immediately criticized the decision and vowed never to apply the court ruling in their states, the decision was applauded worldwide as a "victory for democratic principles and practices" (Goldman, p. 107). On May 31, 1955, the Supreme Court ordered

▲ Marshall on the steps of the Supreme Court, August 1958

local courts to demand a prompt start toward fully applying the decision to their areas.

Marshall knew that it might be some years before the rulings would, in fact, be fully applied, especially in the South, but the decisions heartened him about the future:

> The Court has reaffirmed its pronouncement that segregation is unconstitutional and throughout the opinion stress is placed upon the necessity for full compliance and the earliest practicable

253

date.... We can be sure that desegregation will take place through the United States—tomorrow in some places, the day after tomorrow in others and many, many moons hence in some, but it will eventually come to all. (Marshall in Goldman, p. 111)

Aftermath

Career and personal changes. While professionally life could not have been better for Marshall, his personal life was struck by tragedy. His wife of twenty-five years died of cancer in 1955 shortly after the *Brown* victory. Marshall bore his loss and a year later married Cecelia Suyat, a coworker at the NAACP Legal Defense and Education Fund, Inc.

Brown v. Board of Education

Two *Brown* v. *Board of Education* cases reached the Supreme Court. The 1954 case held that segregation at all levels of public education was illegal. The 1955 case ruled that school authorities were responsible for how fast desegregation was carried out and that it should be done with all deliberate speed.

Marshall continued as the NAACP's Counsel-General for twenty-one years, served as U.S. Solicitor General (trying cases for the government before the Supreme Court), and in 1967 became the first black Supreme Court justice, appointed by Lyndon Johnson. He served on the Supreme Court for twenty-four years. As trials heard in the 1970s and 1980s wiped out some of the earlier civil rights progress, Marshall grew ever angrier and wrote opinions of dissent, or disagreement, with the majority of justices. Marshall retired in 1991 because, he said, of health problems and died in 1993 of a heart attack.

Known as "Mr. Desegregation" and "Mr. Civil Rights," Marshall perhaps had more influence on the interpretation of the Constitution than any other person until his time. Some have called him the most important lawyer of the twentieth century, and his coworkers and former law clerks consider him one of the greatest teachers as well. A former clerk, Paul Gewirtz, described Marshall's impact:

Brown changed the world. And because of that, Thurgood Marshall's life stands for the idea that law can change the world and that the Supreme Court can be a powerful force in fulfilling our best public values. (Goldman, p. 168)

So much to be done. When Marshall died, more than 20,000 men, women and children turned out to pay their respects to the man who brought about desegregation and dedicated his life to promoting civil rights. Never before had so many citizens publicly honored a Supreme Court justice. Marshall not only made huge gains for civil rights during his lifetime but also served as a role model to his own and future generations, whom he urged to carry on his work:

> Some feel we have arrived. Others feel there is nothing more to do. I just want to be sure ... you won't think that's the end of it. I won't have it that way. There's too much work to be done. (Marshall in Kagan and Sunstein, p. 16)

For More Information

Bland, Randall. *Private Pressure on Public Law*. New York: University Press of America, 1973.

Goldman, Roger, and David Gallen. *Thurgood Marshall: Justice for All*. New York: Carroll & Graf Publishers, Inc., 1992.

Kagan, Elena, and Cass R. Sunstein. *Remembering "TM."* Chicago: University of Chicago Press, 1993.

Prentice Hall General Reference. *The New York Library Public Reference*. New York: Stonesong Press, Inc., 1993.

Not Yet!

A big man known for his wicked sense of humor as well as his legal brilliance, Marshall battled all his life against those who wanted him to back down or retire. In 1970, when he visited Bethesda Naval Hospital for a routine checkup, President Richard Nixon sent for his medical files, apparently hoping Marshall might have to step down from the Supreme Court due to a medical problem. Hearing this, Marshall wrote in big, black letters on the outside of the files, "NOT YET" and sent them to Nixon. Marshall endured many such incidents throughout his Supreme Court years. Presidents and reporters continually talked about when he would retire or die.

Cuban Missile Crisis

1956
Dwight D. Eisenhower is reelected as U.S. president.

1959
U.S. missiles placed in Turkey. Fidel Castro leads successful revolution in Cuba.

1961
Bay of Pigs invasion to overthrow Castro fails. Dulles resigns; John Alexander McCone replaces him.

1961
Castro declares his communist beliefs. **John F. Kennedy** becomes U.S. president; approves CIA anti-Castro plot.

1959–1961
U.S. Central Intelligence Agency (CIA), headed by **Allen Dulles,** plans to overthrow Castro.

1962
January–June— Russians decide to place missiles in Cuba.

1962
August— American U-2 spy planes photograph launching pads for defensive surface-to-air missiles in Cuba.

1962
September— Kennedy warns that U.S. will take military action if offensive missiles appear in Cuba.

1962
December— Castro releases the 1,179 Bay of Pigs prisoners for $53 million in medical supplies and goods.

1962
October— Soviet leader Nikita Khrushchev observes blockade; broadcasts news of settlement on October 28.

1962
October— U-2 spy plane detects Soviet offensive missiles in Cuba. Kennedy sets up naval blockade between Russia and Cuba; broadcasts news of blockade on October 22.

Pinar del Rio · Havana · Matanzas · Cienfuegos · Santa Clara · Camaguey · Holguin · Santiago de Cuba

CUBAN MISSILE CRISIS

For one week, October 22 to October 28, 1962, the world stood on the brink of nuclear war. The episode, called the Cuban Missile Crisis, was the most dangerous in the Cold War between the world's two superpowers, the Soviet Union and the United States. It was the climax of a number of events.

World War II saw the United States launch an atomic bomb that became the world's first nuclear weapon. Not yet having an atomic bomb or a long-range bomber, the Soviets set out to develop nuclear weapons and an intercontinental missile. In 1957 Russia developed the first missile that could reach the United States from the Soviet Union. That same year it launched Sputnik, the first satellite to circle the earth. The United States responded by developing an arsenal of long- and intermediate-range missiles of its own.

The United States had been far ahead of the Soviet Union in the nuclear arms race. Now it was rumored that by the early 1960s Russia could have a greater arsenal of nuclear weapons than America. Called the missile gap, the rumor grew into a mistaken belief when Dwight D. Eisenhower was president. Eisenhower had secret information, collected by U-2 spy planes, that Russia was not producing so many intercontinental ballistic missiles (ICBMs) after all. But he chose not to share this secret information with the pubic, and the mistaken belief persisted. Under Eisenhower, some U.S. intermediate-range ballistic missiles (IRBMs), called Jupiters, were positioned in Turkey, near the Soviet Union.

During the 1960 campaign for U.S. president, **John F. Kennedy** claimed that the Soviets had, in fact, outdistanced the United States in nuclear arms. Once elected, Kennedy began a huge military buildup. The goal was to have three times as many ICBMs and four times as many long-range bombers as the Soviets. Fidel Castro had the previous year led an overthrow of the government in Cuba and was on friendly terms with the Soviet Union. In 1961 Castro announced his belief in communism, a system in which the government controls all the industry and there is only one political party. Just 90 miles from the United States, Castro's Cuba brought communism dangerously close to American shores in Kennedy's eyes. The fear was that this made the United States seem weak. Also Castro gave speeches about the need for revolution throughout Latin America, and it was feared that communism could spread to other nearby countries.

Allen Dulles, head of the Central Intelligence Agency (CIA) under President Eisenhower, began a plan to overthrow Castro. Kennedy was informed of the plan and assured that it would succeed. Around 1,200 Cuban exiles were to invade the Bay of Pigs, after which they counted on rebels inside Cuba to take up arms and join them. If Kennedy called off the invasion, it was thought, the United States would be sharply criticized for its loss of nerve. There was also a fear that not invading Cuba would encourage communist revolutions elsewhere in Latin America. On the other hand, if the United States carried out the invasion, it would be breaking international law and its own word about the right of every nation to choose its own government. In the end, Kennedy allowed the invasion to proceed. It failed miserably. Contrary to expectations, no rebels inside Cuba rushed to the aid of the invaders. Castro enjoyed widespead support.

Relations between the Soviet Union and Cuba became even closer after the Bay of Pigs. In the first half of 1962, the Soviet government, headed by Nikita Khrushchev, decided to

▲ Aerial view of San Cristobal medium range ballistic site, Cuba, October 14, 1962. Seven missile trailers with missiles are clustered near two missile shelter tents, while another missile trailer is positioned near an emplacement erector.

place missiles in Cuba. Several reasons have been given for the decision to place the missiles in Cuba. The Soviets were behind the United States in the arms race, and the Americans had positioned the Jupiter missiles near them in Turkey. By placing missiles in Cuba, the Soviets could close the gap. They would, from Castro's point of view, also be protecting Cuba from another Bay of Pigs invasion. And the Soviets

259

could use the missiles as a bargaining chip, to get the Jupiters out of Turkey and maybe to win Berlin. Ever since World War II, Berlin had been divided, with the Soviets controlling only the eastern portion of the city. Perhaps they could exchange taking missiles out of Cuba for getting Kennedy to give up U.S. control of western Berlin.

Some Soviet Weapons Sighted by U-2 Spy Planes in Cuba

1. Medium Range Ballistic Missiles (MRBMs)—48 missiles with a range of about 1,200 miles.
2. Intermediate Range Ballistic Missiles (IRBMs)—12 launchers for missiles with a range of about 2,600 miles. Only the launchers were spotted; the missiles themselves did not reach Cuba.
3. IL-28 Bombers—42 unassembled bombers reached Cuba. Each would have a round-trip range of about 720 miles.
4. Surface-to-Air Missiles (SAMs)—24 sites, each with 6 missiles to provide air defense for the MRBM and IRBM sites. Antiaircraft missiles, the SAMs could hit targets at 80,000 feet altitude.

At the end of August, Americans discovered that the Soviets were constructing launching pads for surface-to-air missiles (SAMs) in Cuba. Kennedy informed the nation in a television broadcast. The SAMs could be there for defensive purposes, to shoot down air-attack craft. If, however, the United States detected offensive missiles in Cuba, to shoot at distant ground targets, Kennedy promised to protect U.S. security by taking military action. The tension was rising. The stakes were high, higher than ever before in history. With all the new nuclear weaponry, the incident could bring on World War III, which could destroy humanity. In October a U-2 spy plane revealed launching pads for Soviet offensive ground-to-ground missiles. Two more weeks of spying brought sightings of the offensive missiles and of other weaponry.

Aside from weapons, some 22,000 Soviet soldiers and weapons operators were spotted. The setup made it possible for a nuclear attack on almost any U.S. city from Cuba.

The president discussed the alternatives with close advisors. He did not, however, consult other European nations that had with America formed the mutual defense North Atlantic Treaty Organization (NATO). Nor at this point did he consult the Organization of American States (OAS). The feeling was that such talk would take too long. His advisors debated far into the night. Settling on a blockade, the president had to call it by another name or else it would be considered an act of war. He described it as a "quarantine" and warned that if the Soviets did not observe it, he would take more drastic military action. After it began, the OAS voted to support it, and Kennedy contacted Khrushchev to say he hoped the Soviets would respect it as well, so that America did not have to fire on a Soviet ship. They did. The world sighed in relief, and a peaceful compromise followed.

The crisis signaled a turning point in Soviet-American relations. There was more acceptance afterward of the idea of peaceful coexistence. That is, the superpowers were more willing to consider leaving alone other governments—whether communist or democratic—and try existing side-by-side in the world. Also they began to limit their arms race, starting with a Soviet-American test-ban agreement to stop atmospheric and underwater nuclear explosions.

There was great controversy in America over Kennedy's handling of events in Cuba. Some said the missile crisis was his finest hour. He made hard decisions. He kept his promises. He stood up to the Russians. Others criticized him for breaking international law in the Bay of Pigs and for not consulting NATO during the missile crisis. It was sheer luck, they argued, that the crisis ended peacefully. The president had risked nuclear war only to end up making a compromise that could have been reached without all the danger. In either case, the outcome showed caution on the part of both the Russians and Americans and was fortunate for humankind.

Allen Dulles

1893-1969

Personal Background

Allen and John Foster. Allen Dulles seemed always to envy his big brother, John Foster, who was the ringleader in their childhood games. The two brothers had very different personalities. John Foster could be cold, calm, and unbending, while Allen has been described as someone given to emotional outbursts. The older brother was conservative and not inclined to favor changes. Allen meanwhile often felt sympathy for the underdog and was a champion of change. Yet the two brothers' lives kept intersecting. Allen followed John foster to Princeton University and worked for him for a time in a law firm. Then, while John Foster was Secretary of State, Allen filled a lower, though highly respected, position as head of the Central Intelligence Agency, or CIA.

The family. Members of the Dulles family distinguished themselves before the birth of Allen or John Foster. Grandfather John Foster had served as secretary of state under President James Buchanan. Robert Lansing (Uncle Bert) had served as chief counsel to the Department of State under Woodrow Wilson. The boys' father, Allen Macy Dulles, was a prominent Presbyterian minister. At the time of John Foster's birth, he was on the move from a church in Detroit to one in Watertown, New York. Five years later, on April 6, 1893, his second son, Allen, was born in Watertown.

▲ **Allen Dulles**

Event: The Bay of Pigs.

Role: As head of the Central Intelligence Agency (CIA) of the United States, Allen Dulles was responsible for American espionage or spy activities on the Soviet Union from 1953 to 1961. He directed both the effort to build the high altitude U-2 airplane and to invade communist Cuba at the Bay of Pigs.

Early life. The conditions surrounding the birth remained a family secret. At the time, it was not uncommon for families to blame birth defects on sins of the family and label them as the mark of the devil. Perhaps Minister Dulles believed in such notions, for he and the family kept it a secret that Allen had been born with a club foot. Just three months after his birth, Allen was secretly whisked away to Syracuse for surgery to repair his misshapen foot. The surgery was successful, but the secret remained in the family. Allen was six years old before his parents told him of the problem.

The Dulles family grew to include five children. John Foster and Margaret were the oldest, then came Allen, Eleanor, and Natalie. Allen and Eleanor became their older brother's most constant followers. Being older, John Foster was usually better at childhood pastimes, but their different personalities gave Allen the edge in one favorite summer activity—fishing. Allen, who believed in being flexible, was far the best fisher as a boy. A fisherman, Allen thought, should try to think like the fish.

When Allen was four years old, the brothers and sisters were separated for a while by disease. John Foster and Margaret caught typhoid, and Allen and Eleanor were forbidden to visit them. Curiosity got the better of the two younger family members, and Allen had to peek into the sick room for a glimpse of his brother and sister. The high temperature of the fever resulted in sister Margaret's losing much of her hair and weight. The sight of her suffering was an emotional experience that Allen would never forget.

Young author. The three companions, John, Allen and Eleanor, all had bright minds, but they showed it in different ways. While John Foster and Eleanor earned top grades, Allen was not always as serious about his school work (although learning was easy for him). On the other hand, events of the day were of great interest to him. When he was eight years old, the whites of South Africa, called Boers, were at war with the British. Allen followed the war in the news and developed strong feelings for the people involved in the combat. At age eight, he wrote a small book, *The Boer War: A History.* His first reader was Eleanor, then five years old. The book was passed around the Dulles family and finally was shown to his grandfather John Foster. Grandfather borrowed the writing for a while and had it printed and bound as a real published book. It was a gift to his grandson. When, years later, Allen Dulles became active in U.S. foreign affairs, the government reprinted this first book.

Education and travel. In 1910 Allen followed John Foster to Princeton University. The end of his college days found the younger brother still undecided about the direction of his life. He decided to look as far away from the family as possible for adventure. In 1912 he accepted a teaching position in an agricultural college in India and then left for China, returning home from there after a three-year absence.

The Foreign Service. Still undecided about his career, Allen took and passed the examination for the U.S. diplomatic service. He joined the Foreign Service in 1916 as third secretary to the embassy at Vienna. A year later, the United States joined the Allies in World War I, and the embassy in Vienna was closed. He was reassigned to Berne, Switzerland. Here fortune directed him into his lifelong career.

There was confusion at the American delegation in Berne. The ambassador was occupied with details of the war, and no one seemed to know why Allen Dulles was there. Finally an assistant told him that he might as well be in charge of intelligence for the delegation since no one else was. Both the secrecy and difficulty of intelligence work made it stimulating and exciting to Dulles. He had found his life's calling but it would be some time before he could become deeply involved in gathering information and carrying on secret activities for the United States.

Marriage. The tour in Berne ended, and Allen Dulles returned home in 1920. Taking full social advantage of this break in work assignments, he began to attend as many parties as possible. At one of them, he met a pretty and lively young woman named Clover Todd, the daughter of a professor at Columbia University. The two fell in love and were married October 16, 1920. Although Clover was less-than-responsible with the family budget, and Allen was said to have had several affairs with other women, the marriage would last until Dulles's death. The family grew with the addition of three children: Clover (1922), Joan (1923), and Allen (1930).

Law. While continuing to work for the government, Dulles began to take evening law courses at George Washington University. He easily passed the bar examinations, though law was not his first interest.

Meanwhile, his older brother had joined the law firm of Sullivan and Cromwell and had risen rapidly to become senior partner in the firm. There were positions open in the firm, but there were also many very capable applicants. Passing over these proven lawyers, John Foster brought his younger brother into the firm.

Allen had no law experience and was not much use to the company as an attorney at first. He did, however, have social skills that his older brother lacked, and they could be used to bring new business to the company. By 1930 he had worked his way to a position as a junior partner of the firm.

The new junior partner soon had one of his few disagreements with his dominating older brother over Hitler's mistreatment of the Jews. Allen joined a staff rebellion that forced the law firm to give up its business in Germany, a decision made much against the will of John Foster.

A brewing war. In 1939 Hitler's Germany marched into Czechoslovakia, and war in Europe began. President Franklin Roosevelt had quickly become convinced that the United States must become involved, but many people in the government wanted to remain neutral. To prepare the nation for war, Roosevelt needed a good international information source. For this and other reasons, he established the office of Coordinator of Information (COI) and assigned General William J. Donovan to take charge of it in 1940. Donovan had been in intelligence work before and had been so imaginative in finding new ways to gather information that he had earned the nickname "Wild Bill." Allen Dulles had worked with him in Switzerland. But it was not until after the bombing of Pearl Harbor in Hawaii, December 7, 1941, that Donovan invited Dulles to join COI.

OSS and World War II. Six months after Pearl Harbor, General Donovan's COI grew to become the Office of Strategic Services (OSS). His activities led to the development of information-gathering stations and plots against supposed enemies of the United States throughout the world. Once again Dulles found himself gathering information from an office in Switzerland.

Dulles contributed greatly to the allied victory over Nazi Germany. One great gain was his recruiting of a German official as a spy for the United States. Fritz Kolbe brought important German documents to Dulles because he thought Hitler's people were destroying the nation that he had loved. Dulles's handling of the matter acquired for the United States valuable information. Toward the end of the war, Dulles used this information to penetrate the German army and to begin the process that led to Germany's surrender.

CIA. Home again after the war, Dulles was at odds with the new Democratic president Harry Truman. The OSS had operated with a free hand and a large budget for its spy work, but Truman felt that the money was wasted in peacetime. He disbanded the OSS, and Dulles returned to law practice at Sullivan and Cromwell. Soon, however, Truman found there was still a need for an intelligence service. In 1945 he started a new service, the Central Intelligence Group. Two years later that organization became the Central Intelligence Agency (CIA). Dulles played no part in this organization until 1950, when General Walter Bedell Smith became its head and asked him to come back into intelligence work. Three years later, Dulles became head of the CIA, once more because his big brother stood up for him and persuaded the president to appoint him.

Many of the actions of the CIA were deep secrets, and it is difficult to know which officer really started some of the actions, especially since Dulles was not a particularly strong administrator. He preferred to get directly involved in the actions in the field rather than control and direct the whole CIA program. From 1953 to 1960, the CIA carried out many successful ventures: engineering the overthrow of a communist president in Guatemala, seeing that the shah of Iran was replaced with one friendlier to the United States, developing and using a high altitude photography airplane to watch over Europe, and designing the first space satellite the United States could rely on for spy information. The secret organization with its nearly

> ## The Germans Approach Dulles to Surrender
>
> "They [Karl Wolff and Viktor von Schweinitz] were coming to surrender ... to arrange for the capitulation of all the German forces, Wehrmacht and SS, in North Italy. They proposed an immediate meeting with me in Lucerne to arrange the details of the trip to Allied headquarters. And I was under the strictest military orders to have no dealings with them!" (Dulles in Mosley, p. 185)

unlimited budget also had its failures: an unsuccessful attempt to remove General Sukarno from power in Indonesia, for example. There was a Cold War on, a struggle between the United States and Soviet Union for world power. And all over the world the Cold War was heating up, or was suspected of doing so. Allen Dulles and his CIA were in the thick of the action, when in 1960 a threat near home demanded attention. Cuba was being taken over by Fidel Castro, who intended to side with Russia. Trying to prevent the Castro takeover became a high CIA priority and resulted in the affair for which Allen Dulles is most remembered, the Bay of Pigs.

Participation: Cuba and the Bay of Pigs

Fidel Castro. In 1960 Fidel Castro was still struggling for power in Cuba. His guerrilla forces were expanding and creating a great disturbance throughout a country that almost seemed to be a part of the United States. American businesses were well established on the island, and American tourists found it a pleasant place to vacation. The United States military frequently visited Cuba.

On one such visit, several navy men decided to travel to Guantanamo Bay for a swim and were caught by Castro's guerrillas and held prisoner. The CIA wanted to immediately launch an attack on Castro's mountain encampments and free the men, but Dulles refused to do so. Instead, the men were quietly ransomed. The incident established Castro as a threat in Cuba, and the CIA decided to do something about him, but world attention was on Berlin at the time.

The U-2. Dulles had supervised the building and use of a superspy airplane, the U-2. It could fly almost unnoticed at 80,000 feet altitude and take pictures of details on the ground. The chief designer of the plane thought it could be flown over Europe and Asia for two years without being detected, but Dulles kept up the flights for four years. On May 1, 1960, on one flight over Russia, a U-2 was shot down and its pilot, Gary Powers, captured by Russian forces.

At the time, the former World War II allies were quarreling over what to do with Berlin. A summit meeting had been called to resolve differences among the British, the Americans, the French, and the Soviets. The Soviet leader, Nikita Khrushchev, did not want to be confronted on the issue. His area of control surrounded Berlin, and he felt that his demands that Berlin be Soviet-ruled should be met. He used the U-2 incident to cancel the summit, and Berlin continued as a hot spot of dispute among the former allies.

Bay of Pigs. Meanwhile, Fidel Castro was rapidly taking control of Cuba. At first, the CIA leaders believed he could be disposed of by organizing small groups of Cuban exiles to be landed on the Cuban coast. A small military unit, Dulles and his men felt, would gather supporters from among Cuban citizens who did not like Castro and, together, they would overthrow the future dictator. But any attempts at using small groups of exiles to stir up the Cuban people failed.

Dulles and the CIA decided that a larger scale invasion must be attempted to unseat Castro. There were many Cuban exiles in the United States. Several hundred of them would be recruited and trained by the CIA. They could then be landed somewhere on the coast of Cuba and establish a foothold on the island, a visible sign of anti-Castro forces that would encourage Cubans to rid themselves of the communist regime.

The men were recruited and sent at first to Panama in Central America for training. Then the operation moved to a base in Guatemala, where several hundred men were trained and led by CIA soldiers.

Of course, no direct action against Castro could be taken unless that action was approved by the president of the United States and, since it was to be a military action, the U.S. military needed to be kept informed. So Dulles held meetings with military officers, members of Dean Rusk's State Department, and others to discuss the action. The army sent several officers to the Guatemala base to see if the training was being done correctly, and they gave glowing reports of the base there. The plan to land forces at a small bay near the city of Trinidad, however, was questioned. Some of the planners felt that the whole invasion needed to be done quietly and that landing so near a center of heavy population would make that impossible. The plan was changed so that the landing was in an isolated area known as the Bay of Pigs.

Finally, on April 4, 1961, the entire plan of the CIA, approved by the Department of State and the military, was presented to President John F. Kennedy. By this time, the chief opposition to the plan came from the CIA itself. The trainers had found that there were too many would-be leaders among the Cuban exiles. There was no unity among them and not much prospect of a coordinated effort.

Dulles Battles the Gout

For years Dulles had a painful ailment of the joints called gout, which seemed to flare up whenever he was deeply worried. On assignment for President Johnson, Dulles braved the thick Mississippi heat in pain, his left foot struck by an attack of the gout. He returned home to suffer the first of six strokes.

But Dulles and his aides went ahead with the presentation to Kennedy. Everyone at the meeting voted to proceed with the project. Without much hesitation, the president approved the invasion of Cuba.

Dulles had never had much interest in managing the details of anything. Now he announced that he had a speaking engagement in Puerto Rico and left the entire invasion of Cuba in the hands of an assistant, Richard Bissell. The landing was attempted on April 17, 1961, and ended in disaster. The mission drew little support in Cuba, while Castro put up stout resistance. At the same time, Nikita Khrushchev threatened to send Russian troops to aid Cuba. Castro's forces easily destroyed or captured the disorganized invaders. In the end, 1,200 CIA-trained fighters were captured by the Castro forces. Dulles was meanwhile not in touch with his men. Returning from Puerto Rico, he wanted to immediately mount a larger offensive to rescue the captured men. The State Department then took charge, refusing to go to war with Cuba, and eventually ransoming the fighters for $58 million in food and medicine for Cuba and $3 million in cash to the Castro government.

Aftermath

Kennedy and Dulles. John F. Kennedy reported to the people of the United States, taking on himself full blame for the defeat at the Bay of Pigs. Outwardly he continued to support Dulles as head of the CIA, but the president sent Dulles a message. The CIA chief could choose his time to resign so long as he did it within a year. On September 28, 1961, Allen Dulles resigned as chief of the CIA.

Dulles did have two more assignments with the government, however. When in 1963 John Kennedy was assassinated, Dulles was appointed to be part of the Warren Commission assigned to investigate the assassination. And, in 1967, President Lyndon Johnson sent Dulles into the southern states to investigate the killings of some civil rights workers there.

Writing. Friends suggested that Dulles document his experiences, and he spent most of his time after leaving the CIA writing books. These volumes began with a handbook on the spy business called *The Craft of Intelligence*.

Dulles died in a hospital in Washington, D.C., on January 29, 1969, after producing a book that was published that same year. He had served his country for much of his adult life. Dulles played an important role in arranging the surrender of the German army in World War II and directed the major government information-gathering agency during much of the Cold War. Although he lacked interest in management and often left important decisions to his staff, he remained an effective agent for most of his career. He had, throughout life, displayed great energy, yet left an impression on some of being lazy due to his indifference to plans once started.

Books by Allen Dulles

The Craft of Intelligence (1963)

The Secret Surrender (1966)

Great True Spy Stories (1966)

Great Spy Stories from Fiction (1969)

For More Information

Halle, Louis Joseph. *The Cold War in History.* New York: Harper and Row. 1967.

Higgins, Trumball. *The Perfect Failure: Kennedy, Eisenhower, and the CIA at the Bay of Pigs.* New York: Norton, 1987.

Johnson, Haynes. *The Bay of Pigs; The Leaders' Story of Brigade 2506.* New York: Norton, 1964.

Mosley, Leonard. *Dulles: A Biography of Eleanor, Allen, and John Foster Dulles and Their Family Network.* New York: The Dial Press, 1978.

John F. Kennedy

1917-1963

Personal Background

The dynasty. John Fitzgerald Kennedy was born on May 29, 1917, to one of the most politically influential families in the history of the United States. The second son of Rose Fitzgerald and Joseph Patrick Kennedy, Sr., "Jack" as he was known by his friends and family grew up with eight brothers and sisters in a Boston suburb called Brookline.

Like all of the Kennedy boys, Jack was from the outset groomed to become a leader. Both the Kennedys and Fitzgeralds had been active in New England politics since the turn of the century, and the Kennedy boys were strongly urged to follow in the family tradition.

Joseph, Sr., who amassed a fortune in the liquor trade and stock market, was a one-time chairman of the Securities and Exchange Commission and served as the U.S. Ambassador to Great Britain during the Roosevelt Administration. But he had greater goals in mind for his sons. He hoped that his wealth and influence would enable his children to succeed in national politics all the way to the White House—a feat that no other Irish Catholic had accomplished up to that point. It was their father's relentless drive for power that fueled the boys' careers and produced three senators, an attorney general, a U.S. president, and a political dynasty that survives to this day.

▲ John F. Kennedy

Event: The Cuban Missile Crisis.

Role: As president of the United States, John F. Kennedy successfully led the nation through one of the gravest international crises it has ever faced. Poised on the brink of nuclear war with the Soviet Union over missile sites in Cuba, President Kennedy succeeded in persuading Soviet leader Nikita Khrushchev to take apart and withdraw nuclear missiles from Cuba. Had this not be done, the crisis could easily have sparked World War III.

Childhood. As the second son, Jack was not his father's first choice to become the president. It was always assumed that his older brother, Joe, Jr., would achieve his father's highest political goals. Still, Jack was strongly encouraged to succeed in all that he did. His father often told him: "We don't want any losers around here. In this family we want winners" (Hamilton, p. 215).

From the time Jack was a small boy, there was a great deal of pressure on him to excel. He was sent to private schools, taught a strict code of behavior by his mother, and encouraged to play sports with a fighting spirit by his father. Though Jack's parents were frequently absent from their home—Joe away on business and Rose traveling abroad—they still exercised tremendous influence over their children. The Kennedy home was run like the military, with Rose issuing orders to the children and organizing all of their activities from attending Catholic church services to where they played, without any great show of affection for them.

Physical weakness, mental strength. Jack was a spunky but small boy. What he lacked in size he made up for in sheer determination. Always in competition with his older brother Joe, Jack pushed himself almost as hard as his father did. He and Joe, Jr. constantly wrestled on the lawn, opposed each other in football, and generally competed for their parents' attention when either was at home.

But Jack was always plagued by ill health. He nearly died of scarlet fever at the age of two, had constant stomach problems, and developed a very bad back, which was finally diagnosed as Addison's Disease. Throughout his life, Jack was in and out of hospitals. Yet he continued to play sports, though it was probably very painful to do so, and did not generally let people around him know how unhealthy he was or how bad he felt.

Boarding school rebellion. When Jack turned thirteen, he was sent to Choate boarding school in Connecticut. Though he was very intelligent—nearly two grades ahead of most children his age—and a tremendous reader, Jack developed a rebellious streak as a teenager. He left his room a mess, dressed sloppily, and often neglected to do his homework. Although he was very well-liked by his classmates, he exasperated his teachers, who sensed that he had great gifts.

Writing and leadership developed. Jack soon developed two of these gifts, abilities that would take him to the highest office in the country. First, he acquired an interest in writing. He penned pieces for his school newspaper and showed such talent that several instructors encouraged him to pursue writing as a profession.

Jack also cultivated his leadership qualities at boarding school. Under his guidance, Jack's friends began a club called "the Muckers," which basically served the purpose of opposing every rule the headmaster made. As "chief mover" of the Muckers, Jack illustrated not only his ability to lead and organize but to challenge the powers that be. However, the headmaster did not quite see the merits of challenging his authority, and Jack was nearly expelled.

This close call marked a major turning point in Jack's life. His father was summoned to the school and quickly donated some money to calm the situation and keep Jack in good standing. Though Joe, Sr., was at first upset with his son, upon learning the details of Jack's actions, he was won over by what the headmaster termed Jack's "misdirected qualities of leadership" (Hamilton, p. 128). He recognized for the first time that his second eldest son held promise of becoming a great leader. To Jack's astonishment, his father told him he had earned his respect. Those words—which he had been waiting to hear all his life—deeply affected Jack. Almost at once, he became more serious about the direction his life would take.

Jack gets serious. By the end of his senior year, Jack's grades improved dramatically as he prepared to follow his brother Joe to the London School of Economics and then on to Harvard University. He began to study history very intensely and developed a deep interest in the causes of war in particular. Jack's study of history would last his entire life and not only lead to a Pulitzer Prize in literature for *When England Slept,* a novel he wrote about the causes of World War II, but enable him to successfully handle the Cuban Missile Crisis of 1962.

College to politics. Poor health prevented Kennedy from studying in London. Instead, he attended Princeton and then Harvard, from which he graduated in 1940 near the top of his class. Kennedy planned to earn a master's degree in business from Stanford University, but his studies were cut short by World War II. In

1941 he followed his brother Joe into the service, volunteering in the navy. Jack's bad back should have prevented him from being accepted but, because of his family's influence, he was made a lieutenant junior grade in charge of a PT (torpedo) boat in the South Pacific.

War. When his PT was sunk by a Japanese destroyer, Kennedy lost three men but was able to save the other ten from death. They managed to swim to an island. Stranded there, Kennedy and his men scrambled to regain contact with American troops. When a rescue party finally arrived, Kennedy was awarded the Purple Heart and the Navy and Marine Corps Medal for bravery. Shortly thereafter, he was discharged from service for medical reasons. His back injury had been aggravated in the encounter, and he could barely walk.

Political rise. Also in the navy, Kennedy's older brother, Joe, Jr., was killed in action in 1945. His death crushed the family, especially Joe, Sr., who had so many plans for his eldest son. Now that Joe, Jr. could not fulfill his political ambitions, the torch was passed to Jack, who was now ready to carry it.

Road to the White House. Campaigning with strong support from his large and highly influential family, Kennedy was elected U.S. Representative of the 11th Massachusetts Congressional District in 1946. He served three terms in the House and in 1952 was elected to the Senate. On September 12, 1953, Kennedy married Jacqueline Bouvier, and by the end of the decade his two children were born, Caroline Bouvier (November 27, 1957) and John, Jr. (November 25, 1960). (A third child, Patrick Bouvier, was born August 7, 1963, but died two days later.)

By 1960 Kennedy felt he was ready to make a bid for the White House. He chose Texas Senator Lyndon B. Johnson as his running mate and on January 20, 1961, was inaugurated as the first Irish Catholic and the youngest man ever to be elected president of the United States.

Participation: The Cuban Missile Crisis

Brave new world. Kennedy's election signaled a dramatic shift in power from one generation to the next, as the forty-three-year-old Kennedy replaced seventy-year-old Dwight D. Eisenhower. It also ushered in a new era in politics.

The nuclear threat, now very real since atomic weapons had been used by the United States to end World War II, added a frightening dimension to warfare and called for increased use of diplomacy, or international discussions and settlements, to avoid conflict. To complicate matters, the Cold War, a struggle for world power between the United States and the Soviet Union, was escalating. The two nations engaged in tremendous nuclear arms buildups and competed on every front from the space race to the arms race.

Kennedy warned that the United States was "in its hour of maximum danger" and called on his fellow Americans to help him keep America strong by asking "not what your country can do for you—ask what you can do for your country" (Kennedy in Richard Reeves, p. 36).

Much like Eisenhower, Kennedy felt that a strong defense was the key to avoiding war. If the United States posed enough of a military threat, he believed, no one, including the Soviet Union, would dare attack. This was the lesson he had learned from studying history and the concept on which he based his foreign policy.

Built for Politics

After World War II, many Americans were ready for a new era to begin. The veterans returning from war, including Kennedy, felt they were on the verge of a brave new world, one in which they, not their commanders, would be in control. As a government leader, Kennedy represented something new in politics: a war veteran with small children and a beautiful young wife. He brought a spirit of change and possibility to a political atmosphere previously dominated by men nearly twice his age.

Bay of Pigs—introduction to the crisis. The Cuban Missile Crisis was preceded by an incident in Cuba known as the "Bay of Pigs" invasion. In 1959 Fidel Castro had led a communist revolution in Cuba, and ever since his victory the U.S. government had been working to oust him from power. U.S. officials were gravely concerned about a communist presence less than 100 miles from the coast of Florida. The Bay of Pigs invasion of 1961, planned by the Central Intelligence Agency (CIA) with military approval, was an attempt to overthrow or kill Castro and spark a democratic revolution. The Kennedy administration authorized the attempt, but it failed miserably. Nearly all of the U.S.-trained Cuban exile invaders

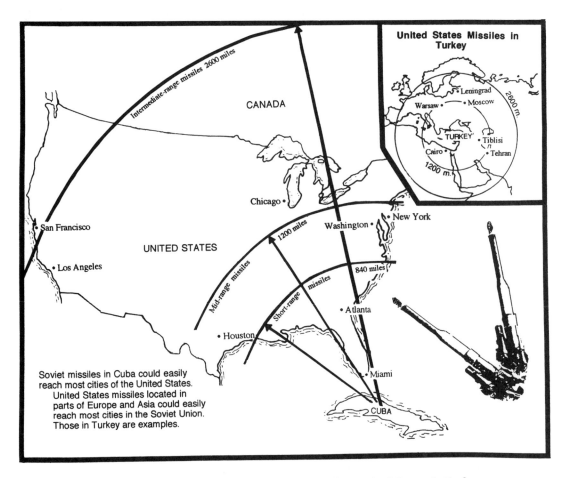

▲ **The missiles game—Soviets in Cuba, United States in Turkey**

were captured when they landed on the beachfront at the Bay of Pigs. The United States was highly embarrassed.

Afterward, Castro sought aid from his communist allies, the Soviet Union, led by Nikita Khrushchev. Castro feared—and with good reason—that the United States was still plotting to overthrow his government and asked for military support in case the United States decided to use all its military might against the tiny island nation.

This was an ideal opportunity for Khrushchev. The Soviet Union had been struggling to keep up in a very expensive nuclear arms race with the United States. Now, thought Khrushchev, by placing nuclear missiles in Cuba, Russia could gain a far less costly strategic advantage over the United States. Though the United States had many more nuclear weapons than the Soviet Union (5,000 U.S. nuclear warheads to 300 Russian ones), the Soviet leader was well aware the United States could be attacked from the South. U.S. radar did not face that direction and therefore missiles could be easily placed in Cuba without detection. Khrushchev also reasoned that missiles in Cuba would pose a strong enough threat to make the Americans cooperate in arms and territory agreements to be made between the two nations.

The crisis. Though it was true that United States radar did not face south, the CIA was surveying Cuba using aerial photography taken from U-2 spy planes. In August 1962, President Kennedy, a great champion of the use of aerial photographs, was informed by CIA director John A. McCone that the Soviet Union appeared to be building missile sites in Cuba. The photographs indicated that the sites were for medium- and long-range nuclear missiles that could reach as far as the Pacific Northwest. Kennedy was alarmed but remained cautious. He knew from the Bay of Pigs disaster that CIA intelligence reports were not always accurate, and he wanted further evidence of a Russian weapons buildup before he did anything rash.

However, it was an election year in Congress and the Republicans were anxious to call Kennedy "soft on the Reds" and use any lack of action by the Democratic president to gain political points for their party (Thomas Reeves, p. 367). Kennedy felt the political heat and immediately called for daily intelligence reports. He also assembled a committee of advisers that met each morning to discuss possible remedies for the situation. Included on the committee, known as the ExCom (Executive Committee of the National Security Council), were his brother, Attorney General Robert Kennedy, McCone, and other national officials. United Nations Ambassador Adlai Stevenson and Vice President Lyndon Johnson also attended the meetings.

By September 1962, U-2 photographs confirmed that six missile sites had been completed and three more were under construction. Kennedy was now deeply concerned and called for a meeting with Khrushchev to discuss the situation. In a letter, Khrushchev told Kennedy that the weapons were strictly for defense, to guard against U.S. invasion. He also assured the president that there were no nuclear warheads on the island. However, as he spoke, forty-two nuclear warheads were en route to Cuba. At the time, Kennedy did not know of the warheads en route but was wary of Khrushchev. Kennedy's brother Robert also distrusted the Soviet leader and urged the president to take a strong stand against him.

Kennedy made an announcement to the press on September 13, 1962, that showed both his cautious approach to what he understood was an incredibly dangerous situation and his firm intention not to back down in the face of a Soviet threat. "The American people defending as we do so much of the free world, will in this nuclear age," Kennedy promised, "keep both their nerve and their head" (Thomas Reeves, p. 368). Kennedy then asked Congress to pass a bill that would grant him the authority to prevent a nuclear arms buildup in Cuba by whatever means might be necessary, including using weapons. The legislation passed that afternoon.

Stop the Presses

A day before President Kennedy was to send U.S. military ships to form a naval blockade around Cuba, the press learned of the plan. Details of the top secret operation had been leaked to both the *Washington Post* and the *New York Times.* Each had front-page stories ready to publish the day before the planned blockade. When Kennedy discovered the leak, he quickly telephoned and convinced the editors of both newspapers to hold the story for a day. He argued that in the interest of national security the Russians must not learn of the plan before it was underway. Kennedy managed in this way to stop the presses and to keep the operation top secret.

Though he remained calm on the outside and in front of the press, the president realized the nation was dangerously close to a nuclear confrontation just off of its southeastern border. By early October he was holding ExCom meetings deep into the night over the crisis. Now thousands of Russian troops were on Cuban soil, with more ships en route transporting soldiers and weapons. Kennedy estimated there were less than two weeks before the missile sites would be ready to operate, and he was still unsure whether or not nuclear warheads were as yet on the island.

ExCom had come up with two possible ways to stop the Soviet buildup—air strikes or a naval blockade—and each of these ways was very risky. Air strikes might not wipe out all of the missile sites and could result in the Russians launching the remaining missiles. A naval blockade, to prevent the Russians from delivering warheads or

▲ Soviet missiles leaving Cuba, December 3, 1962

troops, would be considered an act of war under international law. If the Russians decided to challenge a blockade, it could have the same results as a failed air strike: World War III. The president favored the blockade because he felt air strikes were too final and risky. A blockade could buy time for negotiations, or a peaceful settlement. He and Khrushchev could try to work out a peaceful compromise. ExCom voted eleven to six with the president for the blockade.

As Kennedy ordered the final preparations for the blockade and put the U.S. military on alert, he boldly told the nation of the grave situation. He was willing, he said, to pay the price for U.S.

freedom: "one path we shall never choose, and that is the path of surrender or submission" (Kennedy in Thomas Reeves, p. 378).

On October 24, 1962, 63 U.S. ships, backed up by an additional 120, surrounded Cuba. At 10 A.M., two Russian ships and one submarine approached the naval blockade. Listening nervously to the intelligence reports as the Russians slowly made their way toward the Americans, President Kennedy stared gravely at his brother Bobby. "His hand went up to his face and covered his mouth ... his face seemed drawn, his eyes pained," Bobby said (Thomas Reeves, p. 381). The two nations were but a few hundred feet and one shot away from an all-out nuclear war and Kennedy was well aware of it. At 10:25 A.M. Kennedy received word that the Soviet ships had stopped just short of the blockade and shut off their engines. Seconds later, a second message was relayed to the president saying that the ships were turning back toward the Soviet Union. Speaking first, Secretary of State Dean Rusk said, "We were eyeball to eyeball and I think the other fellow just blinked" (Thomas Reeves, p. 401). Kennedy breathed a huge sigh of relief. The color returned to his face as he realized the threat was over. He had stood up to Khrushchev and won.

Back-up Plan

It is now known that Kennedy was willing to risk his political career to avoid a nuclear war over the missiles in Cuba. If the blockade had not worked and Russian ships had proceeded, rather than fire on them, he had another plan. Kennedy was prepared to offer Khrushchev an even exchange of U.S. missiles in Turkey for U.S.S.R. missiles in Cuba, a trade that did in fact occur.

Kennedy on the Cuban Missile Crisis

"It is insane that two men, sitting on opposite sides of the world, should be able to decide to bring an end to civilization." (Kennedy in Richard Reeves, p. 411)

Aftermath

The crisis winds down. In the days that followed the crisis, Kennedy made a deal with Khrushchev for the Soviets to take apart and remove their weapons and troops from Cuba in exchange for a promise by the United States not to invade the island. Kennedy also quietly later removed U.S. Jupiter missiles from Turkey as part of the agreement.

During the crisis, Khrushchev had sent Kennedy a letter that offered him the deal: "I propose: We, for our part, will declare that our ships, bound for Cuba, will not carry any kind of armaments. You would declare that the United States will not invade Cuba" (Richard Reeves, p. 412). Within hours, a second letter proposed that the United States remove its missiles from Turkey. Not wanting to involve Turkey for the moment, Kennedy chose to ignore the second message and respond only to the first, a tactic that worked. One of his advisers observed that Khrushchev was scared of what might happen. Kennedy agreed. He had been scared, too.

Greatest political victory. The president's life was cut short by an assassin's bullet just a year after the crisis. On November 22, 1963, Kennedy was fatally shot by Lee Harvey Oswald while campaigning for reelection in Dallas. Jacqueline (who died in 1994), Caroline, and John Jr., survived him.

Kennedy has been greatly admired for his handling of the missile crisis. According to many Americans, it was his finest accomplishment in a short bur eventful administration. Critics have meanwhile argued that Kennedy's actions placed the nation in unnecessary danger; the U.S.–Soviet compromises could have been reached without the threat of a nuclear war. Also they blame him for not consulting other nations. His admirers reply that if Kennedy had acted differently, the nation might easily have fallen off the brink into the horror of World War III. Instead, the president handles the crisis in a way that was very responsible, highly successful, and "his greatest political victory" (Thomas Reeves, p. 389).

For More Information

Blair, Joan and Clay. *The Search for JFK.* New York: G.P. Putnam's Sons, 1976

Hamilton, Nigel. *JFK: Reckless Youth.* New York: Random House, 1992.

Reeves, Richard. *Profile of Power.* New York: Simon & Schuster, 1993.

Reeves, Thomas C. *A Question of Character.* New York: The Free Press, 1991.

Bibliography

Bailyn, Bernard, et al., *The Great Republic: A History of the American People.* Vol. 2. Lexington, Massachusetts: D. C. Heath and Company, 1992.

Blair, Clay. *The Forgotten War: America in Korea, 1950–1953.* New York: Times Books, 1987.

Boorstin, Daniel J., and Brooks Mather Kelley. *A History of the United States.* Lexington, Massachusetts: Ginn and Company, 1983.

Brands, H. W. *The Devil We Knew: Americans and the Cold War.* New York: Oxford University Press, 1993.

Carbonell, Nestor T. *And the Russians Stayed: The Sovietization of Cuba.* New York: Morrow, 1989.

Davis, Michael D. *Thurgood Marshall: Warrior at the Bar, Rebel on the Bench.* New York: Carol Publishing Group, 1992.

Degler, Carl. *Out of Our Past.* New York: Harper & Row, 1984.

Dupuy, R. Ernest, and Trevor N. Dupuy, eds. *The Harper Encyclopedia of Military History.* New York: HarperCollins, 1993.

Ferrell, Keith. *John Steinbeck: The Voice of the Land.* New York: M. Evans and Company, Inc., 1986.

Flem, Penna Frank. *The Cold War and Its Origins, 1917-1960.* Garden City, New York: Doubleday, 1961.

Fukei, Budd. *The Japanese American Story.* Minneapolis: Dillon Press, Inc., 1976.

Goldman, Roger L. *Thurgood Marshall: Justice for All.* New York: Carroll & Graf, 1992.

Goldston, Robert C. *The American Nightmare: Senator Joseph R. McCarthy and the Politics of Hate.* Indianapolis, Indiana: Bobbs-Merrill, 1973.

Gunther, John. *The Riddle of MacArthur.* New York: Harper & Brothers, 1951.

Harrison, Barbara. *A Twilight Struggle: The Life of John Fitzgerald Kennedy.* New York: Lothrop, Lee & Shepard, 1992.

Irons, Peter, ed. *Justice Delayed.* Middletown: Wesleyan University Press, 1989.

Irons, Peter. *Justice at War.* New York: Oxford University Press, 1983.

Kinche, Jon. *Spying for Peace: General Guisan and Swiss Neutrality.* New York: Roy Publishers, 1961.

Larrabee, Eric. *Commander in Chief: FDR, His Lieutenants and Their War.* New York: Harper & Row, 1987.

Lash Joseph. *Dealers and Dreamers: A New Look at the New Deal.* New York: Doubleday, 1988.

Leffler, Melvin P. *A Preponderance of Power: National Security, the Truman Administration, and the Cold War.* Stanford, California: Stanford University Press, 1992.

BIBLIOGRAPHY

Louchheim, Katie, ed. *The Making of the New Deal: The Insiders Speak.* Cambridge, Mass.: Harvard University Press, 1983.

MacArthur, Douglas. *Reminiscences.* New York: McGraw-Hill, 1964.

McElvaine, Robert S. *The Great Depression: America, 1929-1941.* New York: Times Books, 1984.

Meyer, Carl Ernest, and Tod Szule. *The Cuban Invasion: A Chronicle of Disaster.* New York: Praeger Publishers, 1962.

Miller, Merle. *Plain Speaking: An Oral Biography of Harry S Truman.* New York: G. P. Putnam, 1950.

Miller, Nathan. *FDR: An Intimate History.* New York: Madison Books, 1983.

Mills, Judie. *John F. Kennedy.* New York: Franklyn Watts, 1988.

Nash, Gary, et al. *The American People: Creating a Nation and a Society.* Vol. 2. New York: Harper and Row, 1986.

Romansco, Albert U. *The Politics of Recovery: Roosevelt's New Deal.* New York: Oxford University Press, 1983.

Salinger, Pierre. *With Kennedy.* New York: Doubleday, 1966.

Scharf, Lois. *Eleanor Roosevelt: First Lady of American Liberalism.* Boston: Twayne Publishers, 1987.

Schlesinger, Arthur M., Jr. *The Age of Roosevelt.* 3 vols. Boston: Houghton Mifflin, 1957–59.

Shamberg, Maurice. *Breaking from the KGB.* New York: Shapolsky Publishing of North America, 1986.

Sharlitt, Joseph H. *Fatal Error.* New York: Charles Scribner's Sons, 1989.

Sheean, Vincent. *Dorothy and Red.* Boston: Houghton Mifflin Company, 1963.

Shepley, James. "How Dulles Averted War," *Life,* Vol. 40, No. 3, January 16, 1956, pp. 70-80.

Smith, Geoffrey S. *To Save a Nation: American Countersubversives, the New Deal, and the Coming of World War II.* New York: Basic Books, 1973.

Smith, Page. *Redeeming the Time: A People's History of the 1920s and the New Deal.* Vol. 8. New York: Penguin Books, 1987.

Thomas, Lately. *When Even Angels Wept: The Senator Joseph McCarthy Affair, A Story without a Hero.* New York: Morrow, 1973.

Truman, Margaret, and Margaret Cousins. *Souvenir: Margaret Truman's Own Story.* New York: McGraw-Hill, 1956.

Urban, George. *Encounters with Kennan.* London: Frank Cass Ltd., 1972.

Watkins, T. H. *The Great Depression: America in the 1930s.* Boston: Little, Brown, 1993.

Wernstein, Irving. *A Nation Fights Back: The Depression and Its Aftermath.* New York: Messner, 1962.

Youngs, J. William T. *Eleanor Roosevelt: A Personal and Public Life.* Boston: Little, Brown, 1985.

Index

Boldface indicates profiles.

MacArthur, Mary Harding 170
Malcolm X 243
Malory, Thomas 24
Manhattan Project 18-19, 119, 122, 129, 220-222, 225
Manzzanar 105
March on Washington 89-90, 92-93
Marquette University 202
Marshall, George 71, 73-75, 143, 154, 168, 208
Marshall, Norma A. Williams 244-245
Marshall Plan 143-144, 161, 168-169
Marshall, Thurgood 229-230, **244-255**
Marshall, Vivian Burney 246
Marshall, William 244-245
McCarran Internal Security Act (1950) 198
McCarthy Era 197-225
McCarthy Hearings 208-211
McCarthy, Joseph R. 129, 199-201, **202-213,** 220-222
McCauley, James 232
McCauley, Sylvester 232
McCone, John A. 279
Meany, George 92
Meeropol, Abel 224
Meeropol, Anne 224
Meeropol, Michael Rosenberg 219, 224-225
Meeropol, Robby Rosenberg 219, 224-225
Mercer, Lucy 51
Messenger 86-87
Migrant laborers 25
"Migrant Mother" 39, 44
Miller, Earl 51
Minidoka Relocation Center 104
Minoru Yasui Recognition Day 106
Missile gap 257
Missouri ex. rel. Gaines v. *Canada* 249-250
Miyake, Shizduyo 96-97
Monterey, California 22
Montgomery Advertiser 239-240
Montgomery, Alabama, bus boycott 230-231, 239-240
Montgomery (Alabama) Improvement Association 240-242

Morgan, Irene 251
Morgan v. *Virginia* 229, 251
Mundt, Karl 211
Musser, Chris 68
Mussolini, Benito 18
"My Day" 55-56

N

Nagasaki, Japan 65, 128, 137, 152-153
Napalm 145
Nasser, Gamal Abdel 194
National Association for the Advancement of Colored People 52, 89-90, 115, 228-230, 235-236, 239, 243, 247-250
National Association for the Advancement of Colored People Legal Defense and Education Fund 248, 254
National Council of Churches' Commission on a Just and Durable Peace 188
National Guard 173-174
National Guardian 223
National Labor Relations Board 17, 218
National Labor Relations (Wagner) Act 16
National New York Packing and Shipping Company 218
National Recovery Administration 16
National Youth Administration 5, 15
Nazism 63-65, 134-137, 114-116, 218, 266-267
Neddermeyer, Seth 126
Negro Urban League 90
Nehru, Jawaharlal 191
Neutrality Acts 18
New Deal 1-5, 12-21, 44, 52, 87, 113, 204
New York State Women's Suffrage Party 132
New York Times 280
New York Training School for Teachers 37
New York Women's City Club 51
Nisei 96
Nixon, E. D. 235-236, 239, 242

PROFILES IN AMERICAN HISTORY

Significant Events and the People Who Shaped Them

Volume 5: *Reconstruction to the Spanish-American War (1863-1898)*

Reconstruction
Andrew Johnson, Thaddeus Stevens
Indians and Government Policy
George Armstrong Custer, Carl Schurz, Chief Joseph
Labor Movement
George Pullman, Samuel Gompers, Mary "Mother" Jones
Struggle for Civil Rights
Ida B. Wells-Barnett, Booker T. Washington, W.E.B. Du Bois
Realism in American Literature
Mark Twain, Stephen Crane, Helen Hunt Jackson
Social Reform
Elizabeth Cady Stanton, Josephine Shaw Lowell, Frances Willard
Spanish American War
William McKinley, William Randolph Hearst, Theodore Roosevelt

Volume 6: *Immigration to Women's Rights and Roles (1880-1936)*

Immigration
Chin Gee-hee, Bartolomeo Vanzetti, Abraham Cahan
Social Welfare
Jane Addams, Herbert Croly, Louis Brandeis, Upton Sinclair, Ida Tarbell
World War I
Woodrow Wilson, John J. Pershing, Oliver Wendell Holmes
Industrial Growth
Henry Ford, John L. Lewis
Scopes Trial
Clarence Darrow, William Jennings Bryan
Harlem Renaissance
Marcus Garvey, James Weldon Johnson, Zora Neale Hurston
Women's Rights and Roles
Carrie Chapman Catt, Margaret Sanger